"After all, what is a garden for? It is for 'delight', for 'sweet solace', for 'the purest of all human pleasures; the greatest refreshment of the spirits of men'; it is to promote 'jucunditie of minde'; it is to 'call home over-wearied spirits'. So say the old writers, and we cannot amend their words, which will stand as long as there are gardens on earth and people to love them."

A GARDENER'S TESTAMENT

A Selection of Articles and Notes
By GERTRUDE JEKYLL

edited by
FRANCIS JEKYLL & G. C. TAYLOR
and illustrated with photographs taken at
Munstead Wood

Macmillan

Gertrude Jekyll (1843-1932) studied painting as a young girl and went on to fulfil many commissions, enjoying considerable reputation as an artist and craftswomen before she became a 'gardener'. A friend and collaborator of Edwin Lutyens, she contributed many articles on gardening to *Country Life*. Her published works include *Gardens for Small Country Houses, Wood and Garden, Home and Garden* (all available in Papermac), *Colour Schemes for the Flower Garden, Garden Ornament, Roses for English Gardens, Lilies for English Gardens, Wall, Water and Woodland Gardens* and *Flower Decoration in the House.*

This book was originally published by Country Life, 1937

This edition, with 24 colour illustrations, published in
hardback 1982 by
The Antique Collectors' Club Limited

Published in paperback 1984 by
PAPERMAC
a division of Macmillan Publishers Limited
4 Little Essex Street, London WC2R 3LF
and Basingstoke

Associated companies in Auckland, Dallas, Delhi, Dublin,
Hong Kong, Johannesburg, Lagos, Manzini, Melbourne,
Nairobi, New York, Singapore, Tokyo, Washington
and Zaria

ISBN 0 333 37655 2

Printed in England by
Baron Publishing, Woodbridge, Suffolk

Contents

		PAGE
I. About Myself	- - - - - -	9
II. Gardens Past and Present	- - - -	17
III. Some Problems of Garden Planning	- -	71
IV. The Water Garden	- - - - -	97
V. The Mixed Border	- - - - -	113
VI. Colour in the Garden	- - - -	153
VII. Wild and Garden Roses	- - - -	185
VIII. The Spring Garden	- - - - -	217
IX. Some Hardy Families	- - - - -	263
X. The Winter Garden	- - - - -	283
XI. The Fern Garden	- - - - -	297
XII. A Retrospect	- - - - - -	307
Epilogue	- - - - - - -	321
Index	- - - - - - -	323

MATRI DILECTISSIMÆ
QUAE NUPER TERRESTREM COLEBAT
IN COELESTEM ENIXÆ PARADISUM
FILIUS

Preface

GERTRUDE JEKYLL died in 1932, leaving behind her, in addition to some dozen published books, a considerable body of notes and articles, mainly on horticultural subjects, contributed to various journals over a period of nearly forty years. To those who appreciate the literary form of her own books the collection and re-issue of these disconnected pieces may appear a questionable undertaking; such a book must, by its very nature, suffer from the comparison, in the absence of a single theme or unifying purpose. Another consideration, however, prevailed. Of the practical articles dealing with plants and their treatment, the greater number date from the last twenty years of her life, following the period 1899-1912 which saw the publication of nearly all her books. These, then, may be taken as reflecting her most mature experience, and it is not unreasonable to surmise that if health and energy had been vouchsafed to her in the closing years of her life, they might have served as material for a kind of testamentary volume, a 'Seven Lamps of Gardening' in which she would have embodied the quintessence of her teaching.

In making this selection and preparing it for publication I have exercised the functions of an editor to the extent of omitting introductory matter and references to passing situations (such as the Great War) and very occasionally, for the sake of greater clearness and concision, altering a word or revising a sentence. Names of plants, since changed under the latest rules of botanical nomenclature, have with one or two exceptions been left as she wrote them.

My grateful acknowledgments are offered to those proprietors of journals who have granted permission to reprint articles originally written for their columns; to Messrs. Benn, the proprietors, and Mr. Robert Jackson, the editor of *Gardening Illustrated*; to the Royal Horticultural Society for reprints from its *Journal*; to Messrs. A. and C. Black for extracts from their *Gardening Dictionary*; to Messrs. Macmillan for an article from the *Empire Review*; to the National Rose Society; to Messrs. Jack for the Introduction to their 'Colour Planning of the Garden'; to the proprietors of the *Edinburgh Review*, the *Quarterly Review*, the *Ladies' Field*, and the *New Flora and Silva*; and lastly to her devoted friend and colleague, Mr. Herbert Cowley, editor of *Gardening Illustrated* during the period of her contributions to it, for many of the photographs which so materially enhance such value as this book may possess.

I

ABOUT MYSELF

SOME EARLY REMINISCENCES
Gardening Illustrated, August 27, 1927

I

About Myself

MY INTEREST in flowers began at a very early age, for my family left London for a country home* when I was four and a half years old. But I had already made friends with the Daisies in the Berkeley Square Garden and with the Dandelions in the Green Park. During the next few years there were the delights of Primroses and Bluebells, and Wood Anemones and wild Violets, besides the carefully kept gardens, and above all the well stocked shrubberies of the new home. Here there were wide turf paths among clumps of shrubs with a general background of *Rhododendron ponticum*; for the hybrids were as yet not generally known. For the date when the shrubbery was made, it was well planted, for besides the usual flowering shrubs there were the sweet *Azalea pontica* and Vacciniums and Andromedas and some of the old Roses; the double Cinnamon with its flat pink bloom, and *Rosa virginiana*, rambling about among the shrubs. The larger things were a number of evergreens of the Arbor Vitae and Cypress class, Ailanthus, Hickory, Cut-leaved Beech and *Taxodium distichum*, ending in a thick plantation of common Laurel, that was by no means devoid of interest because every spring the thrushes built in them.

The soil is deep though sandy, partly peaty and always cool. The place was a good one in which a child might gain early acquaintance with shrubs, and I spent hours and hours in it,

*Bramley Park, in Surrey.

10

getting to know them all intimately by sight and handling, and keenly inquisitive smelling. The kitchen garden was some way off, but that also was full of attractions. There was a bed of Lily of the Valley under a north wall and a quantity of Musk, with the delicious scent that it has now lost, and a narrow border at the foot of another wall of the old double purple Violet, now rarely seen. There were very few hardy plants though there was what passed for a mixed border along one of the middle paths. But the only things I remember in it were a purple Trades-cantia, some Day Lilies, blue *Centaurea montana*, a very poor but sweet-scented lilac Phlox and a quite shocking Michaelmas Daisy. But it had also the variegated sweet-scented Mint (*Mentha rotundifolia*), a precious plant to this day. I think the border was filled up with Stocks and China Asters and any superfluous bedding plants for the summer. But the best thing about this border was the hedge of Sweet Peas at the back, Peas really sweet, though in the four old colours only, one a mixture of bluish and reddish purple, then a pink and white, a sort of grey roan, and a white. It must have been quite twenty years later that an all rosy-reddish one appeared, and it was thought a wonderful novelty. There was a long Lavender hedge close to some Gooseberries, and as the bloom of the Lavender which I was set to cut coincided with the ripening of the earliest Gooseberries, I thought very well of the association. Then there were the plant houses. My father was fond of these and for the time we had quite a fair collection. There were Passion Flowers, Allamanda, Stephanotis and Gloxinias; with Stone Ferns, and in cooler houses Bougainvillea and Lapageria and the usual array of Primula, Cineraria, Cyclamen, Calceolaria and fancy Geraniums. There was a bedded-out garden on each side of the house, one of concentric rings of beds entirely filled with scarlet Tom Thumb Geranium, the other, on the drawing-room side, bedded both spring and summer after the manner of the time.

I had my own little garden with an arbour at the end covered with that lovely Rose, Blush Boursault, which I cannot re-member ever to have seen elsewhere. I am thankful to have kept it for I do not think it is easy to obtain now.

When I was just grown up, though still in my late teens, I had the great advantage of going with friends to the near East —the Greek Islands, Constantinople, Smyrna, and Athens, with several weeks in Rhodes. Though from the sea the Islands look so barren it was delightful to find them clothed with a quantity of sweet herbs besides the usual Myrtle, etc., that we are familiar with on the nearer Mediterranean coasts. There was not much chance of sending home plants, but from Rhodes I brought a root of an Iris of which there was a quantity in the Turkish cemetery. It proved to be *I. albicans*. There was not much in flower then—it was in November—only a good sprinkling of Cyclamens in the nearer wilds, and these not easy of access as there were no roads in the interior, only rather difficult mule tracks.

Some years later I had the good fortune to become ac-quainted with the greater number of that wonderful company of amateurs and others who did so much for better gardening in the last half of the nineteenth century. One day stands out in imperishable memory; a meeting at Mr. Barr's original nursery at Tooting, with Sir Michael Foster and Mrs. Bennett-Poë. It was for the study of Hellebores, of which Mr. Barr had collected all that were then available. He took us round and told us all he knew about them, Sir Michael putting in occa-sional questions. When the tour was over Sir Michael gave a *résumé* of what we had been told—terse and lucid and richly informative—he had not missed a single point. Later Canon Hole, afterwards Dean of Rochester, became our friend and he brought us Mr. Robinson, who came to us often afterwards, and for whose good help I can never be sufficiently thankful. Mr. G. F. Wilson, then planting his Wisley garden,* was another grand helper. He was kind enough to let me come and do

*Now the garden of the Royal Horticultural Society.

actual spade work with him. I remember especially one strenuous day when we formed a mound in about the middle of the position of the present rock garden. But of all these friendly gardeners, the one whom I felt to be the most valuable was the Rev. C. Wolley-Dod, scholar, botanist and great English gentleman; an enthusiast for plant life, an experienced gardener, and the kindest of instructors.

In the early seventies I had a winter in Algiers with my friend Madame Bodichon. Her house was a good way up-hill, quite at the top of Mustapha Supérieur, the inland suburb of Algiers; beyond that was all open country; delightful rambling ground, the home of *Iris stylosa* and *Iris alata*. Hedges of Prickly Pear were garlanded with *Clematis cirrhosa* with its quantity of warm white bell-shaped flowers; in thin grassy places were a number of small Orchises and diminutive Daffodils, and we often had a visit from the good old botanist M. Durando who would name any plant I had collected.

To one who is in sympathy with growing things there is a keen delight in seeing some beautiful flowering plant for the first time in its own home. But it was painful to see a colonist, in clearing the land for cultivation, grub up Dwarf Palm and Cyclamen and the great *Scilla maritima* and other plants that would be treasures in gardens, throw them into heaps to be burnt, and then express his satisfaction by saying the ground was now *plus propre!*

The only carefully tended garden in Algiers in those days was that of our friend Mr. Edwyn Arkwright. It was a glory of good things too numerous to describe, but one of its most prominent features was an immense Poinsettia, a good wide mass of scarlet on a trunk about five feet high—a wonder to see when one's hitherto idea of Poinsettias was the single head of bloom so often seen on London dinner tables. After flowering, Mr. Arkwright used to chop it back with a handbill.

In the early eighties I became possessed of the fifteen acres in south-west Surrey where I have made my home. It is roughly triangular in shape, widest to the south, and slopes down to the north-west. There had been a close wood of Scotch Pine lately felled in the upper nine acres, then a wide strip of Chestnut coppice, and at the narrow end a small field of poor sandy soil. The sandy field is now a profitable kitchen garden, the middle space is the site of the house and surrounding lawn and shrubs and flowers, and the upper, wild part, where the Scotch Pines were cleared, soon became filled with young trees of natural growth; seedling Pines, Birch, Holly, Oak, Mountain Ash and Spanish Chestnut. They all grew up together and my first care was to keep the kinds a little apart in order to get natural pictures of one kind of tree at a time. A space near the middle was cleared for Azaleas and for a bit of Heath garden. Now, after forty years, it has all grown into a state of satisfactory maturity. Daffodils were planted under the trees and many spaces were filled with Lily of the Valley, and more recently with my pure white Foxglove.

There is little else of wild gardening except for a shady region where there are hardy Ferns, Trillium and Solomon's Seal, and a big patch of the beautiful *Erythronium giganteum*; and, further away, a wide undergrowth of *Gaultheria Shallon*, which has taken only too kindly to my sandy soil. I do not want more, for I think that of all kinds of planting for pleasure, wild gardening needs the greatest caution and the most restraint.

If the ways of gardening that seem to me the most worthy and that I have tried to give some idea of in my books, are found of use to others, it is because I have never written a line that was not accounted for by actual work and experience. What I have endeavoured to describe about arrangements of colour and the making of pictures with living plants was helped by some early training; for when I was young I was hoping to be a painter, but, to my lifelong regret, I was obliged to abandon all hope of this, after a certain amount of art school work, on account of extreme and always progressive myopia. But my

Munstead Wood. The approach through the wood

interest in and devotion to the fine arts has always been one of my keenest joys, and, with it, a love of Nature, with all its beauties and wonder. And I am thankful to have been able to cultivate a habit of close observation so that even with my bad eyes I can often detect objects and effects that well-sighted people have passed unnoticed.

II

GARDENS PAST AND PRESENT

THE IDEA OF A GARDEN
Edinburgh Review, July 1896

GARDEN DESIGN ON OLD-FASHIONED LINES
Black's Gardening Dictionary

SOME DECORATIVE ASPECTS OF GARDENING
Empire Review, May 1924

Gardens Past and Present

THE IDEA OF A GARDEN: A HISTORICAL SKETCH

THE INFLUENCES that have determined the development of gardens within the last thousand years must be looked for in those of ancient Rome. In Rome itself gardens of highly wrought architectural character were an actual part of the imperial palaces and of those of the patrician class; and recent examination clearly proves, what has long been vaguely known, that a large portion of the vast area of the Campagna was occupied by villas with their gardens and farms. Professor Lanciani's recent works of exploration and excavation show how this now barely inhabited waste was once a thickly populated suburb, composed of the villas of the wealthier class, with busy streets branching out of the Appian Way and other main thoroughfares. Rome, the all-conquering, subdued not only distant kingdoms, making them her provinces, but, close at home, conquered fever and death, creating smiling gardens and groves where they had lately reigned. As she grew in power and wealth and population, her governing and patrician class required country houses of convenient access, in many cases more than one, for use at different seasons of the year. Marshy hollows were drained and filled up, and permanent roads were built, with raised footways and pleasant fountains and places of rest for wayfarers. Frequent crossroads gave access to the various properties, which increased in size as they lay at a greater distance from the city, till the villa included not a palace and garden mainly, as in those nearer home, but large properties, comprising farms and whole villages of thriving peasant population. An abundant water-

"Surely it is well that gardens should show as many beautiful kinds of treatment as possible; not that any one garden should try for all, but at least for some one or two pictures of lovely form or colour or delightful arrangement."

South front of Munstead Wood with Scotch Briars, and 'Patty' on the lawn

supply, secured by the magnificent system of aqueducts that brought pure water from the hills, and a well-organised arrangement for carrying off surface water, provided an ample supply and an efficient overflow. Not only were houses and gardens built and planted in the plains and small valleys of the Campagna itself, but imperial villas of vast size occupied commanding sites on the slopes of the neighbouring hills. The ruins of the villa of Hadrian, a town in itself, shows terraces, colonnades, fountains, and pools of magnificent design, indicating a garden of the first order; while the remains of the villa of Domitian on one of the slopes of the Lake of Albano point to the former existence of another of great importance. Pliny the younger gives a detailed description of his villa in Tuscany in his 'Letter to Apollinaris' in the year A.D. 62. In these ancient gardens topiary work was in general practice. Trees and shrubs were trained and trimmed into walls, ornaments, and figures of wild beasts; it became a fashion that was carried to a great excess. A certain amount of such work was no doubt in harmony with the architecture, green niches of Box, Yew, and Cypress being admirable backgrounds for the many works of sculpture which decorated the greater gardens. Only in the remoter parts, and in the case of the groves surrounding the family mausoleum, which found a place within the grounds of each great villa, were the Ilex, Pine, Cypress, Myrtle, and Pomegranate allowed to grow into their own beautiful forms. Where the zeal of the *topiarius* or the whim of his master tortured the bushes into extravagant forms, the taste of the practice is questionable, but an explanation may be sought in the excess of slave labour, or in the want of variety of garden material. The number of flowering plants on record as known in these ancient gardens was so limited that they may have sought for as great a variety as possible in the methods of treating what they had. We hear of a wealth of Roses; of Violets, Iris, Poppy, Lily, Narcissus, Hyacinth, and Crocus; of Ivy, Jasmine, Myrtle, and Pomegranate, and of little else.

So great was the demand for Roses that it greatly exceeded the home supply. Rose nurseries were established in sheltered places on the southern coast, and they were even sent from distant countries.

The arrangement of the villa usually followed certain rules. The palace and upper terrace were on the highest ground; then followed a succession of terraces with massive retaining walls, porticoes with niches for sculpture, pools, canals, and fountains. Everywhere the sound or sight of water; rushing or gently murmuring; boldly splashing or falling in finest spray; everywhere the cool quietude of green alleys, some open to the sky between high walls of close-cut greenery; some arbour-like of trellis covered with closely trained Ivy or Vine, direct ancestors of the *pergola* of modern Italy, and distant foreshadowing of the covert alleys of Tudor England.

Happy is a country, as to her present beauty and everlasting renown, when her men of high place and great wealth are, as it were, born artists; when, as in Athens of old, nothing offensive to the eye is tolerated or can be erected; when no commercial considerations are allowed to outweigh the supreme obligation of making every human work that is to be seen sightly and gracious and fit and of due proportion. That such was the happy state of the great centres of Italian civilisation in the end of the fifteenth and beginning of the sixteenth centuries we know to be the case. The princes of Florence of the house of the Medici were at the same time the princes of trade and finance. They were men of strangely mixed character, many of them cruel, tyrannical, licentious; but it was their will and pleasure so to expend their vast accumulation of wealth that it became a precious heritage for all later ages. Then it was that these great bankers and merchants revived the study of Greek literature and of their own classics—that they searched out and chose with just discrimination and fostered the men who have enriched the world with the greatest works of art that Italy had produced for many centuries.

It was among these influences, between three and four hundred years ago, and about twelve centuries after the destruction and abandonment of the ancient villas, when Italy was again the home of all that was greatest in art and literature, that the famous gardens of the Renaissance were built and planted. They followed the ancient villa closely as to their main plan and arrangement, for their purpose was the same; they were for men of the same race and class, in the same climate, under the same sky. The garden was an open-air continuation of the house, the terraces and groves the scenes of state banquets and of gatherings whether social, artistic, political, or commercial. How often have the remains of their fountains, groves, and marble benches, aided by historical record, inspired the painter to bring again to life the personages of noble family giving audience and honour to poet, minstrel, inventor, and discoverer! How often, within our own day, have they been painted, either for their own beauty's sake, or with some incident of human interest of gorgeously cloaked cardinal and old-world liveried lackey!

Happily, enough is left of these great gardens of Italy to show how beautiful they must have been in their maturity. As we see the best of them to-day, they are battered, ruined, weatherworn, neglected; but where enough of the original structure remains there is a unity of design with absence of conscious effort, a princely grace that unites impressive dignity with the modesty that comes of refinement and due proportion; a charm only to be likened to the human charm of a perfect manner. On a steep hillside terrace rises above terrace, with broad easy steps in flights never too long, and spacious landings and resting-places; all with the beauty of proportion and fitness of purpose that mark all good work; nothing jarring or irritating, nothing that makes one wish that anything might be either added or suppressed. Abundance of water, leaping, rushing, spouting, and falling—the fountains and channels fed by copious streams that gush out of the hills above and flow in willing abundance to fulfil the will of the designer.

How much of the charm of these old gardens is due to the magnificent tree-growth, of Cypress as at the Villa d'Este, or of Ilex as in the grounds of the Villa Borghese, or of Pine in other examples, it is difficult to estimate, or whether they can have been as beautiful when 'white from the mason's hand' as now, when their ruin is partly veiled by graceful tangles of wild growth. Probably they were best at from fifty to a hundred years after building, or perhaps even later, when they were on the point of becoming overgrown, but were still in full-dressed and well-kept beauty. The architect may do as he will with stone and marble, but he must wait many years for the green things to grow and be trained to his design, and for the untrimmed trees of the surrounding groves to develop into the fitting background of his dressed work.

The Villa d'Este, near Tivoli, must have been one of the noblest of the gardens of the Renaissance. Even now, in a state of ruin and decay, it is most impressive. The great stairway still towers up, flight above flight, with noble fountains on the wide landings, and refreshing variety of straight or winding steps, till it reaches the highly ornate garden-portico; the whole being the more striking from the severe simplicity of the main building of the palace. The direct ascent of the steep hillside could hardly have been more nobly treated, and through all the defacement and decay, and the mutilation of the original design occasioned by the removal of the sculptures, one cannot help feeling impressed by the nobility and grace of the whole. The almost unchecked growth of wild underwood and the giant stature of the great Cypresses are not out of harmony with the ruined architecture. The great trees, perhaps at first clipped into shape and forming only a subservient part of the design, seem now to guard and protect the old garden, and with the other tangles of wild bushes to strive to hide the ravages of decay and neglect. Kindly Nature clothes the ruin with its own beauty; were it stripped of this gracious mantle, and all its mutilation and decay laid bare, how much of its mysterious poetical charm would be lost!

What a living link with a most ancient past are the ever-flowing waters of these old fountains! Who knows what yet older ones may have been there before them, or what wood-nymph may have bathed in the same rill two thousand years ago? In what other country of the world can one receive such impressions of poetry and mystery as among the waters and groves of Italy? The very names of growing things have a musical sound with an ancient echo—Myrtle, Olive, Vine, Pomegranate! No wonder that such scenes played on the sensitive imagination of Nathaniel Hawthorne as on a sympathetic instrument, inspiring his celebrated story of the present century, whose central figure, both in form and character, shows traces of descent, through centuries of noble lineage, to a woodland ancestor in the dim ages of mythology! Much to be mourned are the old Roman villas that within the last quarter of a century have been wiped out for ever to make room for modern building, and happy are the now living people of middle or advanced age who knew Rome in their youth only, before the time when the greed of owners had destroyed so much that was beautiful of old grove and garden. However, nothing is likely to rob Rome of her waters, and they are the more to be treasured as day by day her other delights are vanishing.

No record remains of any gardening in England during the time of the Roman occupation; we can only suppose that the villas whose foundations and highly decorated pavements have been already discovered, and are still being unearthed, should have had suitable gardens. Certain of our kitchen vegetables are clearly traceable to Roman importation, and a kind of annual nettle with a very sharp sting, which occurs in the neighbourhood of some of the villages on the Sussex seaboard, and is still known as the Roman nettle, is referred to their occupation.

The first English gardens of which we have record are those that were attached to monastic houses; of these one of the earliest and most important was at Ely. Here was also a flourishing vineyard, where it appears that a considerable quantity of wine was made, as well as verjuice, the ancient equivalent of vinegar. But the gardens of the monks were for utility only, the few flowers grown being for church decoration and for the wreaths worn by the priests on festivals and occasions of high ceremonial. We hear of Box and 'Palm' on Palm Sunday—the old country name of Palm for the Willow in flower, showing that this was the accepted substitute—of Rose garlands on Corpus Christi, and of garlands of Rose and of Woodruff on June 11, the feast of St. Barnabas.

The garden made by Henry III at Woodstock in the middle of the thirteenth century was probably one of the earliest pleasure gardens in England; we hear little of anything of the same class till two centuries later, when records concerning them are more frequent both at home and abroad. About the middle of the fifteenth century there are manuscripts with printed illustrations of walled gardens with fountains, arbours, and flowing plants trained on trellis-work. Turfed seats with brick fronts appear to be usual, and the bowling-green, which for the next three centuries was to keep its place in English gardens, came into use. But the greater houses were still castles, or, to some degree, places of defence, so that within fortified limits the pleasure garden could have had but small space. It was only after the conclusion of the Wars of the Roses, when the country had settled down into a more peaceful state, that the beautiful houses arose of which some still remain —houses of brick or stone or timber-framing, no longer fortresses, but delightful and commodious dwellings. In many cases, the need of defence—a need that had existed so long that the thought of it was hard to die—still showed itself in the wall or moat, but the enclosed space was larger, and the house no longer placed in a position as nearly as might be inaccessible for greater ease of fortifying, and no longer fearing to have ample windows on its outer walls.

The ordering of the garden and the greater part of the light labour in early Tudor times seem to have been done by the mistress and women of the house, with hired women labourers; no doubt a survival from earlier times, when master and men were away fighting for their king or raiding on their own account. The still-room was as busy a place as the kitchen. Here a variety of liqueurs, essences, cosmetics, and medicinal preparations were made from the home-grown herbs. One likes to think that the ladies of Italy were as industrious as their English sisters, and themselves prepared the contents of the beautifully decorated majolica jars, whose ornament was formed of the name of the drug and the arms of the family, with enrichment of scroll and figure and arabesque admirably designed and coloured. The garden had also to produce large quantities of honey, to serve all the purposes of the then un-known sugar.

We may assume that the arrangement described by Bacon in his well-known essay was typical of a princely English garden of his day. He advises that in all it should occupy thirty acres, and be in three divisions—namely, the 'green' at the entrance of four acres, the 'main garden' of twelve acres as to its central square, with four acres on either side, and the 'heath' of six acres at the further end. The 'green' is to have 'covert alleys' on its two sides, made of trees trained over a wooden framework in order to give the option of walks in shade. He deprecates the elaborately shaped 'knots and figures' filled with variously coloured earths, and does not care for an excess of topiary work, though he approves of thick box edgings and evergreens trained and clipped into the shapes of columns and pyramids.

The main garden is to be square, and to be encompassed with an arched hedge trimmed on a framework. There are to be pools and fountains, but no stagnant water, and the pools and basins are to be kept cleaned by hand. In the centre is to be the 'mount', an artificial mound of earth surmounted by a banqueting house with three ascending ways of access, wide enough for four persons to walk abreast. A writer of about fifty years earlier describes a mount as having an easy spiral stairway, or, as he says, 'writhen about with degrees, like the turnings of cokil shelles, to come to the top without payne.' Its original intention was as a look-out place, to give a view over the wall or hedge, of the surrounding country. To judge by some remains that exist, it must have been difficult to work them as beautiful features in a garden. A building perched on a steep-sided artificial mound can never have looked quite at home, and one wonders that the plan can ever have commended itself to the minds of our forefathers, who were extremely honest in matters of construction. Still, all this region of the garden was intensely artificial, and one must accept it as a part of the whole. That the fashion for the mount existed for a hundred years after Bacon's time we know by the one constructed at Wotton by John Evelyn.

In other gardens of this date the same purpose was effected in what seems a simpler and better way, by having a turfed terrace raised to the level of one of the outer walls, or with only a slight parapet. Such a one occurs at Rockingham, where the highest level is approached by a succession of turfed terraces and slopes. A beautiful and very simple example is in the large walled garden at Loseley in Surrey, built by Sir William More in the early part of the latter half of the sixteenth century. Here a high wall rises out of the moat on the south, retaining a great mass of earth on the inner side, evidently the excavation of the moat. This forms a wide grassy terrace, whose level comes within a couple of feet of the coping of the wall. A steep turf bank leads down to another long grassy lawn on the general level of the garden, whose ample walled space of four acres is simply and well laid out as pleasure and kitchen garden. Each angle of the wall was enriched with a small

"In the the case of . . . herbaceous borders, these are being arranged . . . with definite intention directed to the forming of a picture of garden beauty and glory. Flowers of delicate cool tints strengthen gradually into warmer, and these lead to a gorgeous mass of richly related colour; after this, again returning to the cooler and quieter."

Madonna Lilies in the wood with Scotch Briars and
LEUCOTHOË CATESBAEI

building of dignified but unobtrusive design, three of which are still in place. Within the walled space nearest to the house is a lawn whose fringe of orchard trees suggests and suitably leads to the vegetable garden beyond; among them is the Mulberry (*morus*), the badge of the founder. Among the vegetable quarters shady alleys of old Filbert trees are grateful walks in summer. One wonders why the Filbert was not oftener used in the pleached alleys of old days; its small tree form, thick shade, and useful fruit would seem to recommend it as better for the purpose than the trees more generally used.

To return to Bacon's garden; the 'heath', its third and further division, was to be planted in imitation of natural wild growth. In his own words: 'I wish it to be framed, as much as may be, to a natural wildnesse.' He would have thickets of Sweetbriar, Honeysuckle, and wild Vine, and the ground planted with Violets, Strawberry, and Primrose, 'for these are sweet, and prosper in the shade,' and little heaps, like the molehills in wild ground, set with Thyme and other lowly plants. One cannot help wishing that his description of the wilder part of the garden had ended here, but he also desires to have some standard bushes trimmed into tidiness. Though he condemns the fanciful beds or 'knots' filled with coloured earths, he allows and even advises other details which to modern taste appear to be incongruous and unworthy trivialities, such as the decoration of fountain basins with 'coloured glass and such things of lustre'. He also recommends as ornaments for the top of the great arched hedge, which is of stately height and noble proportion, over every arch a little turreted space to receive a cage of birds, and over each of the intervening spaces a gilt ornament with plates of coloured glass for the sun to play upon! Quite early in Bacon's century, gardening had already borrowed somewhat in its details from the taste of France and Flanders. Perhaps this may account for what appears to us now too great a jumble of ornamental material.

Such a garden as this one portrayed by Bacon may be taken

"One of the modern French artists has described painting as 'l'art des sacrifices'. The best . . . gardening is also an art demanding constant restraint and constant sacrifice, as well as the knowledge and keen discrimination that can choose. . . what will serve best to make the intended garden picture. . . the opportunities are endless both for sober ranges of quiet harmonies and for rich pictures of culminating gorgeousness."

as a type of the best class of pleasure-ground of his day, and such a one, no doubt, was the garden made at Hampton Court by Henry VIII when, after the disgrace of Cardinal Wolsey, he took it for his royal residence. Here again we read of an abundance of toylike ornaments; figures of heraldic animals, set up on slender wooden columns that rise from stone bases at intervals along the railed edgings of the flower beds; the columns and railings painted in chevrons of green and white, the Tudor colours; also numerous gilt ornaments of lead or of wood. The excuse for the intrusion of the 'king's and queen's beasts' into the garden is to be found in the king's desire to stamp the visible sign of his ownership on the palace and grounds by a constant repetition of his arms and badges, so that the 'beasts' appear not only on the edges of flower beds and fountain basins, but bristle on gateways, parapets, copings, and other salient points of the architecture. Thus he strove to wipe out the remembrance of the fallen cardinal, and by large additions and alterations to impress the place with his own identity.

Sundials were numerous; there are accounts for works still in existence showing payment for sixteen dials for the king's new garden. A portion of this garden was evidently laid out as an elaborately 'knotted' parterre. The term 'knots' or 'knotted garden' came to be used for any grouping of flower beds of other than simple shape; the original designs having been of strap patterns, like a complicated braiding or corded embroidery in a design of loose knots and plaitings; later, these became enriched with scroll and arabesque.

The labyrinth or maze was another distinct feature of the Tudor garden. Occasionally it was laid out with low shrubs, and plants of such stature that they could be stepped over, but more often of clipped bushes grown to a man's height.

When the alterations at Hampton Court were completed, having for some years cost what would now be equal to £50,000 a year, King Henry built the palace of Nonsuch and

An arrangement of Hydrangea, LILIUM SPECIOSUM *and*
Funkia

surrounded it with parks and gardens of great extent. Nothing now remains of what must have been a magnificent royal residence. The palace was pulled down in the reign of Charles II, and the trees were cut down and the grounds destroyed soon after. Had Nonsuch remained to us, it would have been a precious relic, and its garden no doubt the best possible example of a royal pleasure-ground.

The fine green English turf has ever been a source of pride and pleasure in our gardens. The smooth level bowling-green, always a beautiful thing near dressed grounds, must have been an especially reposeful and refreshing place among the many complications of the Tudor garden. Bounded by walls or by a hedge of Yew or Hornbeam, or, as at Berkeley, by a high wall on one side and an ancient hedge of Yew on the other, the bowling-green, whether for summer play or for quiet saunter, must always have been, as it ever will be, one of the most delightful of garden spaces.

While Henry VIII was reigning in England we hear of the planting of one of the earliest of the botanical gardens of Europe—namely, that of Padua. It exists still, and nominally as a botanical garden, but from the overgrowth of some of its ancient trees it has more the appearance of a beautiful private place. Here the great white-flowered Magnolia attains the size of a forest tree, splendid with its ivory-white flowers and solid glossy foliage.

The reign of Elizabeth, so fruitful of varied kinds of learning, research, and enterprise, saw the beginning of botanical classification as conceived by Lobel, also the publication of the great herbals of Hill, Gerard, and Parkinson. Gerard's is a mighty volume of more than sixteen hundred pages, profusely illustrated with vigorous woodcuts. These authors were physicians and apothecaries, and their books treat of the subject from points of view equally botanical, horticultural, and medical. These old herbals are delightful reading, full of keen observation, and even now of practical utility. Their descriptions of familiar plants in the beautiful Elizabethan speech read like the Psalms of David; now and then there is a touch of whimsical humour; while the numerous and lengthy eulogistical dedications, to the queen, to the 'courteous reader', and to each other, though framed in the flowery language of compliment, are unspoilt by the taint of laboured fulsomeness that debased those of a later date, and seem only to give expression to an unaffected and spontaneously courteous kindliness. In the beginning of Gerard's herbal, Johnson's preface of twelve folio pages, in complimentary introduction of the author to the 'courteous reader', passes in review all earlier writers on gardening, beginning with King Solomon, and so, by way of Theophrastus, Aristotle, Dioscorides, Pliny, Galen, and other writers of antiquity, to those of his own day. Parkinson's book, the *Paradisus Terrestris*, which appeared a few years after Gerard's, is not of general botany, but of flowers for garden and medicine, and of fruit and vegetables. His first chapter, 'The ordering of the garden of flowers,' treats of laying out the ground and of the various plants or other material to be used for edgings. The next chapter is of exotic plants: 'The nature and names of outlandish flowers, that for their pride, beauty, and earlinesse, are to be planted in gardens of pleasure for delight.' These chapters are full of shrewd observation and practical detail, useful for all time, even to the trapping of 'earwicks, a most infestous vermine'.

These men were indefatigable in corresponding, and collecting plants and testing them for beauty and use. Their books, of which there must have been very large editions, for even now they are not at all rare, must have had strong influence in spreading a knowledge of flowers and taste for gardening.

The reigns of the Stuarts saw many new gardens in England, of stately house and of homely manor. As to their main design, they remained faithful to the old traditions, of parterre and bowling-green, pleached alley, turfed walk, and clipped hedge, with certain additions derived from foreign influence, those from France inclining to increased stateliness and importance, and those from Holland to an extreme rigidity of treatment, with various matters of petty detail.

But France, the birthplace of so much of accurate design, of delicate fancy, and of just proportion, when at the very summit of her greatness, produced a monstrous garden that remains as a wholesome warning to those who would seek to achieve magnificence by mere magnitude. The spaces and details at Versailles are so large that they are out of scale with humanity. People in crowds of many thousands only look like throngs of ants or other insignificant creatures. All the royal personages in Europe, grouped together in state attire, would be ineffective from the over-large scale of the space. The first impression received from this garden—one of wonderment at mere size—is quickly followed by a feeling of dreariness and depression, from the weight of laboured artificiality, of ruinous cost, of wasted labour, of a garden that is made for display, and not for human enjoyment, 'for state and magnificence, but nothing to the true pleasure of a garden.' Doubtless the intention of the designer was that it should be for display rather than for enjoyment. But the gardens of the old palaces of Italy answered to both of these conditions, and neither at the expense of the other. The saddest of the sights at Versailles are its fountains without water.* A fountain does not justify its existence unless it can always be playing; as well strip the leaves from trees in summer as let a fountain or cascade be seen without water. What can be a greater contrast, either in beauty, in good taste, or in common sense, than the everflowing fountains of Italy and these dry monstrosities that are only brought into play on rare occasions and at great cost? In one case the comforting impression of endless and gracious abundance, in the other the painful consciousness of grievous waste. And it should be remembered that the sound of water is a part of the design or

*[Since their recent restoration this is no longer the case. Ed.]

intention of the maker of fountains, so that if they are robbed of what gives delight to two senses what is left is poor indeed. What wonder that the jaded royalties of the early eighteenth century escaped joyfully for short holidays to the adjoining grounds of the Petit Trianon, there to refresh themselves by playing at sham simplicity, but at least within the healthy influences of real groves and natural streams? It would be unfair to Le Nôtre to judge his work by the exaggerations of Versailles. He has left many noble *châteaux* and gardens, always characterised by the extremely artificial taste of the time, but beautiful and harmonious, and on a reasonable scale as human habitations. Horace Walpole, criticising the redundancy of ornament in the French gardens, says that in one he counted nine thousand pots of China Aster placed along the walks on each side, and describes the trees in the groves as 'green boxes on poles'. These fashions were, alas! soon to reach England, but had not yet arrived, for, writing of the yet untouched English gardens at about this date, Diderot says of them that they are 'the sanctuary of a sweet and placid pleasure'.

Charles II greatly admired Versailles, and wished to have the services of the same designer. It seems doubtful whether Le Nôtre actually came to England; but it is known that a French garden architect of his school laid out the semicircular garden at Hampton Court and the grounds of Whitehall and St. James's Park. The parallel rows of trees that run from Buckingham Palace eastward are all that now remains of this work.

The garden at Levens, in Westmorland, was from the design of a Frenchman in the time of James II, though its general style is rather more Dutch than French. It presents, at the present day, one of the most curious assemblages of cut Yews in England. What the original intention of the designer was with regard to these trees cannot now be traced; he could not have intended them to be cut, as they are, into a variety of quite incongruous forms. This garden appears at its best in

Mr. Elgood's clever picture, one of the collection of garden subjects that this artist has treated with rare sympathy and felicity.*

The decoration of terraces with Orange and Bay trees, trained as standards with round heads and planted in large square boxes, was another fashion introduced from France. The trees being tender, the need arose for the capacious orangeries—large structures lighted on one side only—for their protection in winter. Many of these remain, and can be utilised as winter gardens. In some examples, where a high parapet conceals the roof, the substitution of a glass roof makes the house available as a conservatory that will suit most greenhouse plants, but in cases where the roof is visible, did the gardener but know it, the necessary restriction to the more limited number of plants that will thrive without top light gives a motive for making a winter garden of much less commonplace character. These plants or trees in large boxes, when thoroughly well done, give a garden that full-dress character that was the aim of the French designer. Some fine examples of Oleanders so treated still remain in the gardens of the Luxembourg in Paris. The boxes are painted a delicate light green colour that is decorative in itself, and that enhances the colour value of the foliage by not in any way competing with it. Pepys relates how, on his first visit to a collection of Orange trees in boxes, he surreptitiously appropriated and ate a little orange. Such trees are known as 'fine greens', and their owner as 'a master of curious greens'.

Sir William Temple and John Evelyn were the men whose influence was most strongly felt in gardens in the latter part of the seventeenth century. Temple laid out his garden at Moor Park in Surrey in a way that was adapted from both French and Dutch styles; but his fine taste enabled him to retain the sweetness of the old English garden even while adopting some

*See *Some English Gardens* by G. S. Elgood and Gertrude Jekyll (Longmans, 1904).

of the newer foreign methods. Evelyn's strongest sympathies were with forest trees; but he was none the less a keen gardener, and wrote a book on gardening operations throughout the year, his *Kalendarium Hortense*, full of practical detail and useful matter. Some of his laying out of ground remains at Wotton, and a piece of delightful pleasure-ground at Albury was his work. It is a broad turf terrace some hundreds of yards in length, bounded on one side by a mighty Yew hedge and on the other by the steep rocky bank of the hill that rises just above. Halfway along is a large deep circular basin of cold clear water that comes out of the hill, and at this point a long tunnel-shaped grotto is cut straight into the hill. He seemed proud of this piece of excavation, for he says of it: 'Such a Pausilippe is nowhere in England besides.' The green terrace, as it may be seen now, has simple borders of important hardy flowers on the side next the Yew hedge and for part of the way on the side of the hill, of excellent effect.

At Hampton Court, Evelyn speaks of the planting of avenues of Limes in the park and of the making of the long canal. This canal has been commonly accredited to the time of William III, but that it was made in that of Charles II is clearly shown in Mr. Law's admirable book, where there is a woodcut from a picture painted for Charles II of the east front of the palace, showing the canal and a part of one of the newly planted Lime avenues. Towards the end of his life the King planted the great semicircle of Lime trees, and formed the scheme for the important garden that they were to enclose— now the Fountain Garden. The plan, as projected by him, was carried out by William III under the supervision of the celebrated gardeners London and Wise. Both the King and Queen Mary were ardent gardeners. The King was constantly considering how to improve the palace gardens, while the Queen had several hothouses built, and encouraged the importation of large numbers of tender exotics. The curious pleached alley of Wych Elm still existing, and commonly known as Queen

Mary's Bower, was planted earlier than her reign, and was no doubt the one noticed in 1662 by Evelyn, who says: 'The cradle-work of horn-beam in this garden is, for the perplexed twining of the trees, very observable.'

In the same reign the garden was enriched by the addition of some very handsome stone vases, and by the setting up of the famous wrought-iron gates and screens that have been attributed to Huntingdon Shaw, but have been proved by Mr. Law's recent research to be from the designs of a French artist, Jean Tijou, for whom Shaw worked. They are now in the South Kensington Museum.

The 'Wilderness' at Hampton Court was also laid out by London and Wise. It was admired by Defoe, who says in his *Tour through Great Britain*:

'The vacant ground, which was large, is very happily cast into a wilderness, with a labyrinth, and espaliers so high that they effectually take off all that part of the old building, which would have been offensive to the sight. This labyrinth and wilderness is not only well designed, and completely finished, but is perfectly well kept, and the espaliers filled exactly, at bottom to the very ground, and are led up to proportioned heights on the top; so that nothing of that kind can be more beautiful.'

Mr. Law remarks that Defoe's favourable view was reversed by his editors, for in the edition of 1742 we read:

'As the whole contrivance of the plantations is in regular strait walks, bounded on each side by tall clipped hedges, which divide the whole ground into angular quarters, to every person of taste it must be very far from affording any pleasure, since nothing can be more disagreeable than to be immured between hedges, so as to have the eye confined to a straight walk, and the beauty of the trees growing in the quarters, entirely secluded from the eye. And at the same time as you are walking in this unmeaning plantation, you are denied the benefit of shade, by being confined to these regular walks, where it would be deemed an unpardonable fault, to suffer the neighbouring trees to diffuse their branches over these shorn hedges; so that, in the midst of a wood, a person may faint for shade in a sultry day, the air being excluded from these walks by the taller trees in the quarters; and pent-up air is much more troublesome in hot weather, than the heat of the sun in the most exposed plain.'

The Wilderness, however, was threatened with annihilation, for about the year 1699 there was an extensive project for forming a new entrance court, from Sir Christopher Wren's design, on the north side of the palace. The approach to this would have cut straight through the Wilderness and across the moat. The great avenues in Bushey Park and the Diana basin, as we see them now, were formed as a part of this project, which, however, was never carried into effect. The great Fountain Garden was altered about the year 1730, in deference to the wish of Queen Caroline, by Kent, who substituted large turfed spaces for the elaborate scroll-work of Box which is shown so well in Kip's engraving of the east front. The loss of this garden in its original form is much to be regretted, for nowhere in England, except perhaps at Chatsworth or Blenheim, both laid out by London and Wise, could so fine an example be shown; and though it does not in the least agree with modern ideas of gardening, it would have been precious as a relic of this particular manner of setting out dressed ground, and must have been in admirable harmony with Wren's noble façade.

At Hampton Court may be seen, perhaps as well as anywhere, what may be called the beneficence of overgrowth. In William III's time the canal was no doubt a clean-cut Dutchtown-like piece of water; now it is dappled with Water Lilies, and its side lines, though still absolutely formal, have acquired by time the beauty of an old water-edge, while the neighbouring Lime avenues (probably at first clipped) have grown to their full natural size and shape. In the Privy Garden, the Yew trees bordering the walks, which in the time of George II were small trimmed pyramids of a few feet in height, now form a darkly overshadowing gallery of mysterious and massive shade, giving the highest pictorial quality to the scenes of garden palace, and fountain, of which they are the living frames. Even the Wilderness has at last escaped from the tyranny of the shears, and its component parts assert their individuality as living trees rather than as so much vegetable building material. No doubt much of the charm of Haddon and suchlike fine old places is due to this same beneficence of overgrowth. What precious qualities come by age, both of masonry and vegetation!—the grand form and stature of mature tree-growth; the weather-staining of stonework; and the broken and subdued colouring of brickwork painted by grey and yellow lichen. Even the softening qualities gained by the abrasion of hard edges of masonry and the falling out of surface mortar are a gain, for the lichen laps over the bruised moulding and the mortar is replaced in the joints of the coping by a cushion of moss that harbours little fairy vernal plants that flower and fruit and complete their tiny life within the height of half an inch, while lower joints are clothed with a lacework of Fern or Fumitory. Then there is the perfect turf of the old lawn, and the thought of all the people that have paced it, of the many that have lived and rejoiced and fretted and died in the old place. The lawn is more enduring than stone, for the footsteps that have worn the stairway have left no trace on its green expanse. Infinitely precious are these old gardens, and ever to be regretted are the numbers that were destroyed to make way for the new fashions. The change began to operate under Kent in the reign of Queen Anne, and was in full operation in the time of George I. The poet Thompson was singing the praises of Nature, Horace Walpole had written his essay on gardening, and the deadly thrusts of his brilliant and satirical pen deriding the old method had gone like the point of a rapier into its very heart. It became fashionable to rail at the old ways of gardening, while the buildings of Elizabethan and Jacobean times were voted barbarous. It is true that just before the change came some of the details of the old work had been carried to an excess, such as the topiary work ridiculed by Pope. The 'classical' was still in full fashion, though it was leniently elastic, as we read that in Lord Cobham's garden at Stowe, newly made in the year 1727, in the garden of Venus (one of its many compartments) was a figure of the goddess in her temple with a circle of attendant gods and goddesses, overlooked by a statue of Prince George in his robes. Many classical summerhouses, temples, pyramids, fountains, and statues, as well as gilt leaden vases, adorned this garden, which must have been of great extent. It had no visible fence, a notable innovation, but was bounded by a ha-ha, giving a view into the park and open country. Long avenues of trees were still being planted; sometimes several of them met at a point distant from the house, or, as at Badminton, they diverged from the house.

Bridgman, who carried out the works at Stowe, was followed by Brown,* whose garden training was acquired in the same place. It was through Lord Cobham's influence that he obtained the many important introductions that led to his success and popularity. The long avenues, now just grown to maturity in many of England's greatest parks, fell before Brown's relentless axe, for straight lines were abhorrent to the new 'landscape' school. Everything was to be 'natural'—sham natural generally, and especially there was to be water everywhere. There must be sham-natural ponds on the tops and sides of hills, with their ends concealed to cheat the mind into the idea of their larger extent, and terraces and steps must be abolished, because, according to him, it was not in good taste to have any steps out of doors! Possibly his avowed dislike of stonework arose from his incapacity of designing it; certainly when he did attempt anything architectural, a classical summerhouse or any such structure, his ignorance and want of taste were clearly betrayed. Not only the old English tradition, but the ceremonious full dress of France and the toylike detail of the Dutch, were all cast aside; the latter, it is true, had

*Lancelot, known as 'Capability' Brown (1715—1783).

never taken firm root in England, for it had been felt that its frivolous and petty features were unsuitable in a country already so well furnished with hill and dale and woodland, whereas it was reasonable to expect that diversity, however obtainable, and complexities of close-trimmed sheltering hedges might be acceptable among the treeless wastes and wind-swept flats of Holland.

So the work of destruction and renovation went on, and one knows not whether most to deprecate Brown the destroyer, or to applaud Brown the creator. Certainly the fungoid growth of sham architectural ornament and sham ruins which preceded him, and which infected all Europe, could not be defended, for in France, in the palace gardens of Germany, and even in Italy the sham ruin sprang up and flourished and in some cases even now remains. Only one thing is worse than the sham ruin, and that is the real ruin or ancient stone monument torn up from its historical home, from monastic meadow or bare down, to make an 'interesting point of view' in a garden. There is a case in the home counties where the owner of a large property, when holding the office of governor of a tributary island, was presented with a prehistoric circle of stones. They were duly numbered and shipped to England and replanted on a hillock in this gentleman's park!*

Some such change as that which was effected by Kent and Brown and their followers was inevitable; but that the new gardens should be laid out in the new style is not so much a matter of regret as that the 'improver's desolating hand' should have fallen so heavily on the old ones, then in the beauty of maturity or early overgrowth. Many influences were pushing on the change. For one thing the old ways had become

*This may refer to Park Place, near Wargrave, where a circle of stones from Jersey was set up in the eighteenth century. The author lived near Wargrave as a child and had doubtless seen them. The reader interested in the vagaries of eighteenth-century taste may be referred to *The Picturesque* by Christopher Hussey, and *The Gothic Revival* by Kenneth Clark.

debased by the extravagances of fashion. The taste for the classical had killed the old pleached alley and arbour, and it was fashionable to ridicule in every way the older times and all that belonged to them. It was also felt that the great number of shrubs and plants that had been imported could not find a place in the smaller spaces of the old gardens, and that new methods, giving larger spaces, must be adopted for growing and enjoying them. In working this out it was discovered that a garden need not necessarily be cut off from the ground beyond by a stiff ledge or wall, and so the temptation to extend was increased, until the park and the distant country were included in the garden picture. The first attempt in the later practice to see beyond the garden had been by grilled openings in the walls, coinciding with the long park-avenues or with some desirable distant view. Many of these remain and are of excellent effect.

Brown was followed by Repton, a steadfast champion of his predecessor, but by no means blind to his defects. He was a man of strong sense and of much better taste and education, and though his practice was mainly in the new 'landscape' style, he regretted the destruction of the old avenues and gardens and even laid out some in the old formal way.

As the new system developed, its exponents, differing on many points, produced a critical and controversial literature whose tone makes it dull and profitless reading. Mr. Sedding states it well when he says:

'The writers of the new school of gardening, of which Repton is a notable personage in its later phase, are not, however, on a par with the writings of the old traditional school, either as pleasant garden literature, or in regard to broad human interest or artistic quality. They are hard and critical, and never lose the savour of the heated air of controversy in which they were penned—"I only sound the clarion," said the urbane master-gardener of an earlier day, "but I enter not into the battle." But these are at one another's throats! Who enters here must leave his dreams of fine gardening behind, for he will find himself in a chilly, disenchanted world, with nothing more romantic to feed his imagination upon than "remarks on the genius of the late Mr. Brown", critical inquiries, observations on taste, difference between landscape gardening and painting, Price upon Repton, Repton upon Price, Repton upon Knight, further answers to Messrs. Price and Knight, &c. But all this is desperately dull reading, hurtful to one's imagination, fatal to garden-fervour.'

Within the last few years just such another war of controversy has raged between the exponents of formal and the free styles of gardening, and again it is to be regretted that it has taken a somewhat bitter and almost personal tone. The formal army has hurled javelins poisoned with the damning epithet 'vulgar'; the free has responded with assegais imbued with an equally irritating 'ignorant'. Both are right, and both are wrong. The formal army are architects to a man; they are undoubtedly right in upholding the simple dignity and sweetness and quiet beauty of the old formal garden, but they parade its limitations as if they were the end of all art; they ignore the immense resources that are the precious possession of modern gardeners, and therefore offer no sort of encouragement to their utilisation. If for a moment they leave the safe harbourage of encircling Yew hedge, or let go the handrail of the balustrade, and venture for an excursion into the unknown country of horticulture, they exhibit the weakness of an army that is campaigning at too great a distance from its 'base', and certainly do expose themselves to the shaft of the enemy. They dismiss horticultural knowledge and practice with an airy wave of the hand, holding that the only business of the gardener is to produce so much material; they put him in a position of the brickmaker, or at best the builder—the modern builder, be it noted, who works absolutely to given plan, and can do nothing without precise detail on paper; they do not even concede him the position of the builder of old, to whom the architect gave broad directions, leaving it to his traditional knowledge and personal wit to accomplish the details that the master knew he would find rightly done. Moreover, they do not suggest who is to play the very needful part of artist-gardener—who shall say what is to be planted where, and why, and how. They rightly see the value of the old limitations; but were not these very limitations more a matter of passive safeguard than of active virtue? Give a student of painting three pigments only, and he cannot go far wrong in colour harmony. The old gardeners had confined spaces and small variety of material; even they went wrong when they attempted to increase their resources by means other than horticultural. And who shall say that we are not to extend our gardens, and use in them a right selection of the immense choice of flower, shrub, and tree now at our disposal, and so 'order' them that this beauty may be duly displayed and enjoyed? All who love gardens must value Messrs. Blomfield and Thomas's excellent and beautiful book, *The Formal Garden in England*; but those whose views are wider cannot accept their somewhat narrow gospel. Though true as far as it goes, it is not the whole truth, for do not they seem to mount a high pulpit and pontificate to this effect: 'There is no garden but the formal garden' and one almost hears them add: 'and I am his prophet!' But the book is delightful in itself, and powerful from the tone of genuine conviction in which it is penned. The free gardener will do well to keep it at hand as a wholesome corrective to the exuberance into which his vast resources are likely to tempt him, for the great abundance of material makes it difficult to select and classify and discriminate, and to practise the quiet reserve and dignity that must always mark good gardening. It is here that the work of the artist-gardener comes in. What he has to do is infinitely more difficult than the work of the formalist, because it involves at every point the quality that artists call 'drawing', which is something even more subtle than the equally necessary qualities of balance and proportion that are the chief aims of the garden architect.

The formalists are unjust when they assume that every path

''What is most to be desired in all decorative gardening is that it shall be fitting to its place. Every site, whether great or small, is capable of being suitably treated.'' A brick-paved area left to self-sown seedlings to create a flower picture.

A grass path in the wood, overhung with CISTUS LADANI FERUS

not in a straight line must therefore 'wriggle', and that any shaped or mounded ground must deserve such a term as an 'irrelevant hummock', or that, in general, gardening other than formal is 'vulgar'. It is not to be denied that there are wriggles and hummocks and vulgarities in plenty. The wavy ribbon border of five-and-twenty years ago, with pitiless lines of blue, red, and yellow, was the essence of vulgarity, and in the thousands of cases of mean gardens laid out by incompetent persons, or by the ordinary gardener, there are odious wriggles, and hummocks much worse than merely irrelevant. But it is unfair to assume that these are in obedience to the principles of the free school. On the contrary, it teaches us to form and respect large quiet spaces of lawn, unbroken by flower beds or any encumbrance; it teaches the simple grouping of noble types of hardy vegetation, whether their beauty be that of flower or foliage or general aspect. It insists on the importance of putting the right thing in the right place, a matter which involves both technical knowledge and artistic ability; it teaches us restraint and proportion in the matter of numbers or quantity, to use enough and not too much of any one thing at a time; to group plants in sequences of good colouring and with due regard to their form and stature and season of blooming, or of autumnal beauty of foliage. It teaches us to study the best means of treatment of different sites; to see how to join house to garden and garden to woodland. Repton says most truly: 'All rational improvement of grounds is necessarily founded on a due attention to the character and situation of the place to be improved; the former teaches us what is advisable, the latter what is possible to be done.' The more intolerant of the formalists insist on a clear division, either of wall or hedge, between garden and outer ground; but John Sedding, of wider views than his fellows, in his excellent book, *Garden-craft, Old and New*, advocates the passing of house, garden, and wild from one to the other by well-planned imperceptible gradation. On this he says:

"There is often a paved terrace or some kind of space, with seats either fixed or movable, where a door or French window gives access to the garden. It will probably have . . . steps down to the ground level. If the place is one of careful architecture there may be stone seats, or at least wooden ones, specially designed . . . If the paved terrace is of any width there will be worthy places for the grouping of plants . . . that will carry on a delightful sequence of flower beauty throughout the summer."

'It is of the utmost importance that art and nature should be linked together, alike in the near neighbourhood of the house, and in its far prospect, so that the scene, as it meets the eye, whether at a distance or near, should present a picture of a simple whole, in which each item should take its part without disturbing the individual expression of the ground. To attain this result, it is essential that the ground immediately about the house should be devoted to symmetrical planning, and to distinctly ornamental treatment; and the symmetry should break away by easy stages from the dressed to the undressed parts, and so on to the open country, beginning with wilder effects upon the country-boundaries of the place and more careful and intricate effects as the house is approached.'

The foremost exponent of the free school advocates the bringing up of the lawn without break of any kind to the house itself, at least on one side, but this treatment would seem to be less artistic than that described by Mr. Sedding.

About five-and-twenty years ago, when English gardening was mostly represented by the inane futilities of the 'bedding' system, with its wearisome repetitions and garish colouring, Mr. William Robinson chose as his work in life to make better known the treasures that were lying neglected, and at the same time to overthrow the feeble follies of the 'bedding' system. It is mainly owing to his unremitting labours that a clear knowledge of the world of hardy-plant beauty is now placed within easy reach of all who care to acquire it, and that the 'bedding' mania is virtually dead. Now, by easy reference to his practical books as an aid to personal industry, we may see how best to use and enjoy the thousands of beautiful plants that have been brought to us by the men who have given fortune, health, and often life in perilous travel that our gardens may be enriched and botanical knowledge extended. We cannot now, with all this treasure at our feet, neglect it and refuse it the gratefully appreciative use that it deserves. We cannot now go back a century or two and stop short at the art of the formal gardener any more than we can go back to the speech of our forefathers, beautiful though it was. There is change and growth in all

Attractive plantings for the shrubbery edge, showing Phloxes,
Acanthus, Megasea and Hydrangea

wholesome Art, and gardening at its best is a fine art. For ever true is what Bacon says: 'Men come to build stately sooner than to garden finely, as if gardening were the greater perfection.'

To borrow illustrations from other arts, the champions of the formal garden only would stop short at the music of Bach, which represented the widest scope and highest development of the art in his day. But since then instruments have grown in kind and in compass, and the range of possibilities in orchestral combination has widely increased, so that the music of to-day is no longer the music of Bach, nor restrained within the same limits. The pictorial art of Botticelli is everything that the architects claim for the formal garden; it is full of sweetness and beauty, full of limitations, frankly artificial, frankly artistic. But painting could not remain within the bounds that fenced the art of Botticelli, and a century later we have the work of the great Venetians, and again, in rather less than another hundred years, that of Velasquez and Rembrandt. So near to nature does Velasquez come that Ruskin says of his portraiture, 'He flings the man himself upon the canvas'; and yet so strong within him is the true artistic conscience, the knowledge of right and wrong, the consummate taste that cannot overstep lawful bounds, that his portraits, though perhaps the most absolutely lifelike that have ever been painted, are full of the noble dignity that can only be achieved within the unconscious restraints of the great style.

In one of the collects of the English Prayer Book occurs the magnificent phrase, 'whose service is perfect freedom'; a precious axiom in all religion, morality, and fine art—perfect freedom within certain bounds, liberty but not licence. So, claiming for gardening that it shall be ranked among the fine arts, its resources and its wide field must be free for the uses of the garden artist.

We have now the means of learning not only how to treat the home garden, but how to carry the planting of flowers into further spaces of field and woodland by the naturalisation of rightly chosen and rightly placed exotic plants. The daffodils of the Alps and the Pyrenees easily make themselves at home in our meadows and copses, and many a beautiful plant from North America and Northern Asia and the forest and mountain regions of Europe is not difficult to establish in suitable places. But wild gardening is by no means easy—indeed, it is a kind of pitfall in the path of the impulsive and unwary, for there are more ways of getting into trouble in this than in any other kind of ornamental cultivation.

Even in ordinary gardening there is almost too much to choose from. One of the modern French artists has described painting as *l'art des sacrifices*. The best free gardening is also an art demanding constant restraint and constant sacrifice, as well as the knowledge and keen discrimination that can choose, out of the now boundless wealth of form and colour, what will serve best to make the intended garden picture. It is not so easy to go wrong in the formal garden, because of its limitations, but even here the parterre may be filled with a vulgar and painful glare of clashing crudities such as were frequent in the worst days of 'bedding'. Still the scope for the masterly use of colour is greater in the free garden, and the opportunities are endless both for sober ranges of quiet harmonies and for rich pictures of culminating gorgeousness. Surely it is well that gardens should show as many beautiful kinds of treatment as possible; not that any one garden should try for all, but at least for some one or two pictures of lovely form or colour or delightful arrangement. After all, what is a garden for? It is for 'delight', for 'sweet solace', for 'the purest of all human pleasures; the greatest refreshment of the spirits of men'; it is to promote 'jucunditie of minde'; it is to 'call home over-wearied spirits'. So say the old writers, and we cannot amend their words, which will stand as long as there are gardens on earth and people to love them.

GARDEN DESIGN ON OLD-FASHIONED LINES

When considering the older gardens in relation to those of quite modern times we note that, except in special cases, they were much smaller in size, and for the most part closely walled or fenced. In the early Middle Ages the largest gardens were those attached to the religious houses, almost entirely for food production, with a few flowers only for ceremonial decoration. With few exceptions it is not till Tudor times that we know of gardens purely for pleasure, but then, with the new security of the country and the building of noble houses of the palatial, and many more of the manorial classes, the need was felt for gardens for delight, and every house must have its suitable accompaniment of flowers and blossoming shrubs and trees. The earlier gardens were nearly always of square form, and enclosed by wall or moat, for though the actual need of means of defence no longer existed, the feeling of a desire for safety and seclusion remained, and deer and wolves were still at large. Whether the house was large or small, it was usual to have a quiet forecourt between it and the road, with a paved path to the door passing between plots of grass to right and left, but without any special display of flowers; and perhaps no pleasanter way of access to a house has ever been devised. A large place would sometimes have two such forecourts, with a handsome gatehouse between the two. The flower garden was on the farther side of the house, with a wide terrace running close to the building and overlooking the parterre. It was usual for this garden to be on a level a few feet lower than that of the house, with either a central flight of steps or steps down at each end of the terrace. Later, in Stuart times, came ornaments in stone, marble, and lead. The lines of the garden were kept straight and orderly, and those gardens that remain or that have been designed with the same intention have a kind of homely dignity that accords well with our national character and our English landscape, as also with the houses to which they belong. Such gardens are specially suitable to the dignified style of building of the eighteenth century, when they had settled down into a character that may be described as having the qualities of sanity, serenity, and sobriety. For all good gardening has its foundation in common sense. The old designer accepted the conditions of the place, and moulded them to the most reasonable form; he avoided anything of strain or affectation, and drew no line that was not to some good purpose or definite intention. It is true that, when our gardening began in Tudor times, various accessories were employed that we should now consider frivolous and unworthy, such as gilded bird-cages and hanging objects of coloured glass to flash in the light. But as our gardening grew to more definite form these were cast aside, and our English garden went on its own quiet way, avoiding also in later times the lavish over-adornment of the French and the petty intricacies of the Dutch styles. It would be well in these days, when gardening possibilities are so vast and the designer may be tempted to run wild, that he should restrain himself and strive to regain the older simplicity and charm, remembering that the first purpose of a garden is to be a place of quiet beauty such as will give delight to the eye and repose and refreshment to the mind.

SOME DECORATIVE ASPECTS OF GARDENING

Sixty years ago decorative gardening was in the thraldom of the bedding system, and nothing else found favour. Its one aim was to make a bright display of tender flowers for three or four months of the year, and to ignore everything else. To make way for this, all other garden plants were sacrificed; the Peonies, Columbines and Pansies of May, the fragrant Pinks, the close-scented Gilliflowers and grandmotherly Roses of middle summer; the stately Lilies and all the rest of the old border plants were put aside for the sake of the short-lived tender flowers. The system had its uses, for it satisfied a certain class of lowly aspiration, and had it been practised in the light of modern taste and knowledge might have produced much better effect; but, as the arrangement was generally left to the gardener, who naturally had no definite intention except that of making as bright a show as possible, the result was an incongruous medley of unrelated and often discordant colour.

Now that we have learnt better ways it is of some interest, to anyone old enough to have lived in those days, to look back upon the attitude of mind which would appear to have been one of contentment and self-satisfaction; the method was accepted as the most desirable form of gardening, and nothing further was wished for. My own young days were passed in a place where, on the south-east side of the house, was a garden of three concentric rings of beds in turf, each four feet wide, all filled alike with the same scarlet geranium. In the centre was a round bed of the same with a stone tazza holding a variegated Agave. On the north-west side, facing the series of one large and two smaller drawing-rooms, was another garden, of quite passable formal design, on gravel with Box-edged beds, with a central ornament of a fountain, whose jet rose from another stone tazza of the same design, rising from a wide circular basin. The beds were filled with the usual tender plants of red, yellow and blue without any kind of definite arrangement as to colour. Close against the house were a quantity of flowers in pots, for the building was one of Italian design with a high colonnade on each front, standing on a five-feet wide paving of Portland stone. Between the windows, plants in pots were grouped—Lilies, fancy Geraniums, Petunias, delicate Ferns and tall plants of the sweet-smelling Humea; just anything that was in flower, and again without any thought of arrangement except as to the height of the plants. It all had a kind of pleasant and cheerful brightness, and was much admired, but, looking back, one grieves at the thought of how much better it might have been, if only the thousands of good plants, all admirably grown, had been differently and more intelligently disposed.

There is no occasion to condemn the parterre of summer

flowers; for though there was no such excuse in the case of the garden just mentioned, as it was the one home of the family for nearly the whole year, yet often it is rightly employed, as in the case of the larger country house that is only occupied during the few weeks that come between the end of the London season and the early autumn departure to the moors of the north, or the yachting cruise in southern waters. But there is no reason why the formal parterre should not be beautifully planted, for it has been done, and with our better modern knowledge it can be as well arranged, both for colour and habit of plant, as any other part of the garden. It is true that we have now a much larger number of plants to choose from, but, even if we were restricted to those that were in common use half a century ago, it could still be made beautiful and enjoyable in ways that were never then thought of. It should be remembered that it was not the fault of the plants themselves, for they are still indispensable, and, though with some people there has been so great a revulsion of feeling from the old methods that the innocent plants have been included in their condemnation, yet this is unjust, and the injustice should be atoned for by a careful study of how to use them worthily and well.

There is often a paved terrace or some kind of space, with seats either fixed or movable, where a door or French window gives access to the garden. It will probably have a low balustrade and steps down to the ground level. If the place is one of careful architecture there may be stone seats, or at least wooden ones, specially designed. But though stone seats uncushioned are barely admissible in our climate, yet it may be remembered that in passing to the garden, and especially in returning from the garden to the house, in nine times out of ten at least, it will be the eye only that will repose upon them. And in hottest summer, when they will be actually in use, it is easy to provide such cushions for seat and back and some beautiful mat of oriental weave of quiet colouring for the feet, as may ensure complete and wholesome comfort.

If the paved terrace is of any width there will be worthy places for the grouping of plants in pots; just such plants, only better arranged, as were placed haphazard under the colonnaded spaces of my youth. Bedding and fancy Pelargoniums are now in so many fine varieties that it is easy to make a choice of some two or three kinds whose colours tone well together. Then there are Lilies of several kinds, the most useful being *L. longiflorum* and the varieties of *L. speciosum.* These alone are delightful with Ferns and Funkias and any other green foliage. There are also the graceful, nearly hardy, red and white Fuchsias; and a number of annual and biennial plants will give an ample selection that, by the skill of the gardener in producing and the educated taste of the owner in arranging, will carry on a delightful sequence of flower beauty throughout the summer.

Where there is a conservatory, or any kind of spacious flower room adjoining the house, it is seldom that one sees it made really useful and enjoyable, though this can be done by judicious arrangement. A comfortable bench for sitting should be on the house side, or, better still, if there should be a walled angle, there might be a seat of semicircular or segmental plan. Here, there should be a good clear paved space, enough for a tea-table and several chairs. The usual shelf all round the outside showing the hot-water pipes underneath would be abolished and in front of the pipes and up to their height some rough stone walling will be raised. From near the top of this the ground slopes down to the pavement, and ranges of rough stones run down with it diagonally. These ranges of stones are double, leaving space between for dropping in pots of flowering plants. This opening widens towards the top to allow of a thicker grouping of the pot plants. All the ground in between is a carpet of growing Ferns and Selaginella and anything suitable of neat permanent foliage. A certain number of larger things, such as Hedychiums and Daturas, are planted out, and others that are impatient of pot restraint, such as the sweet

Indian Daphne and the sweet-scented and beautiful Luculia, so seldom seen in good order, because it needs this freedom of root run. The uppermost rocky ridge in places passes right over the pipes, which are entirely concealed. An iron tank is let into the ground for dipping, or a cemented tank is built. Flat stones cover the edges and a rocky bank full of Ferns rises steeply at the back. A way is made through this for the passage of a little alpine torrent, fed by a rain-water pipe outside, whenever rain is falling, or by a supply from a hidden reservoir. It all has to be done to a definite plan, according to the size and shape of the room and the point of view from the resting place, but when cleverly contrived the whole effect is incomparably more pleasing than that of the usual conservatory. It is just the difference between the usual show place to be walked through, and one of complete contentment; of rest and refreshment to eye and mind, where one lingers long, and that one leaves unwillingly.

When a small house of a good type, such as was built in the latter half of the eighteenth century and early in the nineteenth, stands a little way back from the road on the outskirts of a country town, it is usual for the entrance to be through a door into a walled forecourt. A house of this kind, although not large, often has a quiet dignity of its own, and deserves that its approach should have something of the same character. A good plan in such a case is to have a flagged path from the road door to the house entrance with plain unbroken turf on each side, and to keep any planting, and that of a quiet green character, against the side walls, with, perhaps, only a few white Lilies or one or two China Roses, but to avoid anything of strong colour. To come into such a forecourt, passing directly from a busy street or more or less populous road, is like stepping into another world—a comforting world of sympathetic restfulness that shuts out all bustle and hurry, and induces a sense of repose and invigorating refreshment. It is in the sunny garden on the other side of the house that there will be the brightest bloom and the sweetest scents and all the best things with which a living garden, sensibly planned and carefully tended, will repay its thankful owner.

When the better influences were at work to make us see the errors and deficiencies of the worst days of the bedding system, it was not a matter of destruction of the old ideals only, but a happy substitution of something saner and more satisfying; something of living hope and joy, a restitution of all that was best in the older gardening with its scope ever widening as year by year more and more plants were introduced from all the world's temperate regions—from the European Alps, the Cape, the Himalayas, the mountains of Western China, the uplands of South America and other hitherto untapped sources. Raisers of plants and seeds got to work to improve what were already known, and travellers engaged by enterprising firms to secure new species suitable for garden use.

Now that we have a very large number of plants to choose from for every kind of garden purpose, attention is being directed to the best ways of employing them. Among the later developments of horticultural practice the careful study of colour effects is receiving the attention it so well deserves. In the case of what are commonly known as herbaceous borders, these are being arranged, not as of old, with single plants in a haphazard way, but with definite intention directed to the forming of a picture of garden beauty and glory. Flowers of delicate cool tints strengthen gradually into warmer, and these lead to a gorgeous mass of richly related colour; after this, again returning to the cooler and quieter.

It is not in the mixed border only that this careful consideration for colour effect is practised, it is equally applicable to the formal parterre. A notable example comes to mind in the case of a great house in the Midlands. On its southern side is a large parterre in a fine design of Italian character. It was planted in one class of colour only—yellow, orange, mahogany and deep red; the paler colours were in the outer portions, while in the intermediate regions colours of medium strength played about together leading gradually to the richly resplendent tones in the centre. The whole effect was one of easy cohesion, but it was also a glorious harmony, reminding one of the works of the great Masters of the Venetian School, a worthy and dignified decoration in close connection with one of the noble buildings of the Early Renaissance in England.

To what extent it is desirable to have climbing plants on house walls is a question that often arises. In the case of many houses, either of mean or of over-pretentious architecture, the more they are covered up the better; for if their designer has left a building that can only be considered to be in bad taste, it behoves the gardener to do what he can to give it decent clothing, if only of Ivy or a rampant growing Ampelopsis, either of which will save him the trouble of training. But in the case of a good building, though a carefully and duly restrained planting of its walls may give it an added grace, great care should be taken that nothing essential be hidden. Many a noble building has been shamefully buried under Ivy; moulded doors and windows have been reduced to dark holes; beautifully wrought pinnacles look like nothing but May-Day Jacks-in-the-green; buttresses have become shapeless green humps; the whole wall face has lost every feature of plinth, string course and detail of good masonry. Better taste and knowledge are now remedying this desecration of worthy architecture and some of the grandest monuments of the past centuries have lately been relieved of their encumbrances of rampant vegetation. But there are some plants that are singularly sympathetic to good buildings. Many a fine house of the eighteenth century is well graced by the noble foliage of a properly placed Magnolia. Such a house usually has a lesser wing of offices adjoining the main front, but set a little back. Here is the place for this shrub of monumental effect, with its large, lustrous leaves and ivory cups of bloom. And a Wistaria judiciously placed, carefully trained and restricted to a few level lines, is often helpful, and very beautiful with its clear-cut foliage and drooping clusters of light purple bloom.

Against the foot of a house there is commonly a few feet of planting space where, only too often, one may see a weak, temporary show of wallflowers, or whatever it may be. The house foot deserves something better than this, something that is more in accord with its own strength and solidity. If there is a distinct plinth this should not be obliterated, but the border will at least allow of a main planting that has some suggestion of permanence, such as bushy growths of Rosemary and Lavender and other small shrubs; also of the ever-blooming pink China Roses that are so pleasant to see from inside the house as well as from out.

It is not every house that needs a flower garden brought close up to its front. There are dwellings that once were monastic houses or places of study or learning that are best approached by unbroken lawns and groves of trees only. Their ancient character, grave and quiet, telling of centuries of devotion or the studious gaining of knowledge, seems to forbid the near display of coloured flowers. Where such buildings have become modern habitations the flower garden is best kept at a little distance, or in some way so arranged that it is not seen in close connection with the house.

There are some places, unfortunately, only too many, where there were once wide clear sweeps of ancient lawn, beautiful and restful in themselves, that have been sadly spoilt by the intrusion of specimen conifers. It was tempting to plant them, when about fifty years ago they were first brought to England, especially as a young conifer has a certain attractive trimness that commends it to favour. But it is sad to see in what one remembers as a beautiful widespread lawn, already sufficiently furnished with noble cedars and other large surrounding trees, a miscellaneous collection of these conifers, one each of perhaps a dozen kinds, now of forty years' growth and almost meeting and obstructing the garden prospect in every direction. If only they had been given some near spaces of parkland, with time to see how they would develop, they would by now have been well-grown trees of value as specimens for botanical observation.

There are gardens where the original plan has got entirely out of shape; either by the overgrowth of trees or shrubs that were rightly placed when originally planted, or by repeated renewals of bordering material, or by a rather reckless use of the edging tool where lawn meets path. This overgrowth into shapelessness is especially apparent in the case of old gardens in which topiary work formed an important part of the design. Yews that formerly made trim hedges have shot up into tall trees and old topiary forms, even where the shears have not ceased work for centuries, have got out of hand and now show as unmeaning shapes such as could not possibly have been intended by the designer. Paths out of line are easily put right, but one hesitates about meddling with the old clipped work, however much it may have become distorted. It is better to accept it and make the best of it as it is.

What is most to be desired in all decorative gardening is that it shall be fitting to its place. Every site, whether great or small, is capable of being suitably treated. The double strip of flower border from the road to the cottage door is absolutely right, and is often a useful lesson to gardens of some pretension. In the case of houses newly built the garden must closely agree with the style of the house. The designer will follow the architect, accepting from him any main lines he may wish to establish close to the building. It does not often happen, but it is a happy occasion for the one who is to plan the garden when the south or west side of the house, where the main show of flowers is to be, faces rising ground. It is an opportunity for having that beautiful feature of successive flights of steps, seen one above another, giving access to parallel ranges of terraces, with a higher background of dark shrub and tree; beginning at the lowest level with a double flight of half-circular balustraded

A corner of an early summer border, showing Lupins and
IRIS PALLIDA DALMATICA

stairs. The space between these stairs would be paved and have some important sculptured ornament, or a wall fountain and basin or some such decorative treatment.

Even in London there are many opportunities for ornamental gardening—opportunities that have been almost entirely neglected. Nothing is more usual in a London house than that the back room on the drawing-room floor should look into nothing better than a dingy well between sooty walls. The prospect is so uninviting that the window is commonly screened by curtains, or, at best, by a few plants in pots. But such a place, intelligently planned, may be made into something delightful to look at from both the ground and the first floor. Then it is well to consider that, in days of increasing noise and disturbance from street traffic, these back-facing rooms have become the only places of refuge from the outer turmoil, and anything that will give them a pleasant outlook, with the light undimmed, is all the more to be desired and valued. Ways of planning will depend on structural capability, but even in the most difficult cases there will be found some way of bettering the prospect, while in the greater number some kind of pretty garden may be achieved. A few square yards of paving, with borders next the walls, raised a few inches and supported and edged by a boldly moulded stone kerb, may have a planted setting of some of the hardy Ferns and other foliage plants that will endure town conditions. Flowering plants bought in the market or from the coster's barrow are dropped in between and renewed when their beauty is past. At the far end, bounding the view from the windows, there would be some distinct ornament, a raised vase or a *corbeille* of flowers, or the return of the border itself rising in two shaped tiers, or at best a well-designed wall fountain and basin. Figs, Vines and Virginia Creeper all do well in London, and would provide ample wall covering.

There is a matter that is often neglected in gardens, but that deserves careful attention, namely, the colour of the paint used

"The great abundance of material makes it difficult to select and classify and discriminate, and to practise the quiet reserve and dignity that must always mark good gardening. It is here that the work of the artist-gardener comes in."

for any of the several necessary structures or accessories—greenhouses, doors, gates, railings, plant tubs or whatever else may be visible. Many a pretty garden scene in small places is spoilt by the unwelcome intrusion and insistence of the white-painted greenhouse, whereas if the outside paintwork was of some quiet colour, preferably something near what house-painters know as Portland stone colour, it would be unobtrusive. This would not prevent the inside being white in order to preserve light. We all know the well-made wooden seat, startlingly white, that quite unduly dominates the whole garden picture. It is often placed at the end of a wide turf path that has flower borders on each side; the eye longs to look to right and left to enjoy the flowers, but is constantly attracted by the tyrannical seat. It is comforting to know that there is a resting place at the end of the pleasant flower pilgrimage, but it should not be allowed to glare and insist on attracting attention; moreover, its prominence is all the more startling because it is usually backed by dark foliage. Oak, unpainted, weathers to a beautiful cool grey colour, and many a grey tree trunk suggests a suitable tint for the paintwork of seats or doors or railings. Tubs that hold Agapanthus or other plants, or shaped evergreens, are often painted a rather harsh green, and the hoops are carefully picked out with a pitiless black. It is well to remember that any kind of green paint that comes near foliage should be of a less positive colour than the leaves of the plant, or the plant must suffer by the comparison. And there is no need to paint the hoops black; it is better to paint it all out of one pot.

III

SOME PROBLEMS OF GARDEN PLANNING

FORMAL GARDENS

TERRACED GARDENS

THE PERGOLA IN ENGLISH GARDENS, ITS MAKING
AND PLANTING

Journal of the Royal Horticultural Society, vol. xxvii, 1902

Of the 'free school' of gardening, Gertrude Jekyll wrote: "It teaches the simple grouping of noble types of hardy vegetation, whether their beauty be that of flower or foliage or general aspect. It insists on the importance of putting the right thing in the right place, a matter which involves both technical knowledge and artistic ability; it teaches us restraint and proportion in the matter of numbers or quantity, to use enough and not too much of any one thing at a time; to group plants in sequences of good colouring and with due regard to their form and stature and season of blooming, or of autumnal beauty of foliage. It teaches us to study the best means of treatment of different sites; to see how to join house to garden and garden to woodland."

III

Some Problems of Garden Planning

FORMAL GARDENS

WHENEVER I HAVE seen the large formal gardens attached to important houses of the Palladian type that are so numerous throughout England, I have always been struck by their almost invariable lack of interest and want of any real beauty or power of giving happiness. For at the risk of becoming wearisome by a frequent reiteration of my creed in gardening, I venture to repeat that I hold the firm belief that the purpose of a garden is to give happiness and repose of mind, firstly and above all other considerations, and to give it through the representation of the best kinds of pictorial beauty of flower and foliage that can be combined or invented. And I think few people will deny that this kind of happiness is much more often enjoyed in the contemplation of the homely border of hardy flowers than in any of these great gardens, where the flowers lose their attractive identity and with it their hold of the human heart, and have to take a lower rank as mere masses of colour filling so many square yards of space. Gardens of this kind are only redeemed when some master-mind, accepting the conditions of the place as they are, decides on treating it in some bold way, either in one grand scheme of colour harmony or as an exposition of that principle combined with the display of magnificent foliage masses, or by some other such means as may raise it above the usual dull, dead level.

And seeing how many gardens there still are of this type, I

A stone bed in the forecourt, with Cannas and Geraniums

scarcely wonder that our great champion of hardy flowers*
should put himself into an attitude of general condemnation of
the system, though I always regret that it should include
denunciation of all architectural accessories.

For if one has seen the old gardens of the Italian Renaissance, and the colossal remains of their forerunners of still
greater antiquity, one can hardly fail to be impressed with the
unbounded possibilities that they suggest to a mind that is
equally in sympathy with beautiful plant-life and with the
noble and poetical dignity of the most refined architecture—
possibilities that are entirely disregarded in our expanses of formal bedded gardens with their steep or mean flights of steps, bad-
ly designed balustrades, and weary acreages of gravelled paths.

I always suppose that these great wide dull gardens,
sprawling over much too large a space, are merely an out-
growth of plan drawing. The designer sitting over his sheet of
paper has it within such easy view on the small scale; and
though he lays out the ground in correct proportion with the
block plan of the house and is therefore right in a way, yet no
human eye can ever see it from that point of view, and as for
its use in promoting any kind of human happiness, it can only
be classed among those comfortless considerations that perplex
and worry the mind with the feeling that they are too much and
yet not enough.

For the formal garden of the best type I can picture to myself
endless possibilities both of beauty and delight, for though my
own limited means have in a way obliged me to practise only
the free and less costly ways of gardening, such as give the
greatest happiness for the least expenditure, and are therefore
the wisest ways for most people to walk in, yet I also have
much pleasure in formal gardens of the best kinds. But it must
be nothing less than the very best, and it is necessarily extremely costly, because it must entail much building beautifully
designed and wrought. It must also have an unbounded supply

* William Robinson of Gravetye.

of water, for so only could one work out all the best possibilities of such a garden.

There seems to me to be a whole mine of wealth waiting to be worked for the benefit of such gardens, for as far as I am aware, what might now be done has never been even attempted with any degree of careful or serious study. When we think of the very few plants known for garden use to the ancients and to those who built and planted the noble gardens of the Italian Renaissance, and when we compare this limited number with the vast range of beautiful shrubs and plants we now have to choose from, we cannot help seeing how much wider is the scope for keen and critical discrimination. And though some of the plants most anciently in cultivation, such as Rose, Violet, Iris, Poppy and Jasmine, are still among the best, yet we are no longer tied to these and a few others only.

The great quantity we have now to choose from is in itself a danger, for in the best and most refined kinds of formal gardening one is more than ever bound to the practice of the most severe restraint in the choice of kinds, and to accept nothing that does not in its own place and way satisfy the critical soul with the serene contentment of an absolute conviction.

I propose to give presently one example of a small portion of a formal garden such as I hold to be of the most pleasant and desirable kind and such as would present somewhat of the aspect and fill the mind with somewhat of the sentiment of those good old gardens of Italy. And though the initial expense would be heavy—for in work of this kind the artist's design must be carried out to the smallest detail, without skimping or screwing or the usual disastrous necessities of lopping or compromise that so often mar good work—yet the whole would be so solid and permanent that the cost of its after-maintenance would be small out of all proportion with that of the usual large gardens.

These always seem to me as if purposely designed to bind upon the shoulders of their owners the ever-living burden of the most costly and wasteful kind of effort in the trim keeping of turf and Box edging and gravelled walks, with the accompanying and unavoidable vexatious noises of rumbling roar of mowing machine, clicking of shears and clanking grind of iron roller. In the chief portions or courts of my formal garden all this fidgety labour and worry of ugly noise would be unknown, and the only sounds of its own need or making would be the soothing and ever delightful music of falling and running water.

Thoughts of this kind have come to me all the more vividly within the last year or two, when I have seen in the gardens of friends the beautifully coloured forms of the newer Water Lilies. Lovely as these are in artificial pools or in natural ponds and quiet back-waters, it has struck me that they would be still more beautiful, or rather that their beauty could be made still more enjoyable, by their use in a four-square tank in the Water Lily court of a formal garden; one's mind all the more readily inviting the connection because of the recollection of the *nymphaeum* of the ancient Roman garden, of tank or canal form, with stone-paved walk shaded by a pillared portico, and of *Nymphaea*, the botanical name of the Water Lily.

There is a perfectly well-dressed look about these Lilies, with their large leaves of simplest design, that would exactly accord with masonry of the highest refinement, and with the feeling of repose that is suggested by a surface of still water.

All gardening in which water plays an important part implies a change of level in the ground to be dealt with. I am supposing a place where ground slopes away from the house so that it demands some kind of terraced treatment. First there would be the space next to the house, its breadth having due relation to the height of the building. From this space a flight of easy steps would descend to the Water Lily court landing on a wide flagged path that passes all round the tank. On all four sides there are also steps leading down from the path into the water. I cannot say why it is, but have always observed that a beautiful effect is gained by steps leading actually into water; in this case I would have the lowest of the three or four actually below the water-line. Although steps are in the first instance intended for the human foot, yet we have become so well accustomed to the idea of them as easy means of access from one level to another that in many cases they are also desirable as an aid to the eye, and in such a place as I think of the easy lines of shallow steps from the level of the path to that of the water surface and below it would, I consider, be preferable to any raised edging such as is more usually seen round built tanks; it would give the eye the pleasant feeling of being invited to contemplate the Lilies at its utmost ease, instead of the idea of being cut off from them by a raised barrier.

In this kind of impression I am supported by the recollection of an incident in connection with a very happy task I once had of designing and embroidering some satin coverings for chairs that stood in the stair-hall of the late Lord Leighton. When I pointed out that the delicate embroidery in colour silks was not suited for bearing the usual treatment of a chair-seat, he gave me the comforting answer: 'Never mind, nothing but my eye will ever sit upon those chairs.'

On the sides of the path away from the tank there is a slightly raised edge enclosing a flower border not more than three feet wide, backed by the wall that bounds the whole area of the court. But on the three sides to right and left, and across the tank as you stand on the main flight of steps, the wall, midway in each space, falls back into a half-round niche. The niche across the tank is filled with Cannas; the old taller kinds at the back for stately stature and nobility of large leafage; the smaller ones of lower habit and larger bloom being planted towards the front. Coming down the steps you see the level lines of water surface jewelled with the lovely floating blooms of white and pink and tender rose colour; the steps into the tank on the near and far sides still further insisting on the repose of the level line. The eye and mind are thus in the best state of

preparation for enjoying the bold uprightness of growth of the
Cannas. In the narrower flower borders I would have Lilies,
and plants mostly of Lily-like character; Crinums and Funkias,
and of true Lilies a limited number of kinds—the noble white
Lily, *L. Harrisii*, *L. longiflorum*, *L. Brownii*, and white and
rosy forms of *L. speciosum*. These would grow out of groups
of the beautiful pale-foliaged *Funkia grandiflora* and of the
tender green of Lady Fern and of Hart's-tongue.

I would not let the walls be too much covered with creepers;
for I hold that wherever delicate architecture marries with
gardening, the growing things should never over-run or
smother the masonry; but in the Lily court I would have some
such light-running creeping things as can be easily led and
trained within bounds, such as *Clematis Flammula*, blue
Passion Flower, and if climate allows, *Rhodochiton volubile*,
Cobaea scandens and *Solanum jasminoides*. These would be
quite enough and perhaps even too many.

The half-round niches to right and left are partly occupied
by small basins into which water falls through a sculptured
inlet from a height of some feet; from these it runs under the
pathway into the tank. Two overflows pass underground from
this to right and left of the Canna niche and are led out again
below the semicircular stairway to make two little rippling
rills by the sides of the flight of straight steps below.

The border spaces at the angles of the tank would have
slightly raised edges matching the edging on the wall sides of
the path, and would be planted with dwarf flowering Cannas
mostly of one kind and colour. The wall would be about eight
feet high, and as groves of beautiful trees would be in their near
neighbourhood I should wish that any foliage that could be
seen from within the court should be that of Ilex.

Had I ever had occasion to design a garden in what I should
consider the most reasonable interpretation of the good Italian
style, I should have been sparing in the use of such walled
courts, keeping them and the main stairways for the important

and mid-most part of the design, whether it was placed on the next level below the house or, as in the case I am contemplating, at a right angle to it and coming straight down the face of the hill. In this case, wherever flights of steps occurred there would be banks of green shrubs or trees stretching away to right and left, and below them long level spaces of grass. Then where the next descent came there would be perhaps a bank of Cistus and free-growing Roses; never, *never* sharply sloping banks of turf. I always try to avoid the spirit of intolerance in anything, but for these turf banks, so frequent in gardens, I can only feel a distinct aversion. Did such a turf bank ever give anyone the slightest happiness? Did anyone ever think it beautiful? The first of these right and left spaces on the level of the Lily court would no doubt be bounded on the lower side by a wall and balustrade, but as the scheme descended towards the lowest level the architectural features would diminish, so that they would end in a flagged walk only with steps where needful. But the treatment of this would depend on what was below. If it were all pleasure garden or if there were a river or lake, the architectural refinements would be continued though not obtruded; if it were a kitchen garden, it would be approached by perhaps a simple walled enclosure for Vines and Figs, the paved walk passing between two green spaces, in the centre of each of which would stand a Mulberry tree.

On the upper levelled spaces right and left, the formal feeling would merge into the free, for there is no reason why the two should not be combined; and in one level at least the green expanse should be seen from end to end, the flagged path only passing across it. And all the way down there would be the living water, rippling, rushing and falling. Open channels in which it flowed with any considerable fall would be built in little steps or be so transversely corrugated at the bottom as to oblige the water to make its rippling music; and in the same way throughout the whole garden every point would be studied, so as to lose sight of no means, however trifling, of catching and guiding any local matter or attribute, of quality or circumstance, that could possibly be turned to account for the increase of the beauty and interest and delightfulness of the garden. One wants to see one beautiful picture at a time, not a muddle of means and material that properly sorted and disposed might compose a dozen. I do not say that it is easy; on the contrary it wants a good deal of the knowledge that only comes of many forms of study and labour and effort. But the grand plants are now so numerous and so easily accessible that we should consider all ways of using them worthily. As far as I understand the needs of such a garden as I have sketched, with a nucleus or backbone of pure formality, how grandly one could use all the best plants. How, descending the slope, at every fresh landing some new form of plant beauty would be displayed; how, coming up from below, the ascent of, say, a hundred feet, instead of being a toil would be a progress of pleasure, by the help of the smooth flagged path and the wide flights of easy steps. For every step in the garden would be nearly two feet broad and never more than five inches high, no matter how steep the incline. If ground falls so rapidly that steps of such a gradient cannot be carried straight up and down, we build a bold landing and carry the steps in a double flight right and left, and then land again, and come down to the next level with another flight. Then we find what a nice square space is left below for a basin and a splash of water, or some handsome group of plants, or both, and that the whole scheme has gained by the alteration in treatment that the form of the ground made expedient. Then there are frequent seats so placed as best to give rest to the pilgrim and display the garden picture. Where the lower flights of steps occur we are passing through woodland, with a not very wide space between the edge of the wood and the wide paved way, here unbounded by any edging. Here we have in widespread groups plants of rather large stature; Bamboos and the great Knotweeds of Japan, and Tritomas and the Giant Reeds and Grasses Arundo,

Gynerium and Eulalia, and between them the running water, no longer confined in built channels, but running free in shallow pebbly rills. Here we have also other large-leaved plants—the immense Gunneras, the native Butter-bur, the North American Rodgersia, all happy on the lower, cooler levels and gentle slopes, watered by the rill and half shaded by the nearer trees. As the path rises, it comes clear of the wood and the garden spreads out right and left in the lower levels of its terraced spaces. One of these, perhaps the lowest, I should be disposed to plant with Bamboos on both sides of a broad green path.

As the paved path mounts, the architectural features become more pronounced; the steps that were quite plain below have a slight undercutting of the lower part of the front; a little higher and this becomes a fully moulded feature with a distinct shadow accentuating the overhanging front edge of the step, and so by an insensible gradation we arrive at the full-dress of the Lily court and terrace above.

In so slight a sketch as this one cannot attempt to describe in detail all the beautiful ways of using such good things as Roses and Clematis (among hosts of others) that such a garden suggests. But it is perhaps in gardens of formal structure that some of their many uses may best be seen. For the long straight line of the coping of a parapet may be redeemed from monotony by a leaping wave-mass of a free-growing Rose, with its spray showers of clustered bloom; and the tender grace of the best of the small white-bloomed Clematises of spring and autumn, is never seen to better advantage than when wreathing and decorating but not hiding or overwhelming the well-wrought stonework that bounds the terrace and crowns its retaining wall.

TERRACED GARDENS

Many a garden has to be made on a hillside more or less steep. The conditions of such a site naturally suggest some form of terracing, and in connection with a house of modest size and kind, nothing is prettier or pleasanter than all the various ways of terraced treatment that may be practised with the help of dry-walling, that is to say rough wall building without mortar, especially where a suitable kind of stone can be had locally.

It always seems to me important in sharply sloping ground to keep the paths as nearly level as may be, whether they are in straight lines or whether they curve in following the natural contour of the ground. Many more beautiful garden pictures may be made by variety in planting even quite straightly terraced spaces than at first appears possible, and the frequent flights of steps, always beautiful if easy and well proportioned, will be of the greatest value. In this kind of rough terracing the almost invariable fault is that the steps are made too steep and too narrow in the tread. In my own practice the steps are so easy that one can run up and down them. There is no reason or excuse for the steep, ugly and even dangerous steps one so often sees, because space for them can be cut away above, and they can also be carried out free between flower borders beyond the face of the wall below. If for any reason this is difficult or inexpedient, a landing can be built out, and the steps carried down sideways instead of up and down the face of the hill. In fact there is no end to the pretty and interesting ways of using such walling and such groups of steps.

Where the stairway cuts through the bank it is lined on each side by the dry-walling and the whole structure becomes a garden of delightful small things. Little Ferns are planted in the joints on the shadier side as the wall goes up, and numbers of small Saxifrages and Stonecrops, Pennywort and Erinus, Corydalis and Sandwort. And then there will be hanging sheets of Aubrietia and Rock Pinks and Cerastium, and many another pretty plant that finds a happy home in the cool shelter of the rocky joint. In some regions of the walling, Wall-flowers and Snapdragons and plants of Thrift are established, and as they ripen their seed it drifts into the openings of other joints, and the seedlings send their roots deep into the bank and along the cool backs of the stones, and make plants of surprising health and vigour, that are longer lived than the softer-grown plants in the rich flower borders.

I doubt if there is any way in which a good quantity of plants, and of bushes of modern size, can be so well seen and enjoyed as in one of these roughly terraced gardens, for one sees them up and down and in all sorts of ways, and one has a chance of seeing many lovely things clear against the sky, and of perhaps catching some sweetly scented tiny thing like *Dianthus fragrans* at exactly nose-height, and eye-level, and so of enjoying its tender beauty and powerful fragrance in a way that one had never before found possible.

The beautiful details of structure and marking in such plants as the silvery Saxifrages can never be so well seen as in a wall at the level of the eye or just above or below it, and plain to see are all their pretty ways of seating themselves on projections or nestling into hollows, or creeping over stony surface as does the Balearic Sandwort, or standing like Erinus with its back pressed to the wall in an attitude of soldier-like bolt-uprightness.

In place of all this easily attained prettiness how many gardens on sloping grounds are disfigured by profitless and quite indefensible steep banks of mown grass! It seems to me that nothing can be so undesirable in a garden. They are unbeautiful, troublesome to mow and wasteful of spaces that might be full of interest. If there must be a sloping space, and if for any reason there cannot be a dry wall, it is better to plant the slope with low bushy or rambling things; with creeping Cotoneaster, or Japan Honeysuckle, or Ivies, or with such bushes as Savin, *Pyrus japonica*, Cistus or Berberis, or if it is on a larger scale, with the free-growing rambling Roses and double flowered Brambles. I name these things in preference to the rather overdone Periwinkle and St. John's Wort, because Periwinkle is troublesome to weed and soon grows into undesirably tight masses, and the large-flowered Hypericum, though sometimes of good effect, is extremely monotonous in large masses by itself, and is so ground-greedy that it allows of no companionship.

There is another great advantage to be gained by the use of the terrace walls; this is the display of many shrubs as well as plants that will hang over and throw their flowering sprays all over the face of the wall. In arranging such a garden, I like to have a rather narrow border at the foot of each wall. If the whole width of the terrace is eighteen feet I would have the border at the foot of the wall not more than four feet wide, so as to be near it and near all the pretty things in its face and top. Then there would be the paths, six feet wide, and then the wider border, planted with bushy things towards its outer edge, which will be the top of the wall of thé next terrace below. These would be mostly bushes of moderate growth, such as Lavender, Rosemary, Berberis and *Pyrus japonica*, with all the things I could think of for partly hanging over the face of the wall. Among them would be *Forsythia suspensa*, *Phlomis fruticosa* (Jerusalem Sage), the Common Barberry, so beautiful with its coral-like masses of fruit in October, and its half-weeping habit of growth and its way of disposing its branches in pictorial masses. There would also be *Desmodium penduliflorum* and Leycesteria, and above all the many kinds of Roses that grow and flower so kindly in such a position. I never knew till I tried how well many sorts of Roses will tumble over walls and flower in profusion. *Rosa lucida* and Scotch Briars come over a wall nearly five feet high and flower within a foot of the ground; *Rosa Wichuraiana* comes over in a curtain of delicate white bloom and polished leafage. My Capri Rose, a neat and pretty form of *R. sempervirens*, in leaf and habit not unlike *Wichuraiana* but always more shy of flower, hangs over in masses, and in warm exposures flowers more freely than on the flat. If I had to clothe the face of a wall twelve feet high with hanging wreaths of flowering Roses, I should plant at the top a garden form I have of *R. arvensis*, that came originally I know not whence, and that will climb and ramble either up or down or through other bushes to almost any extent. I know it as the Kitchen Rose, because my oldest plant rambles over and through some Arbor-vitæ just opposite the kitchen window of the little cottage that I lived in for two years. When it is in flower the mass of white bloom throws a distinctly appreciable light into the kitchen.

In making the dry-walling the stones should all tip a little downwards at the back and the whole face of the wall should incline slightly backwards; so that no drop of rain is lost, but all runs into the joints. Any loose earth at the back of the stones must be closely rammed; if this is done there is no danger of the wall bursting outward and coming down when there is heavy rain. Any space backward of newly moved earth behind the wall must also be rammed and made firm in the same way.

In many cases it will not be necessary that the steps should be entirely paved with stones. If the front edge is carefully fitted and cemented, the rest can be blocked up with earth and the sides and angles planted with bits of Mossy Saxifrages. This is also a capital way of making steps in steep wood paths. In such places I have a great objection to the use of thick wooden slab as an edging, for in wet or wintry weather it becomes extremely slippery and dangerous.

THE PERGOLA IN ENGLISH GARDENS, ITS MAKING AND PLANTING

It is only of comparatively late years that we have borrowed the pergola from the gardens of Italy. Borrowed is perhaps, in its complete sense, not quite the term to use, for borrowing implies returning or repaying, whereas, having borrowed the pergola, we have certainly kept it for our own.

Its main use in Italy is as a support for Grape Vines and at

A corner of the vine-clad pergola and arbour at Munstead Wood

the same time to give shade to paths. Here we use it, not only for shade, but as an important feature in garden design and for the display of the best plants of rambling growth, whether for beauty of flower or foliage. In the old English gardens of Tudor times there was something that approached the uses of the pergola in the pleached alleys of Hornbeam or some such tree trained on a framework of laths. But these shaded alleys were slow of growth and wasteful of labour, and did nothing to display the beauty of flowers. Our adaptation of the pergola gives a much quicker and better addition to the delights of the garden, for we have our shady walk, and in addition some of the most charming pictures of flower beauty that the garden can be made to show. It is therefore no wonder that a pergola or something of the kind is now wanted in almost every garden.

Before considering how it is to be planted it may be well to give an idea of the different ways in which it is made. The simplest form of pergola in Italy is made of stout poles guiding and supporting the trunks of the Vines, connected across the path by others of less diameter, with a roofing of any long rods laid lengthways along the top. This is repaired from time to time by putting in fresh uprights or other portions in the care-less happy-go-lucky way that characterises the methods of domestic and rural economy of the Italian peasant or small proprietor.

But often in Italy one sees solid piers of rubble masonry coarsely plastered, either round or square in plan, or even marble columns from ancient buildings. These have a more solid wooden beam connecting them in pairs across the path, and stouter stuff running along the length.

For our English gardens we have the choice of various materials for the main structure. If the pergola is to be near enough to the house to be in any sort of designed relation to it, and especially if the house be of some importance, the piers should be of the same material as the house walls—brick or

"It would be well in these days, when gardening possibilities are so vast and the designer may be tempted to run wild, that he should restrain himself and strive to regain the older simplicity and charm, remembering that the first purpose of a garden is to be a place of quiet beauty such as will give delight to the eye and repose and refreshment to the mind." Garden scene of green foliage.

stone as the case may be. Fourteen-inch brick piers laid in cement are excellent and easily made. Such piers may be said to last for ever, and if it is desirable that they should not be red, or whatever may be the normal colour of the brick used, it is easy to colour them in lime-wash to suit any near building. For association with refined brick, building bricks are sometimes moulded on purpose of thinner shape, either square or half-round in plan, the latter being for piers that are to show as round columns. Brick, stone or marble, or wooden columns are also used in refined designs.

For more ordinary work the piers may be of oak trunks of a diameter of eight to ten inches. These if tarred or charred at the butts high enough up to show a charred space of a foot above the ground-line, and put into the ground like gate-posts, will last from fifteen to eighteen years, or have about the lifetime of an ordinary field gate-post. A better and more enduring way is to have the posts of oak eight inches square, set on squared stones that stand a foot out of the ground, with a stout iron dowel let into the foot of the post and the top of the stone. Unless the appearance of the oak post is desired there is little if anything to choose in point of cost between this and the solid brick pier, as the oak has to be squared and the plinth shaped and bedded on a concrete foundation.

In most places local custom and convenience of obtaining local material will be the best guide in choosing what the pergola is to be made of. Larch posts are nearly as good as oak, and larch tops are the best of all materials for the top roofing.

Whatever may be the kind of post or pier, it is important to have them connected by good beams. The beam ties the opposite pairs of posts or piers together across the path. In the case of brick or stone piers it should be of oak or larch seven to eight inches square, not quite horizontal, but slightly rising in the middle. This is of some importance, as it satisfies the eye with the feeling of strong structure, and is actually of structural utility.

It is of course possible to make a pergola of iron with very flat arches, and supporting rods and wires or wire netting for the top; but it is the material least recommended and the one that is the least sympathetic to the plants; indeed in many cases contact with the cold iron is actually harmful.

A modification of the continuous pergola is in many cases as good as, or even better than, the more complete kind. This is the series of posts and beams without any connection in the direction of the length of the path, making a succession of flowering arches; either standing quite clear or only connected by garlands swinging from one pair of piers to the next along the sides of the path, and perhaps light horizontal rails also running lengthwise from pier to pier.

This is the best arrangement for Roses, as they have plenty of air and light, and can be more conveniently trained as pillars and arches, while the most free-growing of the Ayrshires and hybrid *multiflora* ramblers willingly make swinging garlands. Roses are not so good for the complete pergola.

To come to the plants, and to take first the cases in which most shade is desired, with beauty of flower or foliage, the best are certainly Grape Vines, Aristolochia, Virginia Creeper, and Wistaria. They are all, except Virginia Creeper, slow to grow at first, but in four years they will be growing strongly. Vines should be planted a fair size, as large as can be had in pots, or two or three years will be lost at the beginning. Aristolochia, and especially Wistaria, though they grow fast when established, always make a long pause for reflection at the beginning of their new life's journey.

It is therefore a good plan, when a pergola is planted with these as the main things for its future clothing, to plant at intervals several *Clematis montana*, or even the common but always beautiful *C. Vitalba*. These, especially *C. montana*, will make a fine show for some years, while the slower plants are making their first growth; and as *C. montana* has in many soils

"The purpose of a garden is to give happiness and repose of mind, firstly and above all other considerations, and to give it through the representation of the best kinds of pictorial beauty of flower and foliage that can be combined or invented. And I think few people will deny that this kind of happiness is much more often enjoyed in the contemplation of the homely border of hardy flowers than in any of these great [formal] gardens."

not a very long lifetime, the best it can do will be over by the time the permanent plants are maturing and wanting the whole space. The sweet-water Vines of the Chasselas class, known in England as Royal Muscadine, have foliage of excellent form that is beautiful in autumn with its marbling of yellow. The Parsley or cut-leaved Vine is another desirable kind. *Vitis cordata*, the sweet-scented Vine, has large wide leaves that give ample shade, and a strong habit of growth, and flowers that in hot sunshine freely give off their delicious scent; while for gorgeous autumn colouring of crimson and yellow the Vine commonly known as *Vitis Coignetiæ* is quite unequalled. There is also the Claret Vine whose leaves turn a low-toned red in late summer and autumn.

The height and width of the pergola and the width apart of the pairs of piers can only be rightly estimated by a consideration of the proportions of other near portions of the garden, so that it is only possible to suggest a kind of average size for general use. The posts or piers should stand from seven feet two inches to eight feet out of the ground when the piers stand from eight to nine feet apart across the path. In a garden where there is nothing very high close by, this kind cf proportion, rather wider than high, will be likely to be the most suitable; but there may be circumstances, such as a walk through a kitchen garden, where economy of space is desired, or when the pergola has to pass between tall trees at a little distance to right and left, when the proportion that is rather taller than wide had best be used.

In a whole or covered pergola, the pairs of piers would be further apart in the length of the walk than between the individuals of each pair *across* the walk, but in the open pergola, where there is no roof and either no connection or only garlands and level side rails—or garlands alone—they may stand closer.

For the open pergola without top, Roses are among the best of plants; on one post a pillar Rose and on the other a rambler.

To keep the bases of the piers clothed, some strong young shoots of the current year should be shortened so as best to cover the space, when, instead of making the whole length they would otherwise have attained, they will stop growing at the tips and throw their strength into preparation for flowering shoots at the lower levels.

Among some others of the best plants for the open pergola are the free Japan Honeysuckle, the common but always delightful white Jasmine, the new *Polygonum baldschuanicum*, *Clematis Flammula*, the little-known but quite excellent *Clematis paniculata*, blooming in October, the large flowered Clematises, late Dutch Honeysuckle, *Cratægus Pyracantha*, *Rhodotypos kerrioides*, *Kerria japonica*, double-flowered Brambles, and *Forsythia suspensa*.

There is another class of shady covered way made of flowering trees that differs from the pergola in that when mature it has no adventitious supports whatever, the structure being formed by the trees themselves. It may be of shade trees only, when it comes near the pleached alleys of our ancestors. For this the best trees are Plane, Hornbeam, Wych Elm, and Beech. The Planes should be planted ten to twelve feet apart, and pollarded at eight feet from the ground; their after-growth is then trained down to a temporary roofing framework of poles. In the case of this tree the sides are open. Hornbeam, Wych Elm, and Beech are trained as they grow to form both walls and roof. But many of the small flowering trees do very well trained as flowering shady ways, though when they have arched over and form a complete roof the flowers are mostly on the outer sides. One of the best for this use is Laburnum, but the beautiful Japanese flowering Apple (*Pyrus Malus floribunda*), the Snowy Mespilus, the Guelder Rose, the Siberian and other fruiting Crabs, are all amenable to the same treatment.

This leads naturally to covered ways of other fruit trees, and the delights of the fruit garden are much increased by the presence of a naturally formed pergola of Apple, Pear, Plum, Medlar, and Quince trees.

Some adaptation of the pergola, of a temporary kind, is also extremely useful in the case of a garden that is new and raw, or in some place that is held on a short tenancy, when the tenant wishes to enjoy shade without having to wait for the growth of long-lived and slow growing plants. Any poles, from the hop-pole to the bean-pole size, put up as the framework of a covered way, can in one season be clothed with a grand growth of the great Orange Gourds, the Potiron rouge of our French neighbours. These, with others of the ornamental Gourds and quick growing climbers, such as Japanese Hop, *Convolvulus major*, *Mina lobata*, Canary Creeper, and the trailing Nasturtiums, will give ample shade in the hottest months and a glory of autumn fruit and bloom.

Plants that are suitable for the open pergola are equally suitable for verandas, with the addition of some others of the tenderer kinds that will succeed in the shelter and warmth of the sunny house-front, especially in the southern counties. For here we may have, as in Devonshire, Cornwall, and the Isle of Wight, Fuchsia, Myrtle, Pomegranate, *Solanum jasminoides*, and *Solanum crispum*, and even a little further north the beautiful *Bignonia radicans* and the blue Passion Flower. Perhaps a well-grown Wistaria is the best of all veranda plants, for not only does it yield its masses of bloom almost unfailingly year after year, but its foliage is both graceful and handsome, and always looks fresh and clean.

It is well to think out various combinations for veranda planting that will give a good succession of flower. Thus, as one example, the season of bloom might begin with Wistaria, or *Robinia hispida*, a capital shrub for this use; then in full summer would come white Jasmine and, later, *Bignonia radicans*. Wistaria, if allowed to grow at will, covers a very large space, but if rather closely pruned it can be kept within bounds and flowers with astonishing freedom.

The Ayrshire and rambling Roses are beautiful in their season on a veranda, but they have the disadvantage of being for one season only, and they cover so much space that but little room is left for any other plants.

IV

THE WATER GARDEN

THE STREAMSIDE GARDEN
Country Life, February 13, 1909
BOG GARDENS
Country Life, May 13, 1911
WATERSIDE PLANTING
Country Life, May 26, 1923

IV

The Water Garden

THE STREAMSIDE GARDEN

To have water, whether of pond or stream, in a garden is the greatest possible gain, for it enables the ingenious garden owner or designer not only to grow in perfection many beautiful plants, but to treat the watery places, according to their nature and capability, in various delightful ways. The kind of stream that is easiest to deal with is one which has a shallow flow over a stony bottom and that is not much below the general ground-level. Here we have, ready-made, the most desirable conditions, and it is an easy matter to plant the banks and water edges without any work of shifting or shaping ground.

If the little waterway passes through dressed flower garden it may be tamed to take its part in the garden design in rills and pools and basins, bordered with wrought-stone kerbing and planted with such beautiful things as the Japanese *Iris laevigata* and *Iris sibirica*, scarlet Lobelia and the fine double Arrowhead. But if it passes through the outer part of the garden, or near grounds of wilder character, the plants would be, many of them, natives—the Water Plantain with its beautiful leaves, the Flowering Rush (*Butomus*), the lovely Water Forget-me-not, the deep yellow Marsh Marigold, the bright clear yellow Mimulus, so long acclimatised that we class it as a native; then for foliage the common Bur-reed (*Sparganium ramosum*), Lady Fern and Dilated Shield Fern; then the double form of the wild Meadow Sweet and its foreign congeners the pale pink *Spiraea venusta*, the rosy *Spiraea palmata* and the larger white-plumed *Spiraea Aruncus,* native of the banks of alpine torrents. There are others of our beautiful native waterside plants, but these will be enough for a considerable length of planting. It should be remembered that the best effects are gained by some

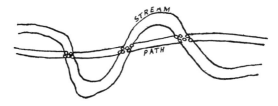

PLAN OF PATH AND STREAM

restraint in the numbers of different kinds of plants used. If in one stretch of twenty to twenty-five feet the plants are blue Forget-me-not, yellow Mimulus and Lady Fern only, one can see and enjoy these lovely things to the full, and far better than

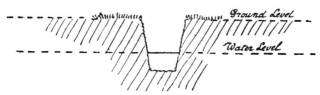

A DEEP DITCH : SECTION

if there were two or three other objects of interest besides. It should also be borne in mind that the plant pictures of wise selection and good grouping are best seen from the opposite side of the stream. If its direction is sinuous, there will be ample opportunity for carrying the path across and across, so gaining different aspects of light on flower and water. The path may cross either by stepping-stones or by some very simple bridge, something much better than the so-called rustic bridge that so commonly defaces garden waters. If the stream is not shallow and stony bottomed, it is worth a good deal of work and trouble to make it so.

Not only is it pleasant to see the clear pebbly bottom, but it makes more movement of water, and the movement brings forth that sweet babbling, the language of the water, telling of its happy life and activity. One may learn the value of this both for sight and sound at many a bridge in country places where a road crosses a running stream or small river. On one side or other of the bridge there is generally a shallow stony place where the water is not much more than ankle deep. However ancient the bridge may be, this shallow is the evidence of a still older ford. The ford must have been made by widening the area of the flow and by shallowing the bottom, putting down stones to hinder its being washed out. It is a useful lesson in the treatment of garden streams.

Sometimes the only stream one has to deal with is running water in the bottom of a straight, deep, narrow ditch, with nearly vertical sides. Nothing can be less inspiring to the planter than such a ditch; yet, on the other hand, nothing is more stimulating to his power of invention, and determination to convert unsightliness into beauty. The ditch, as it exists, is useless except as a drain, but there is the precious running water —the one thing most wanted. In such a case it is often advisable to make an entirely new channel, excavating a good width so as to gain plenty of space down at the water's edge, and to give the stream some other form than a straight one. A natural stream is seldom straight, and though in gardening in general straight lines have great value, yet there are often reasons for departing from them, especially in groundwork of the wilder sort. So with our stream and its accompanying path, the character of the environment must be considered, the general lie of the land, the nature of the places where the water enters and leaves the garden and so on. The path should swing along in one easy line, not straight, but not going out of its way to twist for no reason—an unpardonable offence in all gardening. The course of the stream may be more erratic, and a glance at the sketch will show how such planning gives opportunities for planting and enjoying a limited number of pretty things at

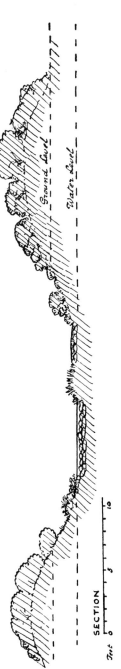

SECTION

Feet 0   5   10

A STREAMSIDE GARDEN ALTERED FROM A DEEP DITCH

Ground Level

Water Level

a time, for each bend of the brook may show quite a different treatment. The soil is taken out not only for the wider, shallower stream, but nearly down to the water-level for a width of some feet to the pathside. The spare earth is thrown up beyond the path and shaped so that it rises first gently and then a little more sharply. The rest of the excavation goes on the other side of the stream, rising easily from rather near the water's edge. In the section the shrubs on the banks are shown by the size they would be about a year after planting; eventually they would be quite as big again. The course of the stream is dug out less than one foot deep, flattish rough stones are laid at the bottom and over them smaller stones. If, as is likely, the path is inclined to be damp, it can be made dry and solid by ramming small stones into the surface, or it can be roughly laid with flat stones in the wettest places. The path must have the character of a wild path, not that of a garden walk—nothing that suggests rolled gravel, and no straightly trimmed edges.

BOG GARDENS

There must be many places in the United Kingdom, and more especially in Scotland and Ireland, where natural bogland either approaches the garden or may easily be included within its boundaries. Such conditions offer an opportunity for making a bog garden of the best kind; for though it is good to see marsh plants got together and well placed in a smaller space, yet the larger area enables the ground to be treated in a more reasonable manner. It is necessarily a kind of wild gardening, for though one may grow Water Lilies and some other beautiful aquatic and paludinous plants in tanks and channels that are severely architectural, yet it is impossible to think of a formal parterre of bog plants. The thought of such plants carries the mind away to stretches of heathy waste and wild places far away from houses and cultivation; therefore the bog garden, if some of its natural expression is to be retained, should be in a place apart from any horticulture of the tamer kind. It is best of all when it can be in some good stretch of rough, wet peatland, cut off from all gardening where the design is of rectangular form, although planting of a sympathetic character may well approach it.

One likes to think of the outer regions of the garden bordering on the peaty waste, set with well-planned groups of Rhododendrons, carefully arranged for colour, and then something that will be a suitable intermediary between these large shrubs and the smaller plants that are to follow—but not yet, for we have first to consider the giant Gunneras, true bog or bog-edge plants, and the Heracleums. The aspect of many a bog garden, even of fairly large size, is rendered ineffectual by the injudicious placing of these gigantic plants. It would be well, after the Rhododendrons, to have some of the Bamboos in large groups, and then a place, not small, but again more or less enclosed with Bamboos, for the Gunneras, keeping the path some distance away from them. The Heracleums would associate with the Gunneras, prominence being given to the fine *H. Mantegazzianum*, a notable improvement in all ways on the older *H. giganteum*. This grand plant is not only larger in all its parts, but, in spite of its size, has an appearance of greater refinement and beauty. This effect is chiefly given by the more handsome toothing of the leaves; but it seems to possess other qualities that can scarcely be separately discerned, but that give it the mien of a specially proud and sumptuous plant. It is a native of Abkhasia, a small Russian province on the Black Sea at the foot of the Caucasus.

A further grouping of Bamboos might screen these great plants from the outer bog garden, and then would come a planting of the true bog shrubs and their allies—Kalmia, Myrica, Comptonia, Ledum, Erica, Vaccinium, and some of that large family of small shrubs broadly classed under the name Pieris. Some of these, with Skimmia and the dwarf Rhododendrons, will be better on slightly raised mounds, for,

though they like cool earth, they are not actually bog plants.
Gaultheria enjoys the same conditions with the addition of
shade or half shade; in fact, if the bog garden is shaded on one
side by wooded, rising ground, it will be all the better for such
plants as Galax, Shortia, the Gaultherias, *Smilacina racemosa*,
Primula japonica and *P. sikkimensis*. The white form of *P.
japonica* should be grown; it luxuriates in black, peaty ground,
so wet and soft as to be almost mud. There is often a mis-
apprehension or want of discrimination about a plant's enjoyment of shade and damp. Kalmias are known to like damp,
but are often planted in the shade, the idea being to secure
some kind of coolness; but though they like damp peat at the
root, they like full sun overhead. Some of the noblest bog
plants are our native Ferns, the graceful Lady Fern and the
Dilated Shield Fern being without doubt the handsomest.
They both enjoy shade, while the Royal Fern likes a sunny
place in wet peat. Struthiopteris, not a native, but European,
is a fine bog Fern, growing to a height of six feet; and the
American *Onoclea sensibilis* should also have a place. As in all
other good gardening, it is best to see one good picture at a
time rather than a confused mixture of the material for five or
six pictures. Thus, on a cool, peaty bank in shade we may have
Galax and Shortia, backed by one of the Andromedas, say, a
straggling group of a dozen Shortia, with some fifty Galax
spreading behind and beyond, and at the back six Andromeda,
or, more properly, *Leucothoë Catesbaei*. This, or some such
grouping, would occupy a length of from three to four yards.
Then the whole bank might have a carpeting of *Gaultheria
procumbens* or of Arctostaphylos, with the tall *Smilacina racemosa* just behind, its thick-plumed white panicles on arching
growths, much like Solomon's Seal; these, as autumn advances,
becoming clusters of curiously speckled berries, whose weight
bends the stem over and makes it sway heavily when moved
by the wind. Such a cool bank in shade would be still further
planted with the tiny Linnaea, with Pyrola and with Trientalis,

and, where the bank comes clear of the shade, with *Dryas octopetala.*

It is well, as a general rule, in planting wild places that are in connection with gardens, to keep exotics nearest to the home end, and to leave the native plants for the further part of the wild. Thus, after leaving the Bamboos and proceeding through the open bog, there would first be a bold planting of the Japanese *Iris laevigata* with the large-leaved *Saxifraga peltata* and the handsome Rodgersia, whose leaves turn such a fine colour in the late summer. This would be quite enough of plant interest for some yards of ground. Then would come the Irises of the *sibirica* class with their larger forms, and the tall yellow and white *Iris ochroleuca*, and, in a place by itself in black, peaty mud, the glorious *Cypripedium spectabile*. A group of *Pieris floribunda* on a mound of peaty earth, just raised above the bog level, would fittingly frame the Cypripedium, and a continuation of the same mound, extending for some fifteen or twenty feet, and kept nearly parallel with the path, at a distance of five or six feet from it, would give space between for the lesser plants of a few inches high, such as the curious Sarracenias. The long mound might well lead to one of larger size for a good group of Kalmias, their roots just raised above the swamp and their heads in full sun. At the foot of these would be groups of the pale pink *Spiraea venusta* and of the double Meadow Sweet, the double form of our native *Spiraea Ulmaria*. After this, in the flat, open bog, there would be a number of plants, all native, and among them some of the best for the wild bog garden. The Water Forget-me-not should have a region nearly to itself, its only companions being the yellow Mimulus and Lady Fern. After that, though before it in time of blooming, would come Marsh Marigold. There are double forms of this, but for fine distinct effect none of them can approach the type plant. With this, and flowering at the same time, should be the double form of the common Lady's Smock (*Cardamine pratensis*).

To all this bog-planting and to what is to follow there will be a general groundwork of wild Heaths, the Bell Heather (*Erica tetralix*) predominating. The bog will have it in abundance to begin with, and in arranging for other planting it would be well to disturb it as little as possible. Its white variety should be planted, also, in drier places, the Cornish Heath and, above all and in quantity, the white variety of the Irish Heath (*Menziesia polifolia*). Out in the more open bog there will be Sphagnum in patches and even in pools, and in these there will be Sundew, Cotton-grass, Parnassia and bog Asphodel, while on the rather drier ground near the path there will be the Marsh Rattle (*Pedicularis*). The native plants are not yet at an end, for there is the yellow Flag Iris and *Orchis latifolia* and the fine blue-flowered Meadow Crane's Bill, and plentiful patches of the Branched Bur-reed (*Sparganium*), and in patches of heathy turf *Gentiana Pneumonanthe*, one of the best of its lovely family.

WATERSIDE PLANTING

There are any number of things that may be recommended for planting along the banks of running water. Some belong to our native flora, but are so distinctly desirable, that if they do not occur naturally in the place, they should be searched for. These are the yellow Flag (*Iris Pseudacorus*) with showy flowers in June and upright sword-like leaves; the Water Plantain (*Alisma Plantago*) with large ribbed leaves, something like those of Veratrum, and a wide-spreading, lace-like panicle of flower; then the beautiful rosy pink Flowering Rush (*Butomus*), looking like something tropical. For a grand plant of stately habit there is a Great Water Dock (*Rumex Hydrolapathum*), with very large leaves that, as the season advances, take on brilliant colourings of yellow and red. The Great Reedmace (*Typha latifolia*), commonly, but wrongly, called Bulrush, should have a place, and there are three fine plants with yellow bloom that should not be forgotten. These are Tansy, the great yellow

A late summer border leading to the pink and grey garden

The pink and grey garden

Loosestrife (*Lysimachia vulgaris*) and the tall yellow Meadow Rue (*Thalictrum flavum*). Buckbean (*Menyanthes trifoliata*), a beautiful native that is sold in nurseries among the choicest water and bog plants, should be planted in some still water edge, or where a wide, shallow ditch joins the main stream. The Great Reed (*Phragmites communis*) should have a place, and the curious and interesting Marestail (*Equisetum Telmateia*), whose simple structure gives the impression of its having been a plant of the earliest evolution. These are best suited for the banks of still or sluggish waters. The Marestail should never be brought into a garden, for it is terribly 'rooty', and soon becomes a troublesome weed almost impossible to eradicate.

The yellow Mimulus is not considered a native, though it has become naturalised by running water in several districts. Its clear yellow bloom is good to see in swamp or water edge, and if it is planted near a patch of Water Forget-me-not each will enhance the colour value of the other. The foaming bloom of Meadow Sweet (*Spiraea Ulmaria*) is always welcome, but the double garden variety has the more effective flower. It is curious that in the double kind the scent, which is so strong and so freely given off by the wild plant, seems to be almost entirely wanting. Others of the water-loving Spiraeas should be planted, especially *S. Aruncus*, with its great creamy plumes, that is so fine by the sides of foaming alpine torrents; and though some of these Spiraeas have a rather rank magenta colouring, these can be avoided in favour of *S. venusta*, which is of a charming quiet pink.

Snowflake (*Leucojum aestivum*), a native bulbous plant with blooms on stems eighteen inches high and looking like a gigantic Snowdrop, should not be forgotten. It should be placed in some clear space of bank where it is not overwhelmed by larger growths.

All these plants will bear occasional submersion by flooding. For positions at the water's edge not actually flooded, and

"To have water, whether of pond or stream, in a graden is the greatest possible gain, for it enables the ingenious garden owner or designer not only to grow in perfection many beautiful plants, but to treat the watery places, according to their nature and capability, in various delightful ways."

especially for cool, quiet places where there is a backing of copse, there should be a free planting of the giant *Heracleum Mantegazzianum*, with its very large leaves and branches of white bloom four feet across. It is a distinct improvement on the older kind of giant Cow Parsnip, *Heracleum giganteum*, for the leaves are larger and a glossier green, more deeply slashed and more sharply toothed, and the massive bloom is larger altogether.

In cool and damp meadowland on the way to the water a few plants of the double Lady's Smock (*Cardamine pratensis*) will soon spread into a multitude. The single kind will probably be already in the meadow. It has a curious method of reproduction by dropping leaflets, each one of which soon forms roots and then develops into a complete plant. A stock can soon be raised by pulling off the leaflets and dibbling them into a pan. Fritillary (*Fritillaria meleagris*), both the purple and the white, should be planted in the meadow, where they will thrive and probably increase. They come in April, a week or two before the Lady's Smocks.

A grouping of white Begonia with Megasea and Yucca foliage for summer effect

Writing of water in the garden, Gertrude Jekyll suggested that if it passes through the flower garden "it may be tamed to take its part in the garden design in rills and pools and basins, bordered with wrought-stone kerbing and planted with ... beautiful things."

V

THE MIXED BORDER

THE HARDY FLOWER BORDER
Country Life, April 6, 1912

SOME PROBLEMS OF THE FLOWER BORDER
Gardening Illustrated, August 16, 1924

SPRING PLANTING FOR THE SUMMER
Gardening Illustrated, March 14, 1926

JUNE AND JULY BORDER FLOWERS

THE AUGUST BORDER
Gardening Illustrated, October 4, 1924

SHORTENING BORDER PLANTS
Gardening Illustrated, October 9, 1926

'BETWEEN' PLANTS FOR THE SPRING BORDER
Gardening Illustrated, June 13, 1925

A SCARLET BORDER
Gardening Illustrated, September 4, 1926

TRITOMAS IN THE FLOWER BORDER
Gardening Illustrated, November 1, 1924

SEASONAL PLANTING
Gardening Illustrated, September 10, 1927

THE NORTH BORDER
The Garden, February 1916

BORDER PLANTS THAT SUCCEED BEST
The Garden, March 12, 1921

BORDERS OF ANNUALS
The Garden, January 15, 1921

SOME DESIRABLE ANNUALS
The Garden, February 2, 1924

ANNUALS FOR SUNNY PLACES
The Garden, January 29, 1921

ANNUALS FOR SHADY PLACES
The Garden, January 29, 1921

ANNUALS TO SOW IN HEAT
The Garden, January 15, 1921

V

The Mixed Border

THE HARDY FLOWER BORDER

THERE IS frequent complaint among horticultural amateurs to the effect that they cannot keep borders of hardy flowers well furnished with bloom throughout the summer. But in an ordinary garden it is quite unreasonable to expect that this can be done. It can only be done where there are the means of having large reserves of material that can be planted or plunged in the borders to take the place of plants gone out of bloom. Owners of gardens should clearly understand that this is so—acceptance of the fact would save them from much fruitless effort and inevitable disappointment. If a really good display is desired, it can only be conveniently done by restricting the season to a certain number of weeks—by devoting separate borders or other garden spaces to a definite time of year. If a border is planted so as to show a good garden picture through July, August and September, it will be quite as much as can be expected, and even then some dropping in of pot plants will be needed. But it stands to reason that the shorter the time in which the border is required to be ornamental, the better it can be done; and if a garden lends itself to plantings of season by season, or can be so arranged that such plantings can be carried out, there will then, throughout the summer, always be some one place that shows a complete and satisfactory garden picture, while the one that is to come next is showing early promise.

The earliest of the season gardens will be for April and early May; the one next to follow for May and June. Then will come the main display for July, August and September. If there may be besides a special border or double border for August and another for September, and even one for October, there will be a succession of seasonable displays, each one of which may be made perfect of its kind. Every border should be carefully considered for colour effect. Without such preparatory care the result will be a mere jumble, of no value to the cultivated eye. For a border of some length it is found best to keep the ends cool in colouring, with a large amount of grey foliage, and to approach the middle through flowers and foliage of increasingly warm colour, with a gorgeous climax of strong reds nearly midway in the length. Thus, taking the July to September border month by month, one end in July—to name some of the more important flowers—would have Delphinium, white Lily, white Foxglove and Eryngium, with foamy masses of the bushy *Clematis recta* and white Tree Lupine, passing to the pale yellow of Thalictrum, Mullein, the tall Œnothera and the pale yellow Day Lily; then onwards in strength of colour in Alströmeria, orange Day Lily and the fine *Lilium croceum*, to the scarlet of *Lychnis chalcedonica*. The sequence of colour would then again proceed by orange and yellow to the far end, where there would be Galega white and purple, *Chrysanthemum maximum*, the tall white Campanulas, *macrantha* and *persicifolia* and white Everlasting Pea, with the splendid purple of *Campanula macrocarpa* and the noble Crane's Bill, *Geranium ibericum*. These will be followed in August by *Anemone Japonica*, white and pink; Echinops, Erigeron, Gypsophila, *Lilium longiflorum* at the cool ends, and Hollyhock, Helenium, Pentstemon, red Phlox, etc., in the middle. September would bring the further succession of the blaze of Dahlia, Gladiolus, Tritoma, Helianthus and Canna for the middle glory, and *Clematis Flammula*, white Dahlia, Hydrangea and the earlier Michaelmas Daisies at the cool-coloured ends. Only the more important of the hardy plants have been named, but besides these and others there will be a wealth of the best half-hardy annuals—dwarf Tropaeolums, African Marigolds, annual Sunflowers, Stocks, China Asters, and a good selection from the hosts of beautiful Snapdragons that are so easily raised and that last so long in bloom.

Although the main occupants of the border are hardy plants, there is no reason why the best of the so-called bedding plants should not also have a place, especially as their blooming time is that of the late summer and early autumn. Therefore we shall look to Geraniums, Calceolarias, Salvias, Gazanias, and Heliotrope to take their places, according to their colourings, in and near the front of the border.

There is one matter that is commonly overlooked, but that makes all the difference between a border that is to be a picture of good colouring and one of lesser value. This is the provision of what may be called 'between' plants. For masses of colour, even if arranged in quite a good sequence, are only truly pictorial if between and among the colour groups there are other masses or accompaniments of neutral colouring. Some of the groups out of flower and the shadowy places under overhanging plants will of themselves do something, but more than this is needed. Especially among the plants of tender colouring there should be a rather full planting of grey foliage, such as Rosemary, Lavender, Rue, Phlomis, Lyme Grass, *Clematis recta* (out of flower), and, towards the front, Lavender Cotton, Catmint, Stachys and Pinks. The effect of the plants of white and tender colouring is greatly enhanced by such a setting, while, when the border is surveyed as a whole, the advantage is quite unmistakable. Even with the permanent perennials, the bedding plants and the annuals, a border is apt, here and there, to show a place that might be better furnished. To remedy this it is well to have some plants in pots in reserve—Hydrangeas, *Lilium longiflorum*, *Lilium auratum* and *Campanula pyramidalis* are among the most useful—ready to drop in where they will make the best effect. No means should be neglected or despised that will make the border handsome and effective, and all such ways of doing it are so many spurs to further beneficent inventiveness. Sometimes the group of warm colouring may seem to overbalance the rest or to be too large or monotonous. In such a case a group of three or four pots of *Lilium longiflorum* dropped in between the growing plants will put new life into it. For though it is undoubtedly best to treat flower borders with consecutive harmonies, yet the garden artist will know when and where to make the exception.

Staking will have to be done with great care and in good time. If a plant that will require support is left too late, its whole form may be lost or distorted. Everyone knows the unhappy appearance of a Michaelmas Daisy whose flowering shoots are gathered together at the last moment and bunched up to one stick; whereas it should have been carefully staked in June with several pieces of branching spray, so that the plant, while amply supported, could grow outwards in all directions in its natural manner. The large flowered Clematises, so useful for training at the backs of borders, through and over other plants, require constant watching and regulating. There is no day in the blooming life of the late summer border, or indeed of any other, when it does not need close watching and some kind of tending. Many people think that to have a good border of summer flowers is an easy thing; whereas to have it well done so as to show a continual picture of plant beauty, even for three months, is one of the most difficult of horticultural feats.

SOME PROBLEMS OF THE FLOWER BORDER

Even when a border is restricted to a certain season—and this is the only way to secure a satisfactory garden picture— some of the plants that are indispensable may be over before the rest, and either become unsightly or, if cut away, leave uninteresting blank spaces. In a border that is carefully planted and devoted to the season that extends from the middle of July to the end of September the fine *Eryngium Oliverianum* will be one of the first to go. To fill its place we have one or two alternative ways of treatment. At the back of the border there is a group of the tall *Helianthus orgyalis*, a plant that, if left to itself, shoots up to a height of seven or eight feet and carries a bunch of small yellow flowers at the top. If it did only this it would not be worth having, but in the early days of August we pull it down and peg it across the border, so that a yard of its upper end comes over the Eryngiums. As with some other plants, this pulling down to a horizontal position causes the plant to throw up a short flowering shoot from each axil, so that the whole becomes a sheet of pale yellow bloom, and the plant that was not worth a place in the border becomes one of its best masses of colour. In another part of the border a second patch of this Eryngium has a white Everlasting Pea trained over it, and as this goes out of bloom a strong growing hybrid Clematis at the back is, in its turn, trained over the Pea.

Another useful device is to plant *Clematis Flammula* at the back of a group of Delphiniums. When the bloom of the Delphiniums is over and seed pods are forming we cut away all the seeding part, leaving the stems standing about four and a half feet high. The Clematis is trained over this and rests on the Delphinium stems and gives a mass of bloom in early September.

The pale primrose Sunflower is planted in happy companionship with *Artemisia lactiflora*. The chief faults of the Artemisia are its rigid uprightness and its considerable show of half-naked stem. The Sunflowers are planted behind. Some of them are let grow to their full height—a moderate height for Sunflowers is about six feet—but some are cut back in July, so that they branch and give a number of smaller flowers at a lower height. These are pulled through the stems of the Artemisia and hide their lankiness. By watching a flower border carefully and noting the ways and wants of its occupants one may invent and practise many such devices, both to the benefit of its appearance and also much to one's own interest and amusement.

SPRING PLANTING FOR THE SUMMER

There are a number of plants in a well-established flower border that can only rarely be moved—deep-rooting things like Everlasting Pea, Gypsophila, Eryngiums, Peonies, Oriental Poppies, and Clematis species—and a certain number that require replanting every two or three years, such as Echinops, *Salvia virgata*, Delphiniums, Hollyhocks, Phloxes and Iris. But the greater number of the good hardy perennials are the better for a yearly shift. In light soils this is best done in autumn, but in many gardens, and especially those on stiff soils, it is either more convenient or more salutary to renew them in the spring. There will already be some large blank spaces where Dahlias and Cannas, Gladioli and other summer flowers, were taken up and put into store for the winter, so that when the plants needing division are lifted, a good two-thirds of the border will be empty. All this ground is freshly manured, the plants divided and carefully replaced according to their needs. Delphiniums will be one of the first cares; the clumps that have stood for three years come up and are carefully divided with a sharp knife into pieces with two or three crowns. Phloxes soon become woody at the base; three-year-old plants will cut up, into a number, and though young plants from spring cuttings, with single shoots, give the handsomest blooms, yet the divisions from the older clumps are too good to be discarded. *Chrysanthemum maximum* increases about three-fold in the year, and is divided so as to have three or four crowns to each piece. *Artemisia lactiflora*, a plant of quick increase, divides in about the same way and is replanted in anticipation of its pleasant association with the pale primrose-coloured annual Sunflower. The tall *Helianthus orgyalis*, so useful for pegging down for an autumn display over earlier plants that have gone out of bloom, is also a plant of ready increase. For some years we had avoided the use of the taller perennial Sunflowers of the *H. rigidus* group, such as the well-known Miss Mellish and the better Mrs. Moon, on account of their root-rambling ways, but the fine colour and handsome bloom of the newer *H. sparsifolius* showed it to be such a grand border plant that it is now admitted. The yearly root growth rambles far and wide, but by careful following up it can all be traced and lifted.

The Thalictrums are left in place for three years. Two kinds are favourites in the border—the tall *T. flavum* and the purple-coloured form of *T. aquilegifolium*. It is interesting to cut down the tall, hollow stems of *T. flavum* while they are still green; each cut gives a distinct musical note. Some sound of the kind may be noticed in a less degree in several plants with hollow stems, but from none that I have known or observed does one get so fully sonorous a note as from *T. flavum*. *Anthemis tinctoria* may stand for two years, but is rather better if yearly divided. This good plant is in several shades of yellow; the paler is the better and more refined, and is the more desirable because there are so many more flowers of the deeper yellow. Œnotheras of the *fruticosa* section are best divided yearly, also that useful front edge plant *Rudbeckia speciosa*, which in all soils is best replanted in spring.

The Spiraeas of the Meadow-Sweet class may be left undisturbed for two years, or three at latest, but by that time their nucleus has become rough and woody, showing need of division. Heleniums are renewed every year. *H. pumilum* is one of the best of the border plants, of strong yellow colouring; the Wallflower-coloured *H. cupreum* is also indispensable, and the late-flowering *H. striatum*, one of the taller kinds, is also desirable.

Tritomas stand for three or four years, but it is well to replant one clump in the border each year. The best way of treating Hollyhocks must depend on the nature of the soil. In strong soils, where they do best and are most likely to resist the prevalent disease, they may stand for two or even three years, but it is well to keep a supply of young plants from seed for spring planting. Michaelmas Daisies may remain for two years, but are best when planted afresh every year. For a proper display they want so much room that, if possible, they should have separate garden spaces to themselves, some of the smaller-growing kinds only, such as *Aster acris* and *A. Amellus*, being admitted to the mixed border. The tall September Daisy (*Pyrethrum uliginosum*) we always grow with them, for it has much the same habit, time of blooming, and rooting system. *Salvia Sclarea*, the Clary of old gardens, is rather best planted in autumn, as are also Mulleins, Foxgloves, Canterbury Bells or any other biennials.

JUNE AND JULY BORDER FLOWERS

The best plants for filling borders for a show during June and July would be: For June, Irises, Peonies of the *albiflora* section, the deep, red form of Valerian (*Centranthus*), Oriental Poppies, Lupines, Gaillardias, and *Œnothera fruticosa*. Delphiniums will begin before the end of June, closely followed in July by Anchusa Dropmore, Erigeron, *Chrysanthemum maximum*, *Salvia virgata*, Galega, Eryngiums (both the perennial *E. Oliverianum* and the biennial *E. giganteum*), the tall *Thalictrum flavum*, Double Meadow Sweet, Canterbury Bells, Alströmeria, and towards the end of the month Day Lilies, Echinops and *Gypsophila paniculata*.

THE AUGUST BORDER

A space of double flower border is devoted to flowers of August and early September, in a restricted colouring of purple, pink, and white, with a whole setting of grey foliage. At the back are groups of pink Hollyhock and bushes of *Lavatera Olbia*, with *Clematis Jackmani* trained over peasticks. There are groups of Echinops and bushy masses of Gypsophila and Gladioli (pink and purple), America and Baron Hulot; also pink and white Snapdragons, with two important annuals, a good Larkspur of selected deep purple colouring and a double rose pink Godetia. Other Clematises are trained into silvery supporting bushes of Sea Buckthorn, and Ceanothus Gloire de Versailles, pruned back hard in spring, shows as a mass of bluish lavender. A pink star Dahlia is in middle places, and taller Dahlias, pink and purplish, stand at the back. There are some purple and white China Asters, and any vacant places quite in the front are filled with dwarf Ageratum. The whole is bordered and intergrouped with silvery foliage of Stachys, *Cineraria maritima*, Santolina, *Artemisia stelleriana* and *A. ludoviciana*.

SHORTENING BORDER PLANTS

The careful gardener is always on the look-out for ways of making plants conform to his needs. Among various devices one of the most useful is the simple expedient of cutting back a tall plant in order to bring its flowers to the height desired. The illustration shows two groups of that excellent border plant *Campanula lactiflora*, which grows to a height of anything up to six feet. Self-sown seedlings are apt to appear near an established clump. One of these had grown into a sturdy plant, but as it was too close to the front edge of the border it was cut down in June to about a foot above ground, and the result was a flowering mass about 2½ feet high. This cutting back does not seem to affect the time of blooming, though it might have been expected to retard it; but if done at the right time the cut-down plant keeps pace exactly with the taller uncut shoot. This useful shortening of height can be practised with several other plants, such as Michaelmas Daisies. Galegas, too, which are apt to be too tall and vigorous in some parts of the border, are benefited by a timely trimming, and even annual Sunflowers can be converted into bushy blooming plants under three feet high. The handsome Japanese striped Maize can be made into a fairly low plant by cutting out the main middle growth. When

A border plant that lends itself to shortening;
CAMPANULA LACTIFLORA

The pink and grey garden: another view

Groups of Begonias with Ferns and foliage plants

Dry wall borders with white Nemesia and foliage plants

this is done the lower shoots, which are always the best striped, multiply and make a beautifully compact plant of quite unusual aspect.

'BETWEEN' PLANTS FOR THE SPRING BORDER

Every year that shows the experience gained by recent observation in the arrangement of plants for colour, confirms the conviction of the great value of a judicious use of what, for want of a better name, I know as the 'between' plants—plants that are not for bloom, but for some quiet quality that shall combine with and enhance the colouring of those that are near. The chief of these among the spring flowers are the purple-leaved Sage, *Heuchera Richardsoni*, and the dark-leaved Ajuga. In the garden of spring flowers, after passing the lively tones of yellow Alyssum, various Tulips and pale Daffodils, closely carpeted with white and yellow Primroses and with intervening drifts of *Myosotis dissitiflora*, the whole of this fresh-looking group is much better seen and forms a better garden picture from the next region in the border having a liberal planting of the purple-leaved Sage. It is the common Sage, but the leaves, instead of being the usual dull green, have a superficial tint of misty purple. If one was planting a group of clear yellow flowers it is just such a colour as one would wish for the background. At the foot of the Sage and for a yard or two along the border there is the richer purple of *Viola gracilis*, a precious spring garden plant. After accompanying the Sage it joins in, quite to the front, with the dark-leaved Ajuga. Here also, towards the back, are purple Wallflowers merging into the purplish red of the darker Honesty. The colour of the border now changes again to yellow, but yellow of a stronger tone, with *Doronicum plantagineum* and the splendid foliage of Veratrum and the fern-like Sweet Cicely (*Myrrhis odorata*) with its wide umbels of creamy bloom. Then come Wallflowers of deep orange and orange Tulips, passing to brown Wallflowers. These are much enriched by a backing and interplanting of another of the good 'between' plants, *Heuchera Richardsoni* (Satin Leaf) with foliage tinted reddish brown and a satin-like lustre. This goes on wherever its quiet colouring will do good among the scarlet Tulips and brown Wallflowers at the far end.

A SCARLET BORDER

A border will often be more effective if Tritomas instead of being dotted singly along the back, are in groups of three each, with Oriental Poppies so placed that the outer foliage of the Tritomas will cover them, for the poppy foliage goes off in July and does not reappear till September. The earliest flowers will be Tulips, *Anemone Coronaria* and *A. fulgens*; then there is necessarily a gap in time till the Poppies are in bloom in early June. Some of the annuals, autumn sown, will be of much use—the scarlet Opium Poppy (*P. somniferum*), *P. umbrosum*, and the brilliant *P. glaucum*—and for the front, the pretty *Collomia coccinea*. Geum Mrs. Bradshaw will be ready in June, and the fine old *Lychnis chalcedonica*. These and the scarlet Bergamot (Monarda) will fill good middle spaces, to be followed by Sweet Peas at the back and by Phlox Coquelicot, *Lobelia fulgens*, and *Lilium chalcedonicum* in the middle spaces. Annuals useful for the front will be *Linum grandiflorum* and *Linaria maroccana*, with a good sowing of dwarf Nasturtiums. Antirrhinums, both tall and intermediate, of the colourings now so near scarlet, will be very helpful; also the fine red forms of China Asters. If there is room for a middle group of blood-red Hollyhocks and scarlet Dahlias they will be good companions for the Tritomas. The quite dwarf Dahlia, Coltness Gem, should not be forgotten. Some patches or drifts of scarlet Gladioli will be needed, and if any quite tender plants are admitted a good patch of Geranium Paul Crampel can be strongly recommended. The whole effect of the border would

Border in early summer

Border in late summer

be much improved by the introduction of some dark foliage, such as the short-growing *Ricinus Gibsoni*, and the tender Iresine towards the front; also the perennial Satin Leaf (*Heuchera Richardsoni*) besides the Heucheras with the red flowers.

TRITOMAS IN THE FLOWER BORDER

The middle part of a long flower border is planted so as to have an effect of strong, rich colour in the late autumn. Here are Hollyhocks, blood-red and darker, and Dahlias, deep orange, scarlet and claret-coloured, with foliage of the dark *Ricinus Gibsoni*, *Atriplex hortensis*, and *Prunus Pissardi*, the last pruned hard in early spring so that the masses of young shoots come at a suitable height among the dark Dahlias. This group of strongest colouring leads away to both sides to orange and yellow, and at these points come the groups of Tritoma. It is a fine border sort, better than the usual *T. uvaria*. The flower spike is tall and of brightest colouring, and the whole plant is robust and vigorous. After the Tritomas the colour of the border proceeds through orange and yellow to cooler tints at the two ends. A mass of the cream-white *Artemisia lactiflora* and a cut-back Golden Elder lead to Delphinium, Anchusa and white Phlox.

SEASONAL PLANTING

To have flower borders in beauty for the whole season at small cost is practically an impossibility. It can only be done by having a large reserve of plants that can be put in to replace those that have gone over, as is done in the gardens of Hampton Court. In a case where you have three separate borders, the best way would be to give each to a season, No. 1 to March-April-May, No. 2 to June-July, No. 3 to August-September-October.

"If a garden lends itself to plantings of season by season, or can be so arranged that such plantings can be carried out, there will then, throughout the summer, always be some one place that shows a complete and satisfactory garden picture, while the one that is to come next is showing early promise."

In No. 1 should be: *Doronicum caucasicum*, Daffodils, Tulips, Wallflowers, Myosotis, Double Arabis, early Irises, *Doronicum plantagineum*, Aubrietia, Alyssum, Pansies, Grape Hyacinths, Primroses, and Pulmonarias.

In No. 2: Peonies, Irises, Lupines, China Rose, Scotch Briars, and many Roses, Foxgloves, Catmint, Centranthus, Rocket, *Spiraeas Aruncus*, *venusta* and double *Ulmaria*, Day Lilies, Gaillardia, *Campanula persicifolia* and *C. macrantha*, orange and white Lilies, Delphinium, Thalictrum, *Œnothera fruticosa*, Pinks, Erigeron, Anchusa, Alströmeria, *Helenium pumilum* and *H. cupreum*, and Border Carnations.

No. 3 should have: Echinops, Gladiolus, Snapdragons, Dahlias, Pentstemons, Clematis, Helianthus, Phlox and a good supply of half-hardy annuals, such as Sunflowers, French and African Marigolds, Stocks and China Asters. Among hardy plants there would also be Rudbeckias, Chrysanthemums in variety and Michaelmas Daisies. Annuals could be sown in May in any vacant places.

THE NORTH BORDER

The possibilities of the north border are often overlooked, but there are many plants that do better there than in any sunny aspect, for many of them come to us from woodland places and the cooler sides of mountain ranges. Solomon's Seal is so well known that no description is needed, but where there is a north border, there it will be best in place. Much like it in its general way of growth, and botanically closely allied, is *Smilacina racemosa*, a North American plant, but in this, the flowers are in close terminal racemes, not in drooping axillary clusters. It is interesting also in autumn, when the weight of the fruit, like little berries curiously veined and marbled, bends the stem over and makes it sway and swing heavily when moved by wind. The little plant that is commonly called *Smilacina bifolia*, but more correctly *Maianthemum Con-*

Tritomas in the flower border

"No one who has seen flower borders or other garden spaces well arranged for colour effect would ever go back to haphazard planting. A garden may contain an ample supply of the best plants, and the gardener may be the most able of cultivators; but if the plants are not placed to good effect it is only like having the best paints from the best colourman. In either case, it is only the exactly right use and right placing that will make the picture, and, in the case of the flowers, show what they can really do for our most complete enjoyment."

vallaria, is another near relation and one of the loveliest plants for the rock edge of the north border. It should be remembered that it does poorly on strong soils, but revels in sand or in peat and leaf-mould. Lily of the Valley must not be forgotten, for though we grow it in greater quantity in reserve ground for cutting and in woodland, yet its beautiful foliage and sweetest of sweet bloom must be near the front edge of this border also. The very beautiful Alexandrian Laurel (*Ruscus racemosus*), a Portuguese Butcher's Broom, will be a fine thing towards the back, and when the plants are well grown—it is slow of increase—a frond or two may be spared for indoor decoration, when it will last in water for some weeks. All these plants are nearly allied. The taller Campanulas are for the most part shade-loving plants. Among them the best will be the white form of *C. macrantha*, and *C. persicifolia* in both the blue and white colourings. Next, shorter in height, will be *C. alliariae-folia*. A beautiful Bellflower that deserves to be better known is *C. eriocarpa*, about a foot high, with a quantity of light purple bloom and greyish foliage. *C. carpatica*, with some of the good garden varieties, are about the same height; and quite in the front, in the joints of the stony edging, the lovely little *C. pusilla*, both the light purple of the type and the white variety, will be charmingly in place. These Campanulas will succeed in any soil, but all are happiest in a chalky one. *Tiarella cordifolia* must not be forgotten, for it is only quite happy in a north border or in slight shade.

If there is a peaty patch, a place near the front should be given to *Galax aphylla* and to *Shortia galacifolia*. In ordinary loam for preference, but in almost any soil, there should be *Orobus vernus*, with its bright crimson and bluish pea-shaped flowers. It is the toughest plant I know to divide. The crowns hang tightly together, and the roots are so strong that it is almost like cutting so much wire. Its fine relative, *Orobus aurantiacus*, follows it later. The pale green leaves and deep orange flowers are so effective that one wonders it is not

Perennial Lupins at the wood edge

The Peony garden with foreground of Candytuft

oftener seen in gardens. Orobus is the older and more familiar name, and convenient to use for garden purposes to distinguish these plants of tufted habit from the taller climbing Peas that have leaf-tendrils, though botanists have now put them all together under Lathyrus. For autumn beauty there should be *Gentiana asclepiadea*, with its beautiful arching sprays of blue flowers in September. All the Meconopsis like shade and a cool exposure, so that both of the tall Himalayan species—*M. nepalensis*, with its drooping sulphur bells, and *M. Wallichii*, with still larger flowers of pale grey blue, a plant of much the same habit—will do well.* A newer kind is the Chinese *M. integrifolia*, a yellow-flowered species.† We should think more of the common Welsh Poppy (*M. cambrica*) if it was a rarity, but it is always a beautiful plant with its fresh-looking foliage and clear, pale yellow blooms; but it seeds about so freely that in many places, it becomes troublesome. It is a capital plant for such a place as the joints of flagstones at the base of a cool wall in any dull yard or court. Pansies of all kinds are never seen to better advantage than in the cool, northern facing border, where all flowers of purple and white colouring look their best.

For the back there will be Foxgloves, of which the pure white may be considered the finest, and Mulleins, that do not open fully in sunlight, and the tall Evening Primrose. Then there are the Columbines, both short and long spurred, absolutely well in place. For the front rock edges there are a number of suitable things. Besides the Mossy Saxifrages, there is London Pride, always one of the most beautiful of plants, although so common; and there is *Asarum europaeum*, with its deep green, highly polished, Cyclamen-like leaves, and Waldsteinia, also with polished leaves shaped something like those of a Geum, and deep yellow buttercup blooms; then, among plants already mentioned, the small Bellflowers and Tiarella,

* These are now both included under the name of *M. napaulensis*.

† Written before the introduction of *M. betonicifolia* and other recent newcomers to the genus.

Smilacina and the Tufted Pansies. At the front edge also there may be Polypody Fern, and back among the flowers other of the hardy kinds—Male Fern and Lady Fern, the beautiful Dilated Shield Fern and Prickly Shield Fern that remains green and in good order throughout the winter, and goodly tufts of Hart's-tongue, happiest in soils containing loam or lime.

BORDER PLANTS THAT SUCCEED BEST ON LIGHT SOILS

Many of the best border plants will do equally well in soils of a light or a heavy character, but it may be helpful to point out a certain number of those that are distinctly preferable for one or the other. It may be taken as a rough rule that plants or shrubs from Southern Europe, the Mediterranean region and the nearer Orient, such as Lavender, Rosemary, Phlomis and Santolina, will be thankful for the warmth of our lighter soils, even though their actual habitat may be on loam or limestone. This will include all the Cistus tribe, embracing the Helianthemums, the greater number of the Artemisias, the Euphorbias and the Eryngiums.

It may be taken as a compensation for the natural poverty of the lighter soils that this quality tends to check over-exuberance of growth and encourages both profusion and good colour of bloom. In fact, if it is reasonably enriched, a naturally light soil is the pleasantest for general gardening, for it can be worked in all kinds of weathers except the heaviest wet; it is not soapy or sticky in the winter months or like a hard brick full of cracks in the dry days of summer; moreover, it is decidedly favourable for the greater number of bulbous plants. The plan gives a section of a flower border showing plants, the greater number of which are specially desirable for light soils. The white Everlasting Pea notched into the back of the Echinops is meant to be trained over and among the branches of the Globe Thistle as this goes out of flower.

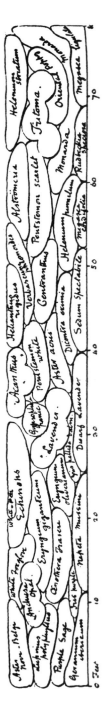

AN ATTRACTIVE ARRANGEMENT FOR A BORDER OF PERENNIALS ON LIGHT SOIL

AN ALTERNATIVE SUGGESTION FOR HEAVY SOIL

ON HEAVY SOILS

Though the best border plants are, as to their greater number, amenable to treatment on any soil that is well cultivated and fairly enriched, there are some that are so closely addicted to their own special requirements that they must have what they want or they 'will not play'. Of important border plants the first that come to mind are the Hollyhocks. It may safely be said that on poor soils it is impossible to grow Hollyhocks without their being attacked and weakened by the fungoid disease *Puccinia malvacea*, while in a soil that is rich in loam or lime the pest is either absent or so little prevalent that it need not be considered. Growing Hollyhocks on a poor soil is a continual struggle, and though rich feeding may give enough strength for the production of a fairly good flower-spike the handsome pyramid of healthy foliage down to the ground cannot be expected; the leaves are pinched and shrivelled with the disease, and the naked spike has to be concealed by a planting of something fairly tall in front.

For general convenience it is usual to group together as heavy soils those that are loamy and calcareous. But it may be well to remember that there are whole families of plants that have a special need of lime. These include the Cruciferæ in general—Wallflowers, Stocks, Rockets, Iberis, Arabis, Aubrietia and Æthionema; also other families, such as all the Dianthus, and the greater number of the Anemones, Clematis and Campanulas. Phloxes of the *decussata* class are apt to be unhappy on light soils, but revel in a rich loam. It is almost impossible to grow the pretty double Primroses in their charming colourings of white, yellow, lilac and crimson on a light soil, even though constantly enriched. Nearly all the Roses are loam lovers, as we know well by experience with their near relatives the fruit trees, almost the only exceptions being Raspberries, the native form of which runs riot in sandy copses, while the cultivated kinds bear heavy crops in the light-soiled fruit garden.

BORDERS OF ANNUALS FOR LIGHT AND
HEAVY SOILS, WITH PLANS

Annuals for Light Soils. There is not always in a garden an opportunity for having special borders for annuals, yet such a chance occurs from time to time, and especially when ground is being slowly restored from unavoidable neglect, or when there are regions infested with Couch or some other troublesome weed, such as cannot be entirely got rid of by one forking over. Here is the opportunity for the bed of annuals, to be used as what gardeners call a cleaning crop. The ground is cleared of the weeds as well as may be during the early part of the year or the previous winter, so as to be ready for sowing in March. The annuals will cover it all the summer, and in the autumn, when their beauty is over, it will receive its final cleaning. It may be taken as a general rule that the plants that are natives of the warmer climates will be the ones best suited to the lighter and warmer soils; we therefore infer that the Californian Eschscholtzia and Bartonia and the Mexican Argemone and Ageratum, and plants from similar climates, will be the ones to use; only avoiding those that, from our knowledge or experience, have shown, by their unwillingness to do well in light soil, that they demand something more nourishing. The plan of a short piece of border shows an arrangement, with some thought for suitable grouping and harmonious colouring, of some of the annuals that do well in light sandy soil with moderate enrichment.

Annuals for Heavy Soils. By a heavy soil is generally understood one that is of a stiffish loam or that has a considerable admixture of chalky matter. A number of our annual and biennial plants have a decided preference for such a soil. It may be taken as a rule that all the Cruciferæ, a large family, including many important garden plants, will only show their best on a rich, heavy soil, preferably calcareous. Here is the place for large plantings of Wallflowers, Stocks, Rockets and

A BORDER OF ANNUALS FOR LIGHT SOIL

A BORDER OF ANNUALS FOR HEAVY SOIL

all the annual Iberis, of which the large *I. coronaria* is so fine a thing when well grown. Sweet Sultan is also a plant that grows in a poor, unwilling way in light ground, but that is grand on a good loam. Sweet Williams, some of the finest and most effective of summer flowers, with all the others of the Dianthus family, are never happy except in loamy soil, preferably chalky, so that the beautiful Indian Pinks, also in their several charming varieties, will be well displayed in our heavy soiled annual border. The Bell Flowers, too, many of them natives of the limestone Alps, are thankful for being grown on such a rich, dark loam as usually clothes a calcareous formation. Of these, Canterbury Bells will be the most important in the annual border, grown, as usual, as biennials; they are all good but perhaps the prettiest are those of the cup and saucer pattern, for the spreading saucer widens the mass of bloom colour. Sweet Peas are never happy in light soils, in which they can only be grown by means of special enrichment, but they revel in a rich loam. The pretty dwarf Phloxes of the *Drummondii* kinds are also loam lovers. In the accompanying plan no Wall-flowers are shown because they are essentially spring flowers and are, therefore, not suitable for a border of summer annuals. But in their own place, in the garden of spring flowers, nothing can exceed their value; also in any places where a spring filling is desired, to be followed later by summer flowers.

SOME DESIRABLE ANNUALS

There are a number of good annuals that may be advised for such a place as a border or bank in full sun—plants from California, Mexico and South Africa. Among them are some of the Poppyworts—Eschscholtzias, of which there are now such gorgeous coloured varieties, and *Argemone grandiflora* with its large white poppy-like flowers, much resembling those of *Romneya Coulteri*. This fine plant stands nearly three feet high, and the prickly-looking foliage is not the least part of its beauty.

The Californian *Bartonia aurea*, more properly called *Mentzelia Lindleyi*, is a shorter plant. Some of the Arctotis have flowers of a fine orange colour and rise to about a foot in height. *Dimorphotheca aurantiaca* is another showy orange Composite. *Thunbergia alata* is a trailing plant with dark-eyed cream and orange flowers that would suit the sunny front edge of the warm border. These last three plants are from South Africa. Arctotis and Eschscholtzias may be sown in the open, and possibly Bartonia, but the others should be raised in mild heat and put out in the first days of June. With the exception of the Argemone they are all plants of strong, warm colouring that will make a fine show if planted in company. There is another desirable Dimorphotheca, *D. pluvialis*; the flowers are white, with the back of the petals of that pleasant quiet colour that is like diluted ink, such as one sees in that interesting plant *Stobaea purpurea*.

Some annuals, of small stature and neat habit, are specially suitable for the rock garden or top edge of dry walling, or anywhere they are brought near the eye. *Asperula azurea setosa* is a charming little plant with lavender-blue flowers, delightful in a still dwarfer setting of *Alyssum maritimum*; both are sweet-scented. Another little blue beauty, *Anagallis caerulea*, about six inches high, may well be in the same company; also *Nolana prostrata* and *N. atriplicifolia*, blue-flowered plants of prostrate habit, natives of South America, that can be sown where they are to flower. One hardly expects blue flowers from any Stone-crop, but the little annual *Sedum coeruleum* certainly has a faint blue colouring. *Grammanthes gentianoides*, another tiny gem, sounds as if it ought to be blue, but the flowers are of a rich deep orange colour almost approaching that of the brightest mahogany. This and the Sedum should be raised in pots and planted out just as they are, straight from the pots without any disturbance. *Nycterinia selaginoides* is a delightful little pale pink starry thing, so small that it would be lost on the level, but a wonder of form when seen close.

There is a splendid Poppy that seems to be always forgotten, the Tulip Poppy (*Papaver glaucum*). The large flowers of deepest scarlet are the most brilliant of its kind; with its grand bloom and glaucous buds and foliage it is a more striking plant than *P. umbrosum*, which is more commonly grown; it is best autumn sown. The Leptosiphons are good plants that are too much neglected; the rich colouring of the red and orange varieties have an effect of being diffused, from the small size of the abundant bloom. When once grown they appear again self-sown. They are not too large for places in bold rockwork.

The night-scented Stock (*Matthiola bicornis*) is too often forgotten. It has no effect in the daytime, for the flowers are of no size and are of a dull, pinkish-brownish colour. They remain closed till dusk, but when the light is gone they open widely and freely exhale their delicious scent, and are quite the best of the night-scented flowers of the hardy garden. *Platy-stemon californicus* has flattish cup-shaped flowers of a pleasant cream colour, with a spreading habit something like that of the better known *Limnanthes Douglasii*. Both of these are best autumn sown, when a single plant will cover nearly a yard of space. Platystemon when once established comes again by self-sown seeds. *Lathyrus sativus* is a pretty little blue Pea of mildly climbing habit, about two feet high; it may be sown in place The better, purplish-blue *L. pubescens* will grow four feet high or more, but is tender and perhaps hardly to be classed with annuals. But the gem of all climbing plants is the splendid *Ipomoea rubro-coerulea*. It should be grown in heat and planted out in June. It is usually seen in a greenhouse, but in a fairly warm summer on a south or west wall, its wonderful and perfect blue is a sight to see. The deep purple blue and a lighter tint of the same, of a good strain of the old *Convolvulus major* (*Ipomoea purpurea*), are also fine things; they are rampant climbers up to seven or eight feet. A beautiful climbing annual that was much in favour about fifty years ago is *Maurandya*

Barclayana. It is raised in heat, potted off singly and put out in June. The foliage is delicate, and the pretty purple flowers are shaped something like a Pentstemon. It should have a place near or against a warm wall. Among annuals of large size there is the fine old *Lavatera trimestris*, with flowers of a good pink. There is also a so-called improved variety of a deeper colour, dangerously approaching an unpleasant quality of rankness. It is a case of progressing backwards! The pure pink Lavatera groups charmingly with white Cosmos, also a plant of some height. The habit of the Cosmos inclines to be straggly, but this can be corrected by stopping the growth at least twice, when it assumes a bushy habit and gives more bloom. Salpiglossis should never be forgotten; the tall kind is the best. The colourings of gold and mahogany, crimson and purple, all tone well together.

Biennials are usually associated with annuals, and one may mention the usefulness of the Purple Rocket and the darker kind of purple Honesty (*Lunaria*). The two plants are much alike, both in colour and habit, and are of great use in the back regions of any garden scheme of which the time is the month of May.

The tall African Marigolds are indispensable for borders in the late summer and autumn. The best are the orange and the primrose-coloured—the latter a much better colour than one of an intermediate yellow that is sold as lemon. Where there is a rather large space to be filled for the summer, the annual Daturas, *D. ceratocaula* and *D. cornucopia*, are grand plants for the purpose; a single plant requiring four or five feet of space. Towering above and behind these, or in an open space among shrubs, where something tall and large is required, the eight feet high Balsam, the white variety of *Impatiens glandulifera*, sometimes sold under the doubtfully correct name of *I. Roylei*, can be recommended.

ANNUALS FOR SUNNY PLACES

So many of our annuals are natives of sub-tropical regions —some even of the tropics—that it is safe to say that quite three-quarters of them are suited to sunny places; in fact, it is comparatively rare to find among them cultivated forms derived from the flora of our own or equally temperate regions, such as the Foxgloves of the woods, the Wallflowers of old ruins, the Poppies and Cornflowers of the arable fields. From the whole region of the Levant, from India, South Africa, South and Central America come the bulk of our annuals, those from the warmest regions being the ones we class as half-hardy. These are too tender to be sown in the early spring in the open ground; it is not that they would not germinate, but that their progress would be so slow that they would not reach their flowering strength till too late in the season. They are therefore raised in heat in early spring, pricked off into boxes and planted out towards the end of May or early in June. These will include the greater number of those that do best in the warmest exposure—French and African Marigolds, Indian Pinks, Alonsoa, Ageratum, *Phlox Drummondii*, China Asters, Portulaca, Zinnia, Salpiglossis, Brachycome, Bartonia, Argemone, Tropaeolum and others.

There are annuals also that are suitable for the hottest places in rockwork; in fact, this is the best place for little gems only an inch or two high, such as *Grammanthes gentianoides*, the tiny Blue Stonecrop and the little Nyctarinia, more properly named Zaluzianskya, a charming little starry flower that should be more often grown in such places as raised rockwork, where it can be brought near the eye and is not in danger of being smothered by plants of larger size.

*With lack of attention to thinning, a border becomes untidy and the
beauty of the individual groups is lost*

*Borders in early and late summer. A garden with restricted colouring
of blue, grey and soft pink*

ANNUALS FOR SHADY PLACES

It may sound rather Irish to say that the best annuals for shady places are biennials, but the statement may be allowed to pass, because for garden purposes the two are commonly considered together. Places in shade other than those sheltered by buildings will be near trees and shrubs and the aspect will be anything between east and north. Such a place and aspect is specially suitable to some of the finest biennials, such as Foxgloves, Mulleins and *Œnothera Lamarckiana*. Where space allows of these being planted in a quantity of one kind at a time, distinct and fine effects may be secured. The pure white Foxglove, seen in shade, is one of the best of summer flowers; *Verbascum olympicum*, a towering candelabrum of pale yellow, and the quicker growing *V. phlomoides*, also tall and pale yellow, are only seen at their best in shade, for except at dusk or in cloudy weather the flowers are never properly expanded in open situations. The tall Evening Primrose also, when in shade, does not wait for the twilight to open its widespread blooms of tenderest yellow.

Of true annuals the finest for a shady place is the tall Balsam, *Impatiens glandulifera*, and especially the fine white variety sold as *Roylei*. It will grow from seven to eight feet high, branching wide with its fragrant pure white flowers of true Balsam form suspended in clusters from the ends of the branches and axillary shoots. There is also the fine *Polygonum orientale*, a tall, vigorous annual; the colour of the type is a strong magenta, but there is a pure white variety of great beauty, though not always obtainable.

Among the Campanulas, many of them shade-loving, there are not many annuals or biennials compared with the numbers of the perennial species; but there is a whole series of fine things in the Canterbury Bells, in purple, light and dark, white and pink colourings. The biennial Honesty (*Lunaria biennis*) is also best in a shady place; so are the Tobacco plants and the Sweet Rockets.

"Every border should be carefully considered for colour effect. Without such preparatory care the result will be a mere jumble, of no value to the cultivated eye." A planned border of golden foliage.

ANNUALS TO SOW IN HEAT

A certain number of annual plants, whose native place is a much warmer climate than ours, would only move very slowly, perhaps not at all, if sown in the open. They are those that we class as half-hardy, and are sown in pots, pans or boxes in a frame or greenhouse, to be pricked off into other boxes when they are large enough to handle, and are finally planted out at the end of May or quite early in June for summer display. Some of them are, in fact, perennials, but have been found to give a good show in their first year, and are therefore suitable for our use as annuals.

Pentstemons and Antirrhinums are examples of such plants. The Snapdragons will be among the first to be sown, in February, so that they may be pushed on and get to flowering strength as early as may be. Lobelias and Ageratums will also be sown early, and some of the large things of fine effect that are so often forgotten, such as the large Solanums and Daturas. The latter are really perennials, but used as annuals with us— grand sub-tropical plants of American origin. *Thunbergia alata*, a trailing plant with buff or orange flowers and a black eye, is more often grown for the greenhouse than the open garden, but will do well on a warm, sunny bank. *Torenia Fournieri*, another old favourite, is also raised in heat as a greenhouse pot plant; it should be more generally grown. The beautiful *Ipomoea rubro-coerulea* (Heavenly Blue) must also be sown in heat and pushed on for planting out in early June with other tender climbing plants such as *Mina lobata*, *Maurandya Barclayana*, *Cobaea scandens* and the blue Passion Flower.

*Hollyhocks, Lavender and double Achillea
(The Pearl) in the border*

Another corner of the same border, with pink Godetia

"Colour, in gardening as in painting . . . means the arrangement of colour with the deliberate intention of producing beautiful pictorial effect, whether by means of harmony or of contrast."

VI

COLOUR IN THE GARDEN

COLOUR PLANNING
>From the Introduction to *Colour Planning of the Garden*, by Tinley, Humphreys and Irving (Jack, 1924)

COLOUR SEQUENCES
>*Journal of the Royal Horticultural Society*, vol. liv, part 2, 1929

BLUES AND MAUVES IN THE GARDEN
>*Country Life*, October 18, 1924

THE GREY GARDEN

A LITTLE AUGUST GARDEN
>*The Garden*, March 26, 1921

VI

Colour in the Garden

COLOUR PLANNING

IT IS a sign of distinct advance in the practice of horticulture
that there is now so strong an interest in the subject of
colour, and so general a desire for instruction or guidance
in its best use. For colour, in gardening as in painting, does not
mean a garish or startling effect, such as may be provided by a
bed of scarlet Geranium in a setting of green turf; but it means
the arrangement of colour with the deliberate intention of producing beautiful pictorial effect, whether by means of harmony
or of contrast. In the old days of sixty years ago, it was simply
the most garish effects that were sought for; the brightest
colourings that could be obtained in red, blue, and yellow were
put close together, often in rings like a target, and there would
be meandering lines, wriggling along for no reason, of Golden
Feather Feverfew, edged with a companion wriggle of Lobelia
and an inner line of scarlet Geraniums, the only excuse being
that such a ribbon border was then in fashion. It was at a time
when endless invention and ingenuity, time and labour, were
wasted in what was known as carpet-bedding; elaborate and
intricate patterns worked out in succulents and a variety of
dwarf plants. When the ingenious monstrosity was completed
the chief impression it gave was that it must have taken a long
time to do; whether it was worth doing did not come in question, for this again was the fashion. This must have been the
time when general taste in horticulture was in its deepest
degradation, when the sweet old garden flowers were thought
not worth notice, and had been abolished in favour of the elaborate display of tender plants for some few months at most.

154

Happily we know better now, and as the new knowledge advances we are learning how to use our plants in the ways they deserve. But it should be remembered that the tender summer flowers that were almost exclusively employed in those unenlightened days, still have their uses. There are some persons with whom the revulsion from the methods of the old 'bedding' days is so strong that it includes a condemnation of the plants themselves, so that they will not admit scarlet Geranium, or blue Lobelia, or yellow Calceolaria into their pleasure-grounds. But, properly employed, these are all good garden plants, and it was not their fault that they were used in uninteresting ways. The sun-loving Geranium is, and always will be, the best thing for vases; and now that there are so many good varieties, there is an ample choice for the exact shade of colour that may best suit the position. The clear, pale yellow of *Calceolaria amplexicaulis* is almost unmatched for purity, and is indispensable in some such arrangement as will be later described. The blue Lobelia—the bluer the better—is of value for jewels of pure colour in the right setting. In fact there is hardly any garden plant, only excepting some that have flowers of a rank magenta colouring, that cannot be worthily employed in some well-considered connection or combination.

It may save confusion to consider some colour arrangements of our garden plants according to their seasons. It is usual that the earliest flowers to appear are the Winter Aconite (*Eranthis hyemalis*) and the Christmas Roses, varieties of *Helleborus niger*. Though they bloom nearly at the same time, it is better to treat them separately. The little Winter Aconite is best planted under some deciduous tree in thin woodland, when this comes near the garden; perhaps for preference under the outer branches of a Beech, as the yellow blooms and the carpet of rusty leaves come so well together. Christmas Roses enjoy a cool place in rich loam where they are never droughted; a quiet dell of their own in a Fern garden is a good place. They look well in a setting of some winter green Fern, such as Poly-

Ayrshire Rose on a wall

A border of single white Peonies in early summer

The south border in late summer showing Yuccas, Hydrangeas, Antirrhinums and LILIUM AURATUM, *with foliage plants (*Santolina *and* CINERARIA MARITIMA) *in foreground*

pody or Hart's-tongue, whose foliage colour is a little more lively than that of their own.

Early in February comes the bloom of the different kinds of the Lent Hellebores. They are the species and garden varieties of *H. olympicus, H. orientalis, H. abchasicus,* and *H. atrorubens.* They are mainly in shades of a quiet purplish red with a darker spotting, and as they intercross freely the variation of tint and marking seems to be infinite. Of several there are white varieties, the patches of white-flowered plants serving as a pleasant break in the general purple colouring. With them may well be grown the little shrub *Daphne Mezereum,* whose bloom, of a low-toned pink, tones well with the colouring of the Hellebores. There are still some flowering plants that may join into the same harmony and that can with advantage be intergrouped with the Hellebores, or be planted in their outskirts. The best of these will be the fine form of *Megasea ligulata* known as *M. l. speciosa.* Its flowering time is nearly that of the Hellebores; its colour, a pleasant, tender pink, is not too clear to interfere with its lower-toned companions, though it is best when massed with the white Lenten flowers. The roundish, leathery leaves are in pleasant contrast to the other palmate foliage. A place that is partly shaded in summer is the best for the Hellebores and also suits the Megasea; such as a border on each side of a path backed by nuts, for the Hellebores are in flower before the leaves of the nuts come, and so get the benefit of the late winter sunshine, while for the rest of the year they are glad of the shade. The nuts, which will be some of the good kinds, Cobnuts or Filberts, will in time arch over the path, so making a pleasant shady way from one part of the garden to another.

Crocuses will be in flower in February. Besides their use in garden ground proper, they are still better in open woodland or any half-shaded grassy places. For the best colour effects it will be found advisable to plant the purples and whites in the shadier or quieter places—though shade in February is barely more than nominal—and the strong yellows in the open, and not to have the three colourings in view at the same time. As in many matters connected with wild gardening this requires more care in the doing than many more regular garden operations. It is certainly best to plant the Crocuses in long-shaped drifts rather than in patches, and, above all, never, as has sometimes been seen, in concentric rings round a tree. The drifts, a little wider in the middle and narrowing into nothing at the ends, may be of any length, according to the space of ground that has to be planted, and they had better be more or less parallel to the path or most usual point of view; each drift or adjoining group of drifts should be of one kind only. In a large space two or three of the purple shades may find a place, with a stream of white here and there, but the white had better be less in quantity than the purple.

Daffodils will be beginning in March and will go on through April and into May. These also, and any other woodland plants, should be in drifts rather than in patches. It is both interesting and instructive as well as being best for colour effect, to plant them in thin woodland in a kind of natural sequence; beginning with the pale *Narcissus pallidus praecox*, then passing to other Trumpets of fuller yellow and then to the bicolour Trumpets, and from these to. the hybrids of Trumpet and *incomparabilis*. The next to follow will be the true *incomparabilis*, and then the hybrids of these with *N. poeticus*—the *poeticus* influence making the colour paler; and ending with the type *poeticus* and its better variety *N. p. ornatus*. This is the white Pheasant-eye of gardens, with a strong, sweet scent. It is, with a few exceptions that need not concern wild planting, the latest of the Daffodils, its blooming time being in May when Sweetbriar is making its fragrant young foliage. The fine double *N. poeticus* should also be planted, and in suitable soils will show as a sheet of white. *N. poeticus* is a plant of the limestone Alps and is not happy in light soils. The greater number of the Narcissi do quite well in sandy ground, though they may scarcely have the size and vigour of those grown on a good loam.

April and early May is the time of Primroses. The wild Primrose, with its rare colouring of a pale yellow that may well be called cool, for it has a greenish quality, is much the best for wild planting, for not only does it look more suitable, but the garden kinds of stouter build and stronger colouring demand regular garden cultivation. It is best to have these in a place of their own—some place that is partly shaded, such as a spacious clearing in a grove of Oaks, where they can be grown in thousands, and where they can have a further irregular shading of Hazels or garden nuts. When space allows, a sort of sequence of Primrose gardens would be desirable, for the true Primroses, with all radical stems, are the first to flower, to be followed by the larger growing bunch kinds. Even these, for the sake of colour effect, should be divided into two or even three sections; one for the rich and dark colours, red, crimson, and brownish, with a few only of the deeper yellows; one for the yellows and whites, robust plants of fine effect; and a smaller section for those whose colour is a tender mauve or pinkish or light purple shade, with whites. This might include the fine old double mauve and double white, now comparatively rare, but these only do well on a strong loam or a chalky soil.

There are a number of small early bulbous plants, such as Scillas and Chionodoxas, that are best used in a place by themselves; they look well carpeted with low-growing things, such as the mossy or the encrusted Saxifrages. The front of a flower border with a rocky edge is a good place for them; they can be planted just behind the stones, with the Saxifrages creeping between the stones and partly between the little flowers; or if there is a bank or border for hardy Ferns, the small plants may well run up in streams or drifts between the Ferns, whose later growth will completely cover them and fill the border.

With April the spring flowers come crowding in. Planted dry walls and rock gardens this month and next are full of bloom, and hosts of bulbous plants are in flower. Iberis, Aubrietia, Arabis, Alyssum, and Myosotis are some of the most conspicuous of the lower-growing plants. They are often placed all together, but it is better to avoid the garish contrast of purple Aubrietia and yellow Alyssum, keeping the Aubrietia only company with the white flowers. Aubrietia is one of the flowers that has of late suffered by the perversion of its proper colouring in the direction of reddish tints. These are bad reds at the best, with the sole exception of a rather pretty one of a pale pinkish tint. The proper colour of Aubrietia is a clear, rather light purple, such as one may get by choosing the best of the produce of a packet of seed of *Aubrietia graeca*. There are some fine things of deeper colouring, of which the best is a well-known kind named after its raiser Dr. Mules. The finest effect of a group of Aubrietia is when it is composed of more than three-quarters of the normal pale colour, with a few plants only of Dr. Mules, in a setting of the pure white bloom and deep green foliage of *Iberis sempervirens*. There is a beautiful variety called Lavender in which the bloom is large and of good colour, but the flowers are not so numerous as in those that are nearer the typical *graeca*. Myosotis is delightful with anything white or pale yellow, such as Primroses or white Tulips, the clear yellow Tulip *retroflexa*, pale Daffodils, and the palest Wall-flowers. Such an arrangement may well have a back planting of the purple-leaved Sage. There are several varieties of Myosotis, and many may be tempted by the stronger blue of some of the newer kinds, but the best for general use is *M. dissitiflora*. The dark Wallflowers, known as blood-red, are fine with the tall scarlet Tulip *Gesneriana*, and the colour effect is all the better for a groundwork of the Satin Leaf *Heuchera Richardsoni*; shorter red Tulips come in front of this, and quite at the edge the reddish-leaved Ajuga. Such a groundwork of related but quieter colour with brilliant flowers is a most important matter in good gardening; and in spring and summer effects this Heuchera, with its ruddy-tinted, satin-lustred leaves, and the purple-leaved Sage above mentioned, are of the greatest use. The Sage, whose leaves have a soft suffusion of pinkish purple, is an excellent setting to anything pink, such as the fine Tulip Clara Butt.

May brings a wealth of bloom not only on hardy shrubs but on a number of good garden flowers. The old Peony (*Paeonia officinalis*) should have a special place, in its three varieties of crimson, rosy red, and white. They are best in good masses accompanied by white flowers only—Solomon's Seal, White Columbine, and little bushes of *Deutzia gracilis* and *Olearia Gunniana*, and they may well be backed by the white Portugal Broom which flowers at the same time. A separate portion of bank or border would be beautiful with purple Pansies, the pink *Dielytra eximia*, and the taller *D. spectabilis* and St. Bruno's Lily (*Anthericum*), with a goodly planting of some of the earlier Flag Irises of white and purple colouring, the dwarf, dark Purple King, the grey-white *florentina*, the stately purple Kharput, with white Foxglove to follow at the back. Some of the common pink China Rose would come in well with this grouping.

June brings the later Peonies, the many beautiful varieties of *P. albiflora*, of which there are great numbers to choose from. These grand Peonies are worthy of an entire garden space to themselves, though they are also in place as either simple plants or as groups of two or three in flower borders. One good way of having them is intergrouped with the Roses in a Rose garden, where the beds are apt to look thin and unfurnished; a weakness that the large foliage of the Peonies tends to correct.

Another great family of June-flowering plants contains the most useful of the Irises, namely, the flag-leaved kinds. A large number of fine new varieties have been produced of late years, and their qualities and colouring can be learnt from any good Iris catalogue. A whole Iris garden is no doubt desirable, but it would have to be carefully interplanted with something of which the foliage would overspread the Irises, because, except in the case of the *pallidas* or varieties with near *pallida* parentage, the leaves wither up and become unsightly. But this does not matter if a special bit of garden can be given to the Irises and a few other flowers of June, and treated carefully for colour effect. Such a place should be rather separate from other garden ground as it would not be of interest either earlier or later in the year. It would begin at one end with Irises, purple and white, purple perennial Lupines, pink China Rose, and the beautiful little shrub, *Olearia Gunniana*, which is covered in June with its myriad of little starry white flowers. Then Irises of a lighter purple, the kinds that are nearest to blue, and the fine white Oriental poppy, Perry's White, and white Lupines. All this region has a plentiful planting of white Foxglove at the back. Then comes the pale yellow *Iris flavescens* with one of the shorter yellow Irises in front, and a goodly planting of yellow Tree Lupine, followed by the deeper yellow *Iris variegata aurea*; all this with a front and middle underplanting of the reddish Satin Leaf *Heuchera Richardsoni*. This underplanting is continued as the Irises darken in colour to those that have claret falls and smoky yellow standards. After this the colour again passes to yellow, with a good deal of interplanting of a most useful plant, *Peltaria alliacea*, about a foot high with a cloud of tiny cruciferous bloom of a warm white colour. Then there are again white Irises and China Roses, and the end of the border has some white Tree Lupines, the tall warm white spires of Asphodel and the creamy plumes of *Spiraea Aruncus*.

The colouring of Roses has been so much altered and extended of late that in planning a Rose garden the separate needs of the newer shades should be kept in mind. For though Roses pink and white, and red and white, and pink and red are fine in company, the whites and some of the cooler pinks do not agree with the salmon and orange shades, although the whites and pure pale yellows inclining to a canary tint go charmingly together.

Of late years we have learnt better ways of arranging flower borders for colour effect. Formerly a border was planted according to the heights of plants only; tall at the back, short in front, and those of intermediate height in the middle, and they were placed, not only without any regard to colour combination, but in single plants, so that the whole effect was like a patchwork of small pieces indiscriminately dotted about. It is a good plan, before planting, to settle on a definite scheme; and one that can be recommended is to keep flowers of tender colouring at the ends of a border and to work gradually towards a grand effect of gorgeous colouring in the middle of the length. There is one thing to be noted, that whereas all the strong warm colours, deep yellow, orange, scarlet, crimson, and any deeper kinds of rich colouring are best suited for a gradual progression of intermingling shades, the cool colours, and pure blue especially, demand a contrast. This being so it is convenient, in arranging a long border, to have the blues at one end and the purples at the other. When in these notes blue is mentioned it is to be understood that a true pure blue is meant, not any of the cool purple or violet colourings such as are so frequent in, for instance, Asters and Campanulas, and that are so often miscalled blue. Thus, at the blue end, the border will begin with Delphinium and Anchusa, enough of each to make a good show, for the true blues are not too many. Farther forward there will be the shorter hybrid Delphiniums and the beautiful still dwarfer Belladonna and *Commelina coelestis*, with *Salvia patens* dropped in for the summer. At the front will be the pretty Cape Daisy, *Agathea coelestis*, and the bright little *Lobelia erinus*. A strong plant of *Clematis Flammula* is at the back of the Delphiniums; when their bloom is over, the fast-growing seed-pods are cut away and the white flowered Clematis is trained over the Delphinium stems which now stand between four and five feet high. Here at the back are also white Dahlias and creamy Spiraeas and tall Snapdragons of palest yellow, half-way between yellow and white. Pure pale yellow Snapdragons are delightful with the blue flowers. Following this comes a beautiful combination near, and at the front, some yards in length, of the old garden plant, *Mentha rotundifolia*, whose leaves are variegated with warm white, with the warm white striped grass *Glyceria aquatica*; and at the back of these the fine old pure canary yellow *Calceolaria amplexicaulis*. Now there are yellow Hollyhocks and yellow Dahlias at the back and the tall yellow *Thalictrum flavum*; even a bush of the brightly gold variegated Privet is not out of place. Now we come to the region of the stronger yellows; *Helenium pumilum* in a large, important drift and *Œnothera* of the *fruticosa* section, leading to the orange colourings of Helianthus and *Coreopsis lanceolata*, and the still deeper orange African Marigolds. Dwarf Tropaeolums and orange Pot Marigold and Gazania are now in front, with Tritonias in the middle spaces and towards the back, and Dahlias of deepest orange colour approaching scarlet. Then we come to actual scarlet and rich blood red of Dahlia and Hollyhock, with a softening setting of the annual *Atriplex hortensis*. Here also are the brightest scarlet Phloxes, Pentstemons, and Gladioli and in front a dozen or so of the grand bedding Geranium Paul Crampel. The whole of this region of gorgeous colouring is softened and tempered by an interplanting of deep reddish foliage—Iresine, the Atriplex just mentioned, and among the red Dahlias at the back, the red-leaved *Ricinus Gibsonii*, and some bushes of *Prunus Pissardii*, yearly pruned so that the deep reddish shoots may accompany the Dahlias and provide something that tones well with the whole gorgeous mass, and that is better than the dull green of the Dahlia foliage. At the back of the Dahlias is a tall old kind of a blackish crimson colour, and the blood-red Hollyhocks also have a companion of the same deep claret tint. The strong colour then passes again through orange and full yellow to white, with palest green foliage. Here are white Dahlias and white Everlasting Pea and foliage of striped Maize, and then a group of pink Hollyhock. After this the accompanying foliage is mostly grey—*Cineraria maritima*, Santolina, and Stachys; the colour passes from pink to mauve and on to the strong light purple of *Aster acris*. Echinops and Erigeron are grouped with the white of *Chrysanthemum maximum* and Paris Daisy, and white and pink Gladioli, and these are backed by taller purple Asters, white Dahlias, white Hollyhocks, and the creamy white of *Aster umbellatus*. Here also, at the end, are some tall Yuccas, *Y. gloriosa* and *Y. recurva*, with the lower-growing *Y. filamentosa*; all with a deeply dusky background of Yew which comes forward from the high wall that is at the back of the whole border. The flowers on the wall agree in colour with those in the border. The grey-blue of Ceanothus Gloire de Versailles tones in with the flowers at the blue end; then comes the white of *Laurustinus lucidus* and of Japan Privet, with dark foliage of Bay backing the yellow group. Where the mass of strong colour comes in the middle there is a *Fuchsia Riccartoni* and the showy orange-scarlet trumpets of *Bignonia radicans*, while the pink and purple at the farther end are accompanied by the pink of *Robinia hispida* and *Clerodendron foetidum*, and the purple of *Buddleia Veitchii*.

The same general rule of colouring is followed in a separate garden set apart for the better use of the tender things formerly known as bedding plants, including some already named in the flower border. But here in the brightest part there are more Geraniums, toning away to right and left from strongest vermilion to palest pink, and Cannas and a host of Snapdragons, with again Dahlias, Gladioli, and Pentstemons. But at one end of this garden, forming a background to the whole, there are raised banks of grey and glaucous foliage—Yuccas, Phormium, *Senecio Greyi*, *Cineraria maritima*, Euphorbia, Othonnopsis, and Cerastium, with pink and purple flowers only.

This combination of grey foliage with pink and purple flowers is so important that a whole double border may well be given to it. Such a border is in existence and is every year a source of greater pleasure. Here are bold clumps of tall pink

Hollyhocks and tumbling masses of *Clematis Jackmani*, the shrubby pink-flowered *Lavatera Olbia*, a lavender-coloured Ceanothus trimmed to bush form, Echinops, purple and white China Asters, Ageratum tall and dwarf, the mist-like Gypsophila, a fine purple form of the annual *Delphinium consolida*, and another valuable annual, the double pink Godetia, with tall white and palest pink Snapdragons. All these, with the silvery *Eryngium giganteum* and a plentiful filling of *Cineraria maritima*, Santolina, and *Stachys lanata*, form a most satisfactory picture of good garden colour in and about the month of August.

The Michaelmas Daisies are so important in September and October that it is well worth while to give them a separate place, in addition to their use with other flowers in the mixed border. And though their colouring is restricted to shades of purple and pinkish, yet whole borders of them, if rightly arranged, are full of beauty and interest. It will be found better to concentrate on a few good kinds and have them in bold masses, than to try to accommodate a larger number of varieties. A few other plants may well go with them, especially the September-blooming *Chrysanthemum uliginosum*, a big white Daisy that makes a better show among the Asters than any white variety of their own kind. The large pink-flowered *Sedum spectabile*, beloved of butterflies, will also be welcome, and some of the latest China Asters. The front edges may well be filled with the silvery Stachys and purple Ageratum both tall and dwarf. The tendency of growers who specialise in these excellent Asters seems of late to incline to the production of more of the pinkish kinds, but the use of these had better not be overdone, for the true character and chief beauty of Michaelmas Daisies must always be in those of the clear purple colourings.

The practice of good colour arrangement in gardening is full of delightful potentialities. In the foregoing notes it has only been possible to put forward some general principles and their application in one or two more or less definite schemes. But to anyone who delights in the beauty of flowers, and has, either by natural endowment or by the education of perception, acquired some knowledge of how to use colour, they may serve as an early guide or substructure on which to build further, according to their own desire or inclination. In any case the study and practice of good use of colour in the garden cannot fail to be a source of abiding interest and unfailing inspiration.

COLOUR SEQUENCES

Fifty years ago, when the bedding-out of tender plants for a summer display was the general garden practice, if any thought was given to arranging them for colour, it was to produce the crudest and most garish effects; such as a round bed of a vivid scarlet Geranium with a border of blue Lobelia, or a wavy ribbon border of scarlet, blue, and yellow. Now that all that concerns the planning of our gardens is engaging the attention of our best designers, the better use of colour is being carefully considered, and is already being gloriously practised. For when colour is rightly used the various portions of the garden will have the highest pictorial value as living pictures of plant beauty.

An example of the better arrangement may be quoted in the case of a large flower border, nearly 200 feet in length. It begins with flowers of tender and cool colouring—palest pink, blue, white and palest yellow—followed by stronger yellow, and passing on to deep orange and rich mahogany, and so coming to a culminating glory of the strongest scarlet, tempered with rich but softer reds, and backed and intergrouped with flowers and foliage of dark claret colour.

The progression of colour then recedes in the same general order, as in its approach to the midmost glory, till it comes near the further end to a quiet harmony of lavender and purple and tender pink, with a whole setting of grey and silvery foliage.

"The practice of good colour arrangement in gardening is full of delightful potentialities ... to anyone who delights in the beauty of flowers, and has, either by natural endowment or by the education of perception, acquired some knowledge of how to use colour, they may serve as an early guide or substructure on which to build further, according to their own desire or inclination. In any case the study and practice of good use of colour in the garden cannot fail to be a source of abiding interest and unfailing inspiration."

A picturesque association of GYPSOPHILA PANICULATA *and Megasea at the edge of the shrub border*

Another attractive combination of Megasea and ASTER CORYMBOSUS *at the shrubbery edge*

No one who has seen or carried out such a scheme, and whose desire it is to have the best effects that the flowers can give, will be contented with a haphazard mixture. Such an arrangement in harmonies is not only satisfying as a whole picture, but, though perhaps unconsciously to the observer, it follows natural laws relating to sight; for the cool and tender colouring is the best optical preparation for the splendour of the warmer masses, and, when the eye has had its fill of this, it receives a distinct sense of satisfaction when it comes again to the cool and restful colouring of flower and foliage. It is like passing from some shady place of half-light into the brilliant glow of hottest sunshine, and then, when this is almost too burning and oppressive, coming again to the quiet comfort of coolest shade and perhaps the sound of running or splashing water.

Some garden space is often devoted to the satisfaction of a desire for a special colour such as blue. There is some curious quality, not easy to define, about flowers of pure blue, such as Delphinium, Anchusa, Cornflower, and the useful dwarf Lobelia, that demands a contrast rather than a harmony; for though in a blue garden the colouring can, with more or less success, be made to pass from the pure blues into those of purpler shades, such as those of the Campanulas, yet it is a duller thing than if the pure blues only are used, with the companionship of something of white or pale yellow, such as white or yellow Lilies, white Phlox or pale yellow Snapdragon; or the creamy white of *Artemisia lactiflora* or *Clematis Flammula*.

It is much to be advised that there should be some such special place put aside for the best of the Michaelmas Daisies—especially for those of the purest purple colouring—with white. In late September and October, just at the time of year when the beauty of the garden is over, when the general impression is of dissolution and decay, and when leaves of trees are turning towards yellow and brown, it is a rare pleasure and a delightful surprise to come into the clear fresh colouring of

The "Problems of colour arrangement are becoming an engrossing study; every year some new or better combination suggests itself, with its certain reward in the following season. Something of the satisfaction of a good conscience rewards and encourages the designer; for surely one of the objects of a good garden is that it shall be pictorially beautiful — that it shall be a series of enjoyable pictures painted with the living flowers."

purple and white. There are now many fine kinds of the pinkish shades and also some good whites, but for the best enjoyment of the Michaelmas Daisy garden, the cool colouring of the purples is to be preferred; and for white, *Chrysanthemum uliginosum*, with its large pure white bloom, is more effective than the white of any of the Aster varieties—after all it is a Daisy and blooms at Michaelmas and may therefore make an honest claim for inclusion.

These problems of colour arrangement are becoming an engrossing study; every year some new or better combination suggests itself, with its certain reward in the following season. Something of the satisfaction of a good conscience rewards and encourages the designer; for surely one of the objects of a good garden is that it shall be pictorially beautiful—that it shall be a series of enjoyable pictures painted with the living flowers.

BLUES AND MAUVES IN THE GARDEN

It is easy enough to dispose the warm colours—red, orange and deep yellow—so as to form important and telling effects in flower borders and elsewhere; but the cooler colours, blue and mauve and all the many shades of purple, require rather special arrangement for the forming of satisfactory garden pictures. For the purpose of these notes I should like to define what is meant by blue, and especially by mauve, a colour word that has come into common use, but that is so loosely applied that it is impossible to know, in the very wide range of what may be called purple colourings generally, what kind of tint is intended. The word itself is the French name of the Wild Mallow, *Malva sylvestris*, and is an obvious and rather near corruption of the Latin generic name. The colour is a purplish pink rather low in tone, and far from that of the Wild Thrift, and can be matched by some of the pinkest shades of the common Lilac. A rather purpler tone is rightly called lilac. Our language is so rich in colour words for this range of tints that

A border showing Nepeta, STACHYS LANATA *and other
plants with distinctive foliage*

the common slip-slop in their use is the less justifiable. Then we have the useful word 'lavender', for a lightish purple of cooler quality. The bloom of common Lavender is so constant in tone and kind that when the word 'lavender' is used it may be taken to have a quite definite meaning. For deeper, richer tones we have the word 'violet'. It is true that violets themselves vary in colour from the pale lavender of the Parma to kinds of a strong reddish purple, but when we use 'violet' as a colour word we consider it to mean the deep, rather cool purple of the Czar Violet. Thus we may describe the splendid colour of *Iris reticulata* as a strong and deep bluish violet; for having all these useful colour words for purple flowers, it is easy to connect or modify them by combination. Heliotrope is another useful colour word, for, though there are heliotropes both light and dark, yet the type colouring that the word brings to mind has some softening of grey about it.

It is much to be desired that our seedsmen would be as careful and as nearly accurate in their description of colour as are our foreign neighbours. There is no class of garden flower that has a wider range of purple colourings than the China Aster, but I look in the catalogues of our two premier seed houses and find only very rare mention of the word purple, while varieties in each class are described as light and dark blue. This is extremely misleading, as it may safely be said that there is no such thing as a blue China Aster. Equally, there is no such thing as a blue Campanula, and hardly such a thing as a blue Iris. The little pale grey-blue *Iris pumila coerulea*, whose tone of colouring is so entirely different from that of the many kinds of bluish purple Flag Irises that are so commonly called blue, is perhaps the only one that may properly claim to be really blue.

When blue is named in these notes, what is meant is a perfectly pure blue, a colour that is perfect and complete in itself —that has no inclination whatever to a reddish or purplish tone. It means the blue of Commelina, of *Salvia patens*, of

Lithospermum and some of the Gentians; of Ipomoea Heavenly
Blue, of *Anagallis Phillipsii*, of Anchusa and the best Delphiniums, with the lighter blues of Forget-me-not, *Omphalodes
verna* and Nemophila. These, and a few others, may all be
described as perfectly pure blues. They are none too many and
are, therefore, all the more precious in garden use. There is a
quite indefensible colour word that has somehow crept into
plant lists, for which there would seem to be no kind of
justification. It is the word 'amethystine'. It is so familiar in this
connection that when we see a flower described as 'a brilliant
amethystine blue' we know that a brilliant pure blue is intended. But why 'amethystine'? An amethyst is not blue at all,
it is reddish purple. Did it, perhaps, originate in a muddle
between sapphire, which is really blue, and amethyst, which is
always purple? Did the original muddler think he was saying
'sapphirine' when he said 'amethystine'? It would appear to be
so. In any case, it is time to protest against the misuse of what
would be a useful colour word if it were rightly applied.

There is some curious quality about pure blue flowers that
obliges one, if one would have them at their best and happiest,
to satisfy them by the companionship of a distinct contrast,
either of white or of palest yellow. No border of blue flowers is
quite satisfactory without this. There are some who desire a
blue border or a whole blue garden, who make it a kind of case
of conscience that if it is called a blue garden there shall be
nothing in it that is not absolutely blue, whereas the flowers
may be praying for the company of white Lilies or palest
yellow Snapdragons or sulphur and white Hollyhocks. To deny
them this is to spoil the garden for the sake of a word!

If a border for the special display of blues and purples and
mauves is desired it may begin at one end with a group of
Delphiniums combined with Anchusa Opal. It is a good plan
to plant a *Clematis Flammula* behind these, for the blue flowers
will be over by the middle of July and the Clematis will grow
over them and give a sheet of sweet-smelling white bloom in

September. White Phloxes will come in the middle and white and palest yellow Snapdragons. Some tender plants are also wanted—the deep blue *Salvia patens* and the pale blue *Plumbago capensis*, the latter grown in pots and dropped in where required. Two of the Hydrangeas will also come well here, *H. paniculata* and *H. arborescens grandiflora*. Both have the fresh, pale green foliage that is so becoming to blue flowers, and the same effect is continued to the front with that of *Funkia grandiflora*. Here in the front will be the blue Cape Daisy, *Agathæa coelestis* and *Lobelia Erinus*, planted close enough to form a complete sheet of blue. White Dahlias are now at the back and white Lilies in the middle spaces, and some of the dwarf bedding Dahlias, both white and pure pale yellow, come towards the front. The colour now passes to purpler tones, first by the light bluish purple of the dwarf Agapanthus, *A. Moorei*, and its white variety, then by the Eryngiums—steel blue and silvery white. Here in front we have the large glaucous foliage of *Funkia Sieboldii* and the still larger and more glaucous *Crambe maritima*—the Seakale of the kitchen garden and a plant of much value in such colour combinations. At the back of these is the splendid *Iris pallida dalmatica*.

Now we come to flowers of pure lavender colour, Lavender itself and Echinops at the back. Behind the Echinops is a plant of *Clematis Jackmani* trained over pea-sticks and so placed that the sheet of pure purple bloom comes over the dimmer colour of the Globe Thistle. We are now at the middle point of the border, with the most intense of the purple colouring. For here are China Asters of the miscalled blue colourings both light and dark, and a fine violet-purple form of *Delphinium Consolida*, sown in place. The whole of this central group and what follows has a setting of grey foliage with a great group of Globe Artichoke at the back, quite the noblest of the Thistle family and much too good a plant to be left to the kitchen garden only. Then there is the good grey of *Artemisia Ludoviciana*, a most useful thing, for it can be allowed to grow to its full height of three and a half feet or it can be cut back to any height desired. The fine silvery foliage of *Cineraria maritima* comes in the middle and towards the front, and quite at the front are *Artemisia stelleriana* and Stachys. *Aster Amellus* and *A. acris* are here among these silvery greys, setting each other off to perfection. Nepeta in plenty is in the foreground. Bushes of Gypsophila with their mist-like clouds of tiny flowers form a backing to the deep violet purple Gladiolus Baron Hulot, and all vacant spaces are filled with tall and dwarf Ageratums. Now the colouring changes to softer, pinker shades—the true mauves, with a bush of *Lavatera Olbia* at the back and several fine Dahlias all with the continued grey setting.

THE GREY GARDEN

It is not the first time that attention has been drawn to the importance of grey and silvery foliage in the arrangement of flower borders for the late summer; but this aspect of gardening has of late aroused so much interest among amateurs, and such unqualified encouragement from artists, that some notes about its planting may be helpful to those who desire to make their gardens pictorially beautiful. The best season for such an arrangement is the six weeks during the months of August and the first half of September. It is unfortunate that these weeks coincide with the time when so many are away on holiday, and when the owners of large gardens are absent; afloat, or fishing, or on the Scottish grouse moors; but there are many good gardeners who are at home and able to enjoy not the grey garden alone, but all the splendid border flowers whose best effect seems to culminate at just the same season; for it is the time of Dahlias and Hollyhocks, Pentstemons, Snapdragons, Zinnias, Salpiglossis, the grand French and African Marigolds, and the rest of the good plants that are glorious in the late summer. Of these the most important in the grey garden are Hollyhocks and Dahlias, those whose colouring is right with the other flowers of purple, pink, and white, in the complete setting of silvery-white foliage that is the keynote of the grey garden's harmony. The Hollyhocks are the clear pink Pink Beauty, which is almost identical with the one known as Palling Belle; the Dahlias are white and pink varieties of the Star class, with one or two of light and full purple colouring. Any Dahlias of this kind of colouring will serve well. *Echinops ruthenicus* is of use, not only from its abundant heads of purplish bloom, but also because the foliage is of so quiet a green that it goes well with the grey plants. Eryngiums would be of much use, but the best kind, *E. Oliverianum*, the Silver Thistle, is just too early in season; but *E. planum*, though less showy, is just right in time, and should be included. There are not too many pink flowers available, but among the best are some of the Phloxes, especially the cooler of the pink-toned varieties, and one or two of the pale lilacs. It is best to avoid any pink flowers inclining to the salmon tints; the cool colours are better with the purple flowers. A bush of *Lavatera Olbia* should be in the background, for though it naturally flowers a little too soon, yet if it is cut back early in June it makes a quantity of flowering shoots for the right time. Also in the background are some bushes of Sea Buckthorn, valuable not only for their own silvery foliage but also as supports for purple Clematises, which ramble over them in delightful fashion. This was a valuable hint from an artist. Another precious bush for the back of the grey border is Ceanothus Gloire de Versailles. Cut hard back, it makes a quantity of flowering shoots for the middle of August.

A good supply should be provided of China Asters and Ageratum. The Asters of either the Victoria or the Comet classes, in the colours miscalled blue, and the fine deep purple Sutton's Purple Prince. There should be both kinds of Ageratum, one of the good dwarfs and the tall *A. mexicanum.* Snapdragons, white and pink, will also be included, with a good short-growing one called Mauve Beauty, of a true mauve colour, a low-toned purplish pink. Annuals, to be sown in place, are Godetia double pink, and a fine violet form of *Delphinium Consolida*. *Campanula lactiflora* is useful, preferably cut over early to retard the bloom and to shorten those that would grow too high. *Gypsophila paniculata* is indispensable. It is useful to keep a reserve of standard Heliotrope to drop in as may be required, and also Hydrangeas, but these should be arranged so as to show as little as possible of the bright green foliage, which does not go well with the cool grey setting. This consists of *Stachys lanata* and *Artemisia stelleriana* at the front, with *Cineraria maritima* and Santolina; the yellow bloom of the Santolina is cut away. But the most effective of the grey plants is *Artemisia ludoviciana*. It is a most accommodating thing, for at the back it may be let grow to its whole length of four feet or more; in the middle spaces it is cut back to any height required, and it may even be reduced to four inches, when, as often happens, a plant strays to the front edge. It must be transplanted every year, as it is what gardeners call a very rooty thing; each plant throwing out sheets of roots all round. Some of the earlier of the perennial Asters may also be in the grey garden; the tall creamy *A. umbellatus* at the back, *A. Amellus* in the middle, and, quite to the front, the little known *A. corymbosus*, with its quantities of starry white bloom and dark, wiry stalks.

A LITTLE AUGUST GARDEN

It has been a great pleasure and interest during recent years to make out a plan for a little garden of restricted colouring for the month of August, and it has met with so much appreciation and encouragement from those whose opinion I most value, and so much simple admiration from many who have no special understanding of colour combinations, but who cannot help seeing that it is pretty and distinctly effective, that I am now year by year trying to improve it in detail. The accompanying sketch of its general arrangement will serve as a suggestion to

a Clematis Jackmanni

Top-left bed

Hollyhock pink · Leonotis · Echinops · Snapdragon tall white · Gypsophila · Santolina
Clematis · Echinops · Artemisia ludoviciana · Delphinium consolida · Convolvulus maritima · Stachys
Hollyhock pink
Dahlia · Lilium · Eryngium · Artemisia stelleriana · Snapdragon tall white · Ageratum
Clematis

Top-right bed

Santolina · Echinops · Aster tall white · Hollyhock pink
Ageratum · Cineraria maritima · Aster Victoria Blue · Delphinium consolida · Snapdragon tall white · Echinops · Clematis
Stachys · Godetia Double rose · Cineraria maritima · Gypsophila · Delphinium Tall white
Artemisia stelleriana · Eryngium · Lilium · Delphinium consolida · Snapdragon Tall white · Artemisia ludoviciana · Hollyhock pink
Hippophae · Clematis

Lower-left bed

Lavender
Hollyhock pink · Hippophae · Hollyhock · Ceanothus · Dahlia
Echinops · Artemisia ludoviciana · Echinops
Gladioli · Gypsophila · Godetia Double rose · Snapdragon tall white · Delphinium consolida · Soft-blue
Cineraria maritima · Gladiolus America · Yucca · Lilium
China Aster Victoria Blue · Snapdragon tall white · Ageratum · Artemisia stelleriana
Stachys Lanata

Lower-right bed

Lavender
Stachys · Ageratum · China Aster Victoria Blue · Artemisia stelleriana
Cineraria maritima · Godetia Double Rose · Ch. Aster Tall white · Convolvulus maritima · Lilium · Gypsophila · Yucca
Delphinium consolida · Snapdragon tall white · Delphinium tall white
Gypsophila · Artemisia ludoviciana · Echinops · Ceanothus · Hippophae · Clematis · Hollyhock pink
Clematis · Hollyhock pink · Santolina

any who may feel an interest in such a plan, and may like to continue the experiment for themselves. The colouring is of purple, pink and white flowers, with a good deal—in fact, a general setting—of grey foliage. The plants that make the greater part of the effect are a good clear pink Hollyhock, *Clematis Jackmani* and a bright purple form of *Delphinium Consolida*. What may be called the secondary plants are Snapdragons (pale pink and white), China Asters (purple and white), and good double pink Godetia, and purple and pink Gladioli. As the little garden consists of four long-shaped beds with an axial path and a cross path, the ends nearest the intersection are treated alike with a *Yucca filamentosa* and a group of *Lilium longiflorum*. I have not been able to indulge myself with the Lilies of late years, but as they made a good show in happier times I have put them in the plan. The grey plants are the low-growing *Artemisia stelleriana* at the angles, and a good deal of the tall *A. ludoviciana* in other parts of the border. This is a most accommodating plant, for it can be used up against the Hollyhocks its full height of five feet, or it can be cut down to any height that may best suit its neighbours. Then there is the fine silvery white of the best form of *Cineraria maritima*, and, for front edges, the ever-useful *Stachys lanata*. Some well-grown plants of *Gypsophila paniculata*, that spread to nearly four feet, also come in as grey colouring. As there are not many pink flowers available, I had hoped to use *Lavatera Olbia* in the back parts of the border, and had planted some last year. They have been a disappointment, for I only learnt too late that there are two forms of this bush, and it is evident that the one I have is the wrong one—a rank, lush-growing thing ten feet high with a great mass of leaves and small, poor-looking flowers. One Lavatera only is shown on the plan, but more, if of the right kind, would be desirable. The Dahlias are of the Star kinds, white and cool pink.

As with all other border gardening, it is not enough to plant and then expect it to do all that we wish without further care, for to have it right it must be constantly watched and guided and tended. The first thing will be to see that the *Clematis Jackmani*, which makes growth early, is trained in the right direction on pea-sticks in the case of those near the Echinops, so that it will come just over it and finally lie on its tops when the colour of the Globe Thistle begins to go; for the Clematis is much the longer lasting of the two. Any other August blooming Clematis of purple or lavender colour can be used, but there are not many that give the mass of bloom of the old *Jackmani*. The beautiful Perle d'Azur is noted for trial. The *Jackmani* is the original kind, of bright purple colouring; not the so-called improved, which is redder and darker. Some of the Clematis are trained into the Sea Buckthorn (*Hippophaë*); this is kept trimmed to a suitable height and gives the setting of grey foliage that is desired. The next duty will be to cut out the blooming shoots of the Stachys, for it is the carpet of silvery leaves that is wanted, not the lanky, ineffective bloom; as soon as this is cut away the plant spreads at the base. Then as the *Artemisia ludoviciana* grows, it is topped and topped again at about fortnightly intervals, to make it do exactly as one wishes. The two annuals, the pink Godetia and the *Delphinium Consolida*, are sown in place. After the first year the Delphinium probably comes up self sown, but it is better to save selected seed and to sow early in March. As soon as flower buds show, the whole tops are cut off, and this cutting back is repeated till the middle of July. This is not only to make the plants bushy and more densely bloomed, but to keep them back till August. The bushes of Ceanothus are the fine variety Gloire de Versailles; they are kept in compact bush form by being pruned back after flowering.

VII

WILD AND GARDEN ROSES

A CLASSIFICATION AND SURVEY
    Quarterly Review, October 1914

DESIGNING A ROSE GARDEN
    Country Life, August 23, 1919

SUGGESTIONS FOR THE DECORATIVE USE OF
    SOME GARDEN ROSES

WEEPING STANDARD ROSES
    Country Life, February 24, 1912

ROSES IN WILD WOODLAND
    National Rose Society's Annual, 1908

THE OLD GARDEN ROSES
    The Gardener's Year Book, 1928

ROSA GALLICA
    Country Life, February 3, 1923

VII

Wild and Garden Roses

A CLASSIFICATION AND SURVEY

IT IS FOUND that the Roses of the world fall into twelve groups or sections, the individuals of each section agreeing in exhibiting some characters in common. In some cases it needs the close scrutiny of the trained scientist to determine the place of a specimen but, broadly and generally, there are well-known features by which the group to which any Rose belongs may be fairly well estimated. Even in every-day horticulture, those who are much among plants, and notably those who specialise, are able to recognise some faint trace of resemblance—what may be called a trick of physiognomy—so that among the hosts of hybrids and crosses that are now being produced, a very fair guess at probable parentage may be made. In Roses it is the leaf, or the fruit, rather than the bloom, that is the more usual indication of relationship; while for definitely placing in one of the primary groups the botanist has often to be guided by some less obvious character, such as the stipule, the leaf-like attachment at the base of the leaf-stalk; noting whether it is toothed or fringed or otherwise edged, and how it is shaped and set on; noting also the form and arrangement of the style and the extremely variable form of the prickles. In the case of Roses that climb, these are curved or hooked or set facing diagonally backward; some are very wide at the base, others are straight needles or even only bristles. It is a common error to speak of the thorns of a Rose; no Rose has thorns. A thorn is a hard, woody structure growing out of the wood of a branch, that can only be severed by actual cutting; a Rose prickle is attached to the bark or outer skin only, and can easily be detached by side pressure.

To note briefly some of the more prominent of the Roses in the twelve groups, the first group, Simplicifoliae, has the Persian Rose (*R. persica*). It stands alone in appearance and some of its characters. It is the only Rose that has simple leaves, that is to say, a leaf of one leaflet only; a frugality that is further emphasised by there being only the faintest trace of a stipule. The bright yellow flowers have red-brown blotches at the base of the petals. Its only cognate is *R. Hardii*, a hybrid of *clinophylla* and *berberidifolia*, roses of China and Japan, raised by Hardy, the curator of the Luxembourg gardens in Paris. This is the nearest representative of *persica* in gardens, and is just hardy in England. Like *persica*, it has bright yellow, brown-blotched flowers.

The second group, Systylae, has *Rosa arvensis*, the loveliest of the British Roses. It grows as a weak bush about three feet high, trailing until it meets with something it can clamber into, when its growth is increased, and it is better able to display its clusters of snow-white flowers. The old garden favourites known as Ayrshire Roses have *arvensis* for one original parent, the other being supposed to be the South European *sempervirens*. The blooms were at first single, but already in the early years of the eighteenth century some more distinctly climbing and double forms were in cultivation in Scotland.

Rosa multiflora, a Japanese species, was first described by Plukenet in 1700. Sir Joseph Hooker says it was not known in England till 1875, though it had already been grown in France for thirteen years. The Seven Sisters Rose, formerly a favourite in gardens, is *R. multiflora, var. platyphylla*. Its pretty name is said to come from the variously tinted flowers in the panicle, seven different shades of pink and rose being noticeable. The type *multiflora* is an extremely vigorous rambling Rose; the yearly branches are from fifteen to twenty feet long. It is one of the best Roses for rough wild gardening. The garden Rose

Crimson Rambler, which came to England from Japan in 1878, is apparently *R. multiflora* crossed with *R. chinensis*. The origin is a mystery; it is very hardy and easy to propagate. Its brilliant effect soon gained it a wide popularity, though this has of late years been modified by the appreciation of the more refined beauty of various Roses that have been raised from it. Other hybrids of *multiflora* have also enriched our gardens, some of a strong rambling habit and others quite dwarf; charming little garden Roses flowering in dense clusters, that are commonly known as Polyantha hybrids.

Rosa moschata, the Musk Rose, is an Indian mountain plant. From its great beauty it would naturally be one of the earliest Roses known. It was described by Theophrastus of Mitylene, a contemporary of Alexander the Great. In our own Tudor times Gerard had it in his garden at Holborn in no less than three forms; Parkinson also figures it. Hakluyt, writing in 1599, says it came to England from Italy; Bacon speaks of it as giving off its scent in the air. The varieties of the Musk Rose may all be known by the central column of styles, which are more united in this than in any other of the Systylae. In an unpublished diary Sir George Watt writes thus of this beautiful wild Rose:

'This is by far the most obvious and most characteristic Rose of the Himalaya. It climbs over the bushes by the wayside and over the small trees of the forest. It thus produces dense roundish masses, which, when in bloom, look like patches of snow. Its bright flowers are the delight of bee and bird, and it perfumes the air in a manner few people could realise who have not lived in the invigorating atmosphere of the early months of summer on the outer ranges of these mountains. The Western Himalaya, without the Musk Rose, would be without half their charm.'

Rosa Ruga, a hybrid of *arvensis* and *chinensis*, is one of the most beautiful climbing Roses. It is an old favourite in gardens, having been in England since 1830. There are not many Roses that are distinctly unbeautiful, but this may certainly be said

"One cannot attempt to describe in detail all the beautiful ways of using such good things as Clematis ... the tender grace of the best of the small white-bloomed Clematises of spring and autumn, is never seen to better advantage than when wreathing and decorating."

Garland Rose on a Holly in the wood

of *R. Watsoni*, a curious plant from Japan. It has small, mean, colourless flowers in rather shapeless trusses that have the appearance of being stunted or blighted; the leaves are twisted and attenuated, and their set and action have an aimless character; they also look as if some enemy had been at work upon them or as if they had been passed through boiling water.

Rosa wichuraiana came to England in 1890. It is distinguished by its trailing habit and its glistening foliage with Box-like leaflets. It was at once perceived that here was a species that should be the parent of useful garden Roses. Many beautiful kinds have been raised from it, and their number is always increasing. Nearly all retain the brilliant polish of the foliage. *Rosa setigera*, the Prairie Rose, that ranges through the southern and middle United States, is said by botanists to be the only American representative of the section Systylae.

In the third group, Indicae, the China Rose (*R. chinensis*) is the most typical. It was brought to this country by Sir Joseph Banks in 1789, and has ever since been one of the best loved Roses of English gardens. The French know it as Rose Bengal. The beautiful dark variety of French origin, Cramoisie Supérieure, should be in every garden. Fellenberg is another of the garden Chinas of deep colouring; it forms a good-sized bush and is always in bloom. The green Rose, a curious freak, with all the floral organs transformed into leaves, is also a China. *Chinensis* var. *semperflorens* has slender stems, dainty leaves, and double deep-red flowers; its whole appearance is of distinguished refinement. Another miniature China, like a dwarf copy of the type plant, is known as Miss Lawrence's Rose. It is a favourite in the Paris markets, where it is charmingly grown as a pot plant.

The wonderful Rose commonly known as Fortune's yellow is *R. chinensis Pseudo-indica*. It was found by Robert Fortune when he was travelling in China for the Horticultural Society of London in 1842-1846. He thus describes his first sight of this Rose in a Mandarin's garden:

"Some garden space is often devoted to the satisfaction of a desire for a special colour such as blue. There is some curious quality, not easy to define, about flowers of pure blue . . . that demands a contrast rather than a harmony." Bluebells in a wild garden against a background of greens.

'On entering one of the gardens on a fine morning in May I was struck by a mass of yellow flowers which completely covered a distant part of the wall; the colour was not a common yellow but had something of buff in it which gave the flower a striking and uncommon appearance. I immediately ran up to the place and to my surprise and delight found that I had discovered a most beautiful new yellow climbing Rose.'

He expressed a hope that it might prove hardy in England, as it came from Northern China. A superb picture of this wonderful flower is in *The Genus Rosa*. Except in the most favoured parts of our islands it is scarcely a plant for the open, but it is one of the best of Roses for cold-house treatment.

A cross of *chinensis* with *moschata* resulted in the beautiful *R. Noisettiana*; and from this have been obtained a limited number of garden forms, all showing something of the Musk Rose's peculiar grace and charm. They do not seed freely, but some beautiful hybrids have resulted, of which the well-known old Roses Lamarque and Aimée Vibert are examples. A later cross gave the orange-coloured William Allen Richardson. It would be well if raisers paid more attention to the Noisette class; for, though it may be more difficult to work upon than others, yet the probability of producing Roses of refined beauty is relatively greater. From Upper Burma came, in 1888, the great *Rosa gigantea*, with white bloom five inches in diameter. It is not hardy in England, but is admirable in the gardens of the Riviera.

The fourth group, Banksianae, begins with the Chinese Banksian Roses. Both the double-white and double-yellow are well known, though the yellow, of a rich butter colour, is the one oftenest seen in gardens, where, when it is in soil and site that suit it well, it blooms with extreme profusion. It was first brought to Europe in 1807. The type plant has white flowers; it grows in great hanging bushes in the gorges of the Yangtse. It is curious that in cultivation there are no prickles, though it always bears prickles in a wild state. The large white Cherokee

ROSA BLUSH GALLICA *planted on the top of dry walling*

Rose (*R. laevigata*), though best known in the Southern United States, is believed not to be a native, but to have come from Japan. It can be grown in the south of England. The very beautiful Rose Anemone (*R. laevigata* × *chinensis*) was raised in Germany in 1896.

The fifth group, Bracteatae, has the remarkable Macartney Rose. It is quite unlike any other Rose, from its extremely characteristic foliage, of stiff texture, brilliantly polished and evergreen, and its large single white flowers with a mass of bright yellow anthers; the whole appearance of singular nobility. The double flowered kind in general cultivation is disappointing, for, though it grows vigorously—much more freely than the type—and forms masses of healthy looking buds, they do not open satisfactorily. Still, the foliage is so handsome that it would be worth growing for that alone.

The sixth group, Microphyllae, is represented by *R. microphylla* and its double form; a very distinct flower, with globular, extremely prickly buds and large fruits also densely armed and crowned with the stiff, deeply toothed calyx-lobes. The flowers open wide and flat and are of a lively pink deepening to the centre. The leaves are remarkable for their many leaflets, a single leaf having sometimes as many as fifteen. Except for the better development of the curious fruit, the double flowered form is the only one worth growing.

Group seven, Cinnamomeae, with one exception, that of the one that follows, occupies a wider geographical area than any other, though it appears neither in Britain nor in the Himalaya. It contains a large proportion of American species. *R. cinnamomea* is best known in the double form; in the older days it was frequent in gardens. It has a peculiar sweet scent supposed to be like cinnamon, though the resemblance is difficult to trace. It has small flat flowers and wide-winged stipules that are sometimes an inch across from tip to tip. *R. laxa* is a handsome species with pink or rosy flowers nearly three inches across; it is a native of Siberia and the Altai Mountains, and is not yet in cultivation in England. *R. Fendleri* is a pretty Rose of the Rocky Mountains.

R. rugosa, one of the most distinct of the Rose species, is also one of the hardiest. It ranges through northern China and Japan, Kamchatka and Siberia. It was first known in England in 1796, but it is only of comparatively late years that it has come into general cultivation. It is the least exacting of Roses, thriving in the smoky atmosphere of large towns and also on sea-shore sandhills. It hybridises freely, imparting its strong constitution to its descendants; the remarkable potency show-ing in distinct traces of the rugose-reticulate leaves, even to the fourth generation. A fine hybrid, the pure white Blanc Double de Coubert, is of great value in gardens, its good bushy habit and handsome deep green leaves fitting it for quite special uses in garden design. *R. calocarpa* is a beautiful hybrid of *rugosa* and *chinensis* of French origin. *R. Iwara*, a hybrid of *multiflora* and *rugosa*, is a white Rose of much beauty.

Rosa virginiana, a North American species, extending from Newfoundland to Pennsylvania, is more commonly known in gardens as *R. lucida*. It is an extremely useful bush for wild planting, spreading by suckers. It is best in slight shade, as the pretty, faintly scented pink bloom is apt to burn and shrivel in hot sunshine. The abundant clusters of scarlet fruit are hand-some in autumn, when much of the foliage assumes a fine colouring of red and orange. The double form of *R. virginiana*, the Rose d'Amour of old gardens, known in England since 1768, is one of the most charming of small Roses. *R. humilis* is a low, spreading plant of Virginia, Eastern Tennessee and Carolina; several other American species, of which the more noticeable are *Caroliniana*, *nitida* and *foliolosa*, are mainly of botanical interest. *R. Californica* is so variable that some botanists have been inclined to make several species. *R. gymno-carpa*, of the North-western States and British Columbia, and also *R. Webbiana* have some affinity to the European *spinosis-*

sima, while *R. granulosa* forms a link between Cinnamomeae and Rubiginosae.

The eighth group, Spinosissimae, has first *R. spinosissima*, the *pimpinellifolia* of Linnaeus. It is a plant of poor land, often, near the sea-coast, occurring over a wide extent of Europe and temperate Asia. It has the widest range of any wild Rose and is the most northerly, as it has been found in Iceland. The popular English name Burnet Rose comes from the close resemblance of its leaves to those of the herb Burnet (*Sanguisorba*). It is the origin of the Scotch Roses or Scotch Briars so well known in gardens. It is said that they are hybrids with some double garden Roses, but, except for the colouring and doubling of the flowers, they retain all the characters of the wild plant, so that they might be supposed to be garden sports rather than intentional hybrids. Before the middle of the nineteenth century no less than seventy-six varieties were catalogued. Stanwell Perpetual, with larger flowers, and blooming for a longer season, is certainly a hybrid. The colour of bloom of the type-plant is a beautiful lemon-white—*Rosa altaica* resembles it exactly but is a little larger both in bloom and bush; *ochroleuca* and *hispida* are both yellow species. *R. spinosissima myriacantha*, the Rose of a Thousand Thorns, a native of Spain and Southern France, is densely set with prickles as the specific name implies.

Rosa foetida, or *R. lutea* of some botanists, the yellow Austrian Briar, ranges from the Crimea through Asia Minor to Turkestan, and thence to Thibet, and has occasionally been found in Southern France and Switzerland. The colour is a fine yellow, but it has a heavy, unpleasant smell. The Copper Austrian Briar, the only Rose that has a colouring of pure scarlet, was known in England in the sixteenth century; it is probably a natural variation from the yellow, as flowers of both colours are occasionally found on the same plant. Its distribution is through Asia Minor, Persia and Turkestan. It is interesting to observe that the scarlet colour on the petal is an extremely thin film laid over the yellow; also that in painting there is no other way than this of getting the same kind of brilliancy. The Persian Rose, *R. persica*, which came to England in 1838, is a beautiful double yellow Briar; *R. Harrisoni*, produced in America, much resembles it but is paler in colour. *R. hemisphaerica*, formerly called the yellow Provence Rose, with large double yellow flowers, is now rare in gardens. It was a favourite of the Dutch flower painters. *R. xanthina*, *R. Hugonis* and *R. Ecae* are nearly related yellow-flowered species, ranging from the Altai Mountains to Western China. A natural hybrid of *R. spinosissima* with white bloom, named *R. involuta*, is found in the Hebrides; a variant with pink flowers grows by the Menai Straits. Some of the sub-species are so various in character that they are difficult to distinguish, botanists classifying one group together as Sabiniae. *R. hibernica* connects *spinosissima* with *canina*.

Rosa pendulina, more commonly known as *R. alpina*, extends from the Pyrenees, through the alpine chain, to Greece. It is said to have come to England in 1683. A cross with *R. chinensis* resulted in the Boursault Roses. The old Red Boursault has a rank crimson colour that is not now much in favour in gardens. The variety Amadis has a better red colouring, as has also *Lheritieranea*; Blush Boursault, with flowers of a pure pinkish white deepening to a rosy middle, is one of the most charming of garden Roses. The Labrador Rose, *R. blanda*, has rather large single pink flowers—*R. pratincola*, of the Northwestern United States and Canada, is remarkable for being almost herbaceous; the yearly shoots rise to nearly two feet, bearing handsome red flowers in a terminal panicle.

The ninth group, Gallicanae, contains Roses of the most supreme importance. To the botanist—as botanist—one species may be as worthy as another, but this group of Roses has, within the whole space of time of which we have written record, been intimately associated with the history, poetry, painting, literature and lives of civilised nations. It may safely be said that no one group of plants has ministered so closely to human sensibility or has so greatly promoted human happiness. Joy in the beauty of Roses and thankful enjoyment of their varied sweetness has ever been one of the best and purest of human pleasures; and it is these flowers of France and Southern Europe, carefully tended and made better by patient skill, that has made them first favourites in all gardens where the best kind of beauty is sought and cherished. These were the Roses that so often appear in the pictures of the Dutch flower painters; and in more recent years it was these flowers, now old-fashioned but always adorable, that, amid all the thousands of more modern kinds, held the admiration and inspired some of the most beautiful work of Fantin-Latour, whose genius and sympathy enabled him to show on his canvases not only their intrinsic beauty and dignity, but a pathetic suggestion of their relation to human life and happiness.

Early in the eighteenth century the Dutch were the first raisers of hybrids. Till then garden Roses were but few, as may be seen by the limited numbers described by Gerard, Parkinson, and other early writers. It was within the first twenty years of the nineteenth century that the French took up rose growing. This was, in the beginning, largely due to the influence of the Empress Josephine, when an extensive collection was made in the garden of the Luxembourg under Dupont. About the year 1815 rose growing went on apace in France, growers vying with each other in the production of new flowers; and England soon followed. The names of the earliest raisers should be recorded in honour: Vibert, Laffay, Prévost, Desportes, and Hardy in France, and, following them, Mason, Loddiges, Lee, and Kennedy in England. Between 1820 and 1830 there were as many as 2500 Roses enumerated in catalogues, the greater number being *gallicas*. The red Rose of Lancaster could only have been a variety of *gallica*; the mixture of the two colours in *R. gallica versicolor* accounted for the name York and Lancaster for this very old garden Rose, which is striped and splashed with pink and red on a white ground, though the same name is often applied to a Damask that is also parti-coloured and marked in much the same way. The Bourbon Rose is a hybrid of *chinensis* and *gallica*; it originated in a garden in the Isle of Bourbon. Its most noteworthy descendant is the well-known Souvenir de la Malmaison, a handsome pale pink Rose with a strong scent of a rather unpleasant quality.

Rosa centifolia, the Cabbage Rose, was of all others the best loved flower of old English gardens. It is now, as ever, the sweetest scented Rose known. Herodotus extols it as the most fragrant Rose existing. It was in English gardens in the sixteenth century, though no record remains of its actual introduction. The Moss Rose, *R. centifolia*, var. *muscosa*, is a Cabbage Rose with a dense moss-like growth—pubescent and glandular—on the calyx and stem. This growth has a special and delicious scent, of a cordial quality which mingles with, and much enhances, the excellent sweetness of the flower. *R. pomponia* is a diminutive Cabbage Rose in a few varieties, of which the best known is De Meaux; to this the Burgundy pompons are nearly related. The Provins Rose, *R. provincialis*, is a native of Spain, Italy, and France. The names Provence and Provins for Roses of the *centifolia* and *gallica* classes have been often confused, but botanists are agreed that Provins is a variety of *R. centifolia*, and Provence of *R. gallica*.

Of the Damask Rose, *R. damascena*, the origin is uncertain, but it is widely cultivated in the East. *R. damascena rubrotincta* is an old garden favourite of strong *gallica* character. It has the two names of Hebe's Lip and Reine Blanche. The origin of *Rosa alba*, another excellent old garden flower, is doubtful, but it is supposed to be a hybrid of *canina* and *gallica*. It was the White Rose of York, a red *gallica* being the badge of Lancaster. It has been found wild as a natural hybrid. William Paul in his *Rose Garden* accounts for fifteen varieties. It is the White Rose of English cottage gardens, where it may still, in some districts, be found in some abundance. It must always be one of the most charming and individual of garden

Roses. Though some of the older varieties may be lost, we still have the white, nearly single and full double, the double pink Maiden's Blush, and the very beautiful pale pink Celestial. All the *alba* varieties may be known by the distinct character of the foliage; the whole leaf has a wide, flat shape with the blunt leaflets handsomely toothed, and a quite peculiar bluish colour.

The tenth group, Caninae, has the Dog Roses. At least a hundred species have been defined, but it has been found convenient to group them under certain typical forms. It ranges through Europe, North Africa and North-western Asia, but is absent in the Himalaya and Japan. The species of most use in gardens are *R. rubrifolia*, a plant with smooth, glaucous, red tinted leaves, formerly regarded only as a curiosity, but now found useful for certain colour effects in gardening; and *R. macrantha*, a beautiful Rose found wild in France early in the nineteenth century. It has pale pink flowers three inches wide and is a valuable plant for half-wild gardening.

The eleventh group, Villosae, contains a few species that are mainly of botanical interest, but two are of some value in gardens from their handsome fruit, namely *R. Hawẓana*, a Hungarian plant with large red hips densely bristled, and a near species *R. pomifera*, the Apple Rose, with still larger fruits that endure far into the winter.

The twelfth and last group is Rubiginosae, the Sweetbriars. *R. Eglanteria*, the well-known Sweetbriar of gardens, is wild throughout Europe and extends to Persia. It is said to be one of the eight Roses known to classical authors and is the only British species that from old times has been welcomed in gardens. It is extremely long-lived. An old Sweetbriar cut down in Touraine near the middle of the last century showed in the stem section a hundred and twenty annual rings. In old English still-rooms, where the women of the better families made many good things, the young shoots were candied.

It remained for an amateur, the late Lord Penzance, to recognise the possibilities of the Sweetbriar in hybridisation. After an arduous life of legal toil he devoted the years of his retirement to the raising of hybrid Roses; specialising in Sweetbriar. The kinds he produced, all more vigorous than the type, are a lasting benefit to gardens. In the work of professional Rose-growers the last decade has seen astonishing progress; those of France, England, Germany and America taking part in an international contest of skill and judgment that is yearly enriching the already bewildering store of good things that awaits the choice of those who desire the best and most beautiful in their gardens.

DESIGNING A ROSE GARDEN

A Rose garden may often be made much more delightful by having some one point of interest besides the Roses, for nothing is more usual than to find that, except in the few weeks of its fullest bloom, the Rose garden is rather a dull place. There are several ways in which such an object of interest may be secured; either by a sundial or fountain, or a raised stone flower bed, or a piece of ornamental sculpture in stone or lead, whether central or defining certain points of the circumference in prepared niches in the bounding hedge. In the case of the garden shown, this variation of interest is given by a tank for Water Lilies twenty feet across, giving good space for at least three kinds of beautiful Water Lilies. The low, flat kerb, which in an unbroken circle of this size would be a trifle monotonous, is varied on the four sides opposite the paths by a square projection, which gives width enough for the placing of four pots or small tubs of flowers in pairs. The four beds nearest the tank are also treated with a certain symmetry, and are planted with Lavender and China Rose, thus securing some permanence of effect and good clothing for all seasons, and so also joining in with the enduring and unaltering stonework of the tank. The small circles in the four diagonal angles are trained weeping Roses, of such a kind as the pretty pale pink Lady Godiva.

The large clumps have a middle mass of five plants of the fine Rugosa hybrid Blanc Double de Coubert. This is chosen because of its handsome dark green foliage and for its way of forming a dense, bushy mass of solid character, quite different

PLAN OF A ROSE GARDEN WITH LILY POOL IN THE CENTRE

A Blanc Double de Coubert
B Zephyrine Drouhin, or other deep pink
C Bright Red
D White
E, F Light Pink
L Lavender in round bushes, with edges of China Rose

to the thinner habit of most Roses. The coloured Roses will come well in groups as shown, using four kinds in each clump.

The names of the actual kinds are not given, because the choice will depend both on the character of the soil and climate and on the taste of the owner. But as a general suggestion as to colour arrangement, it would be well to have in the space B some good Rose of a deep pink or a clear rosy red such as Zephyrine Drouhin, in C a bright red, in D a white, and in E and F a light pink. The whole garden is much beautified by a complete edging of *Stachys lanata*. The flower stems are cut out when half developed; then the plant at once spreads at the root and forms a silvery carpet. It is kept fairly even on the side next the turf, but runs freely into the bed where there is space between the Roses. This edging is not only most becoming to the Roses, but serves a useful purpose by defining the form of the design. Thorough preparation of the soil is, of course, essential for success.

SUGGESTIONS FOR THE DECORATIVE USE OF SOME GARDEN ROSES

Considering the large number of different kinds of Roses now in cultivation there seems to be hardly enough care and attention given to using them to the best advantage in our gardens. For however various may be the forms, or conditions of spaces of garden ground, there are none, if only they be away from the smoke of towns, where a number of the good Roses now available may not be used; and if used intelligently, that is to say, by first studying their nature and habits and then favouring their likings, and making those likings fit our wants, we may secure the very best service that any particular kind is capable of rendering. Often in gardens where money is not grudged in suitable outlay, one sees with regret the best possible Roses planted apparently without thought or knowledge. The words 'Rose garden' call up thoughts of what should be one of the most delightful spots on earth, but how seldom is it really beautiful, just because we do not use rightly the Roses that are ready to our hands.

For there are Roses for every purpose, for beds and clumps, for simple points, whether as standard or pillar, for banks and mounds, for screens and fences, for great isolated fountains, for arches and garlands, for wall draperies, for impenetrable thickets or hedges by themselves, or for rambling over and through hedges of other growths, for tumbling from heights or for trailing over ground.

Sometimes even a Rose will run wild, and of its own accord show some way of treatment that one had never thought of.

The limits of such a paper as this do not admit of describing in detail all the various ways of using Roses so as to exhibit and render enjoyable the highest beauty of which they are capable, neither does it allow of naming many of the kinds suitable for each purpose. I will therefore only name a few of those that for special decorative use have come most prominently under my own observation.

Leaving aside, for the present, the bulk of the splendid show Roses, the Hybrid Perpetuals and the more compact growing of the Teas, I should like to begin by suggesting a larger use of the free growing Roses such as are catalogued under the general headings of Ayrshire and Sempervirens, adding to these, single, double and large flowered Polyantha and the Himalayan *Rosa Brunoniana*.

For places where garden joins rougher ground or well-established shrubbery, especially if the shrubbery is mainly of evergreens such as Box, Yew, Holly or Ilex; by training a good selection of these Roses among and through and over the dark-leaved shrubs a surprising number of delightful pictures of free Rose growth and bloom may be produced; moreover the Roses when encouraged to grow in this way, and when once established, seem to take the matter into their own hands; for I have noticed that they do their climbing in several different ways; some will run a little way up the supporting tree or bush and then shoot out the flowering branches, draping the tree's whole surface, while others, such as the vigorous Dundee

Rambler, will rush up the whole length of twenty feet or more and throw out a great crown of bloom around the top.

Much may also be done by assorting the colouring of the Roses and their foliage with that of their ground of larger growth. I am now preparing a piece of ground for this kind of well-thought-out planting. It is a small area, roughly circular, among Yew, Holly and Ilex of about twelve years' growth. Near the foot of one Ilex I am planting a group of *Cistus laurifolius*. The leaves of both are approximately of the same quality of cool dark colouring, and I judge that they will form an admirable ground for the almost blue leaves and milk-white bloom of *Rosa Brunoniana*, while among the Cistus will again be the bluish foliage and white bloom of *Rosa alba*, a kind that though scarcely a climber is excellent for straggling through bushes seven to eight feet high. This group will lead to Maiden's Blush and the lovely Celeste, still with bluish foliage. On the further side, where the Yews give place to *Bambusa Metake*, the Roses are of pale green leafage. Here is already a huge bush of *R. polyantha*, more than thirty paces in diameter, whose fresh green nearly matches that of the Bamboos, while through these the Crimson Rambler pushes its bright flower-laden sprays.

Of the old Cluster Roses, the one I have found the prettiest and most generally useful is the Garland, for it is beautiful in all ways, on arches or for hanging wreaths from post to post; for covering an arbour, or best of all as a natural fountain, growing without any restraint or support. Year after year its graceful branches spring up and arch over and are fully laden with the lovely clusters of pink-white bloom, which in this natural way of growth are perfectly displayed to view.

For rambling through low tree growth and indeed any of the more free uses there are two Roses, a red and a white, of extreme beauty, namely, Reine Olga de Wurtemburg and Madame Alfred Carrière. Reine Olga will make shoots fifteen feet long in a season, and has the added merit of holding its admirable foliage in perfection for some weeks after Christmas. Madame Alfred Carrière, with its beautiful pale Tea Rose foliage and loose yellow-white bloom, soon becomes leggy below and is therefore all the more suitable for pushing up through bush and tree. The Boursaults delight in the same treatment, for it is exactly that of their alpine ancestor that grows on the fringes of woodland and in wild bushy tangles.

Another of the ways in which some of the garden Roses and half-tamed species can be used to the best advantage is by planting them in an elevated place such as the edge of a terrace and letting them droop over and be seen from below. Even the Scotch Briar, which has in general the appearance of a rather stiff little bush, will hang over a terrace wall in a charming way and display much of its bloom at a level some way below that of its roots. I have it in a double dry wall four feet six inches high with three or four feet width of earth between the two walls, falling over to within a foot of the ground. Another Rose of bushy growth (*R. lucida*) in the same wall, falls over, and the lower branches bloom near the ground, while the luxuriant growth of both this and the Scotch Briar completely clothes the wall, so that taking Rose and wall in section, the Rose would show as a complete circumference, all but about one-sixth at the bottom represented by the thickness of the wall.

There are Roses that like nothing better than to trail over the ground, rising very little above it. Such a one is *R. wichuraiana*, neat and glossy of leaf and beauteous of its single white bloom. No plant is a better covering for a sunny sloping bank, and it seems almost more willing to grow down the bank than up it. I have a very neat growing South Italian form of *R. semper-virens*, with unusually glossy leaves, that a good deal resembles *wichuraiana*, and has a prostrate habit of nearly the same character, but this Rose though of excellent foliage, enduring a good way through the winter, is very sparing of flower.

WEEPING STANDARD ROSES

Among the various ways of growing the free Roses this is an interesting and pretty one. It is well suited to the habit of growth of many of the newer rambling Roses, especially to that of those that have *R. wichuraiana* for one parent. This also ensures the neat, well-dressed, polished foliage that adds much to their refinement and ornamental quality. The old Ayrshires can also be treated in the same way, that is to say, be grafted on tall stocks and trained downwards. The design of gardens, governed by the circumstances of site and space and other considerations, vary so greatly that many different opportunities may be found for the use of these pretty weeping standards. One of the best and simplest is where, in an outer part of a garden, they are made to stand in straight ranks on either side of the path, on a wide verge of mown grass with rough grass and trees beyond. Here there is the best opportunity of seeing the charming Roses close at hand, of enjoying their individual beauty and inhaling their sweet scent and of studying their varied characters of leaf and stem, bark and prickle, closely and conveniently. Another important way of using these Roses is as accentuating points in some definite design, such as that of the Rose garden given herewith, where they are denoted by the small shaded circles. Here they not only show to the best advantage backed by the dark Yew hedge, but are in pleasant variety of form from the lower-growing Roses in the beds.

ROSES IN WILD WOODLAND

Now that every year brings an increase in the number of free growing Roses, descended, for the most part, from *R. polyantha* and *wichuraiana*, we have the pleasant task of thinking out ways of using them to the best advantage.

A Rose garden, even one of the most formal design, is never so beautiful as when it nearly adjoins, on one side at least, ground of a woodland character. Where this occurs it should

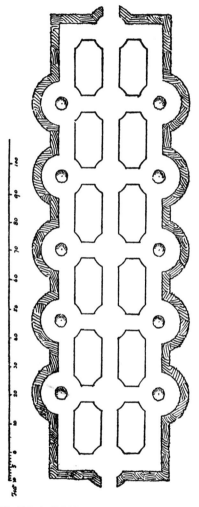

PLAN OF A ROSE GARDEN ENCLOSED BY
YEW HEDGES. THE SHADED CIRCLES DE-
NOTE RAMBLERS OR WEEPING STANDARDS

be an easy matter, first to join the Rose garden to the fringe of the wood, and then to carry on a beautiful planting of suitable Roses into the very wood itself. A clearing must be made from twenty to thirty feet wide, or perhaps even more if the wood is of very tall trees, and here and there the clearing may well be extended to form a deeper bay. Then the trees might close over the path, the space opening out again beyond, so giving a pleasant change of aspect while passing either way, and a view of sunlit roses while standing in the shade.

The nature of the wood itself would suggest details of treatment, but it would seem desirable that in general the Roses should not be planted nearer to the path than from six to eight feet, and that they should be encouraged to form brakes or bushy masses as wild Brambles do in so much of our grassy common land. But here and there a Rose might be led into a little Tiller Oak, or a Holly, or through a Thorn bush; or be planted so as to join an already formed mass of Bramble and wild Honeysuckle.

If at any point the path could be lowered so that it would pass between sloping banks, so much the better for the planting of Jersey Beauty or Dorothy Perkins, or any of the pretty descendants of *Rosa wichuraiana* that delight in trailing over banks. But the possibilities of beautiful wild planting, with the great number of Roses we can now choose from, is almost endless.

The common Sweetbriar should also have its place in some quantity by the woodland Rose walk, and the bushy *Rosa lucida* that loves half-shady places.

It would be prettiest if the path itself were of the nature of a true woodland path, not like one in a garden with hard edges, but just such an easy way, carpeted with its own wild flowers and grasses, as would occur naturally in such a place. In forming it at the beginning it would only need to have tree stumps and roots removed from the actual walking space, and to have the ground made firm and fairly level.

THE OLD GARDEN ROSES

The number of beautiful Roses, especially among the hybrid Tea section, is now so great that it is almost bewildering, and it is with a feeling of repose and refreshment that our thoughts turn to the quite old Garden Roses, so comparatively few in number, so full of individual interest and beauty, and some of them with a scent so delicious that the perfume of no modern Rose can excel. Happily it is not in thought only that one can have fellowship with the old Roses, for so much interest has been aroused in them of late among the leading amateurs, that growers are collecting them and already a good many are appearing in trade lists. First and foremost comes the old Cabbage Rose (*R. centifolia*). It may be taken to be our oldest Rose, for it was in English gardens of the sixteenth century, and nineteen hundred years before that, Herodotus speaks of it as the most fragrant Rose existing; in spite of the many beautiful new-comers it may still claim this delightful predominance.

This and some form of *gallica* were probably the Roses best known in English gardens till early in the eighteenth century, when the Dutch began to hybridise. Some of the *gallicas*, single Roses of French native origin, and the Damasks are among our earlier garden kinds. The old white Rose of cottage gardens (*Rosa alba*) was supposed to be a hybrid of *canina* and *gallica*. It was the White Rose of York; a red *gallica* being the badge of Lancaster. There are several varieties of *Rosa alba*, all desirable; among the best known are the double white, a double pale pink named Maiden's Blush, and another near form called Celeste, a tender pink in colour, and one of the loveliest Roses in the opening bud state. Nearly related to the Damasks is an old Rose, known both as Reine Blanche and Hebe's Lip. It has the low bush form of the Damask, and is very slightly double; it opens a warm white, like the colour of old ivory, and has a kind of picotee edge of crimson, the unopened bud showing as

The spring garden, showing groups of Tulips, Candytuft and double Arabis

An excellent and well-furnished Candytuft (IBERIS GIBRALTARICA HYBRIDA)

IBERIS CORONARIA *with bold upstanding spikes*

almost all red. There are other varieties—one of the dark purplish colour called the Velvet Rose, and Village Maid, which is splashed red and white about equally. Some of what we take to be Damasks are so near the *gallicas* that it is unsafe to ascribe them definitely to either section. The old Blush *gallica* is one of the best of plants where a free flowering Rose of bushy growth is wanted, not in formal Rose beds, but in places among, or in front of, low shrubs. It has a fully double flower, not unlike a small Cabbage Rose, and has the same colouring of pink, deepening to a fuller tint in the centre.

For the same kind of place, rambling among shrubs or in the wilder part of the garden, the Rose known as *Rosa lucida* is most desirable. It is one of the few kinds that like a little shade, for the deep pink single blooms may burn in hot sunshine. It has much beauty in autumn, both from the abundant bright red hips and from the brilliant colour of the foliage—a deep gold, with some branchlets almost scarlet. There is a delightful double form with the old name Rose d'Amour, very beautiful in bud, and more disposed to grow into shapely bushes than the more robust single form.

The old pink China Rose is always a treasure, beginning at the end of May and flowering almost continuously the whole summer, with special bursts in early summer and autumn. It is one of the best Roses to have near the windows of a house, and delightful when associated with the quiet greys of Lavender and Rosemary. The rather less vigorous red variety, Cramoisie Supérieure, should not be forgotten.

Sweetbriar should be in every garden, and close to the paths, so that its sweet scent should not be lost.

The Boursault Roses, derived from the unarmed *Rosa alpina*, are perhaps the oldest of the rambling cluster kinds. The one best known, the Crimson Boursault, is not the best, although it is the easiest to grow and the most floriferous; for the colour has a rather rank quality. The Blush Boursault is a lovely thing of rare and most charming colouring—milk white, shading to a deep rosy centre. Madame Sancy de Parabère is another well-coloured kind.

Although there are now so many good rambling Roses with the parentage of *R. multiflora* and *R. wichuraiana*, there are some of the old Ayrshires that are quite as well worth growing. The Garland, Dundee Rambler, and others of this class hold their own well, and are not excelled in freedom of growth and generous clusters of bloom by any of the new-comers.

ROSA GALLICA

Quite the brightest Rose for general effect that has been in my garden this year is a bush of the common type of *Rosa gallica*, such as one may come upon here and there in an old garden, but such as the show rosarians would certainly condemn as utter rubbish. The flowers are not much more than 2½ inches across, but are in generous clusters of nine or thereabouts at the ends of the shoots, and the whole bush is a wonderfully showy mass. The bright effect is increased by the variety of tint, for they open a deep rosy crimson and gradually pale to almost white. Its sweetness and abundance make it a useful pot-pourri Rose. Another of these old Roses, the Blush *gallica*, is also a great favourite. It blooms about a month earlier, in the middle of June. This is rather more of the Cabbage Rose (*R. centifolia*) form and colour. The Cabbage Rose itself, with its incomparable sweetness, which no modern Rose has ever surpassed, and its crested variety the Moss Rose, are nearly related to the *gallicas*. They are derived from Roses native to France and Southern Europe, and through the skill and patience first of Dutch and then of French raisers were the original material, with later additions of Indian stock, from which our modern Roses have been evolved. But there is still an attractive charm about these older flowers that anyone who truly loves a garden must needs feel, though it may be hard to define.

VIII

THE SPRING GARDEN

GROUPING OF HARDY BULBS
The Garden, October 11, 1913

GROUPING SPRING FLOWERS FOR COLOUR
The Garden, May 31, 1913

SNOWDROPS
Country Life, February 19, 1916

SPRING CROCUSES
Country Life, February 26, 1916

SPRING CYCLAMENS AND GRAPE HYACINTHS
Country Life, April 8, 1916

LENT HELLEBORES
Country Life, March 10, 1923

THE EARLY ANEMONES
Country Life, March 18, 1916

MISTLETOE AS A SPRING PLANT
Country Life, March 25, 1923

IBERIS SEMPERVIRENS AND OTHERS
Country Life, October 28, 1922

PRIMULAS FROM A GARDEN POINT OF VIEW
Journal of the Royal Horticultural Society, 1913

MUNSTEAD BUNCH PRIMROSES
The Garden, June 22, 1918

EARLY IRISES
Country Life, March 11, 1916

THE IRIS GARDEN
Country Life, June 24, 1922

VIII

The Spring Garden

GROUPING OF HARDY BULBS

IT WILL be the Daffodils that come first to mind when it is a question of arranging and grouping hardy bulbous plants. For these there is no better place than a stretch of thin woodland, where they can be seen both far and near. For the manner of the planting, on which much of the success of the display depends, it may be confidently recommended that they should also be placed in long drifts, more or less parallel, and that these should also be more or less parallel with the path from which they will be seen. A pattern something like long-shaped fish is advised, all going in one direction in a thin, open shoal, and the actual bulbs clustered or scattered within the fishlike outline.

When ample space has to be dealt with, there may be three or four of these drifts of the same kind, and it is interesting and instructive, as well as good to see, to have the whole arrangement of kinds in a proper sequence as to species and hybrids. Thus, at one end of the plantation there would be *N. poeticus*, single and double, followed by the older hybrids of *poeticus*— the Barrii group; then *incomparabilis* and some of its varieties, and lastly the Trumpets. For these large plantings, as to the *poeticus* hybrids and *incomparabilis*, the best for landscape effect are the paler kinds rather than those that have the more brightly coloured eyes.

When it comes to the Trumpets, the grouping would begin with the finest of the older bicolors, *Horsfieldii* or Empress, and would then pass on to the full yellows, such as Emperor. The Pyrenean *N. pallidus praecox* should not be forgotten, for,

The handsome GALANTHUS FOSTERI

A good form of GALANTHUS ELWESII

CROCUS VERNUS

CROCUS TOMMASINIANUS

though from its very early blooming it is not an actual companion to the later kinds, yet it delights in wild planting. It may be the experience of others, besides that of the present writer, that whereas this charming Daffodil dwindles and dies out in garden cultivation, when planted in woodland it thrives and increases, not only at the root, but by a multitude of self-sown seedlings. It is pale in colour and would come best at the place where the *incomparabilis* hybrids join hands with the Trumpets.

If in the wood there are any spots of damp ground, there would be place for the tall Snowflake (*Leucojum aestivum*), a plant that groups well with the Daffodils. Nearly all the ordinary Narcissi will succeed in a variety of soils, but where the ground is distinctly chalky, *N. poeticus* and its hybrids will thrive amazingly, for the type is a native of the limestone alpine pastures. These might well be intergrouped with *Colchicum autumnale*, a plant that belongs to the same soil and region. It cannot, of course, be regarded as a companion to the Daffodils, for its flowering season is September, but meanwhile the great tufts of large polished leaves are handsome objects, and the bold, crocus-like, mauve-pink flowers are a joy in the late summer. In obtaining them, the type plant should be asked for; there are garden varieties of deeper colour and others, but the paler, purer tint of the old plant is much the best for planting in the wild.

Besides the Daffodils, there are one or two classes of bulbs that are better suited for growing in quantity by themselves, than in lesser numbers in combination with other plants. The Dutch Crocuses, now so cheap and plentiful, are seen at their best in a half-wild place, such as where garden gives place either to open or to thinly wooded parkland, and where they are beyond the influence of the mowing machine, for they need the full growth of the foliage that goes on after the bloom is over. Moreover, they are so bright and showy that they would outshine and overpower others of the smaller bulbs that flower at the same time, and therefore, as a main rule, they are better kept apart.

In the cases of Crocuses it is best that they should be planted in drifts of one kind, or at least of one colour at a time, and preferably in the way described for Daffodils. Many a good place has been spoilt by an unwary planting of a quantity of cheap bulbs in mixture. Like all else in good gardening, there should be a definite intention towards some aspect of pictorial beauty. Thus the purple Crocuses might come first, followed by, or at one end intergrouped with, the white. If Crocus space is limited, the yellows could follow, but they would be better apart, in a generous planting by themselves.

The common Snowdrops, in the heavy or chalky soils that they prefer, are also good in large sheets or groups by themselves. In such places they increase and spread and form such lovely pictures of plant beauty that one does not wish to add anything that would distract the attention from the one complete and simple effect. It should be remembered, in establishing a plantation of Snowdrops, that they are thankful for deep planting.

But there are other of the smaller early bulbs that may be brought together with delightful effect. Thus, the early Scillas, *S. sibirica* and *S. bifolia*, and the Chionodoxas, *C. Luciliae* and *C. sardensis*, with their slightly varying shades of blue, are all beautiful with the pure white of *Leucojum vernum*, that looks like a handsome Snowdrop, and with some of the best of the true Snowdrop species such as *Galanthus Elwesii*, and the broad-leaved *G. plicatus*. With these there should be some of the Anemones, which, though not bulbous, come naturally as garden companions and may well be noted here. The first to bloom, with the earliest of the little Squills, will be the Hepaticas, soon to be followed by *A. coronaria*, whose fine white variety, The Bride, is a fitting companion to the early bulbs. But, as its flower and whole habit is larger and more robust than that of the Squills, it should be kept well to the back, with some drifts of *A. apennina*, a beautiful species that is not nearly enough seen in gardens. Its blue is not pure enough, though lovely in itself, to go well with the Scillas, but they do not clash as its season is just a little later. It is a capital thing in strong soils, increasing and spreading into wholesome-looking sheets in half-shady places under the edges of shrubs. It pleasantly recalls some springtime rides of many years ago in the Roman Campagna, where its blue stars are sure to be seen among the herbage at the foot of thin bushy brakes—such spots in England would be the places to look for the earliest wild white Violets.

There are others of the spring bulbs that may be used in happy colour combinations, with some of the earliest shrubs and plants. Dog's Tooth Violets (*Erythronium Dens-canis*) and *Corydalis solida*, the latter a favourite in old cottage gardens, are happy in combination. The Corydalis, also known as *Fumaria bulbosa*, has solid little round yellowish tubers that go down a good depth. The flowers of both these plants are of colours nearly alike and that merge pleasantly one into the other; a low-toned purplish pink, very near that of *Daphne Mezereum*, which, with *Rhododendron praecox*, may well stand in the background. The picture may be made more complete by the addition of some of the Lent Hellebores that have the same kind of purple-pink colouring—hybrids of *H. colchicus*, *H. olympicus* and *H. orientalis*. There are other beautiful Erythroniums that are best treated separately, such as the tall *E. giganteum* from California and Vancouver Island. This capital plant is at its happiest in the half-shade of thin woodland, where, when a wide patch is well established, it is a sight worth seeing in April. The pale yellow flowers, on stems a foot high, look like little turncap Lilies; they are not only beautiful when seen in the mass, but they well repay close examination for the delicate pencillings and markings of the under part of the flower. The leaves also are handsome, with a whitish marbling on a quiet green.

It is with such variations of plants and colour that the floor of the wild garden is most suitably covered. It is not enough to say that in a wild garden anything looks well, even indiscriminate planting. Successful planning and grouping of varieties and colour forms will turn even a dull stretch of thin woodland into a place of beauty.

GROUPING SPRING FLOWERS FOR COLOUR

No one who has seen flower borders or other garden spaces well arranged for colour effect would ever go back to haphazard planting. A garden may contain an ample supply of the best plants, and the gardener may be the most able of cultivators; but if the plants are not placed to good effect it is only like having the best paints from the best colourman. In either case, it is only the exactly right use and right placing that will make the picture, and, in the case of the flowers, show what they can really do for our most complete enjoyment.

I give here some suggestions how this may be achieved with spring flowers and, for the sake of those who are beginners in this kind of arrangement, name examples of good grouping.

It will be convenient to take the groupings in four sections. Each group or section should merge imperceptibly into the next, and, whatever the shape of the spring garden may be, it would be well to keep the sequence of colourings in the order here given:

1. *Myosotis dissitiflora*, double Arabis, pink Tulip Rosa Mundi or Cottage Maid, white Primrose, white double Daisy, *Tiarella cordifolia*, Tulip White Hawk (early) and White Swan (later); Veratrum at back.

2. Palest Aubrietia, again double Arabis, *Phlox amoena*, *Nelsoni, stellaria* and *divaricata, Corydalis ochroleuca*, Alyssum, *Tulipa retroflexa*, palest yellow Wallflower, yellow Primrose, Tulips Chrysolora (early) and Golden Crown (later), *Doronicum plantagineum*; at back Sulphur Crown Imperial, Solomon's Seal, Veratrum and *Myrrhis odorata*.

Snowdrops in a bank of Ferns

CYCLAMEN COUM, *a charming plant for ground cover*

The white form of MUSCARI BOTRYOIDES

3. *Orobus vernus,* purple Wallflower, Aubrietia (middle and deep purple), purple Tulips, especially Rev. H. Ewbank (pale, moderate height) and the taller double Bleu Celeste and the fine single Morales; dark purple Honesty, and again Solomon's Seal and Myrrhis. A few white Tulips.

4. Tulips Thomas Moore, La Merveille and *Gesneriana lutea* (they are named in the right succession for season and height, the first-named being the shorter and earlier); brown Wallflower in plenty, both tall and dwarf. At back *Berberis Darwinii* and one or two of the red-leaved dwarf Maples; a drift or two of scarlet Tulip, beginning with such as the early Artus, and ending with the splendid tall *Gesneriana major.* Near the front, between the drifts, some of the reddish-foliaged *Heuchera Richardsoni.*

These suggestions suppose a space of garden ground that can be given to the spring flowers and is not required for later gardening; for many of the best spring flowers, and all the plants of large foliage, such as Veratrum, Solomon's Seal and Myrrhis, that so greatly enhance the appearance of the flowers, have to remain some years in the ground.

It will be seen that several of the groups, or main parts of groups, are in close colour harmony. The comparatively slight difference of related colouring gives that most important quality of gradation that is a prime necessity in any good picture, while the fairly large spaces of each kind of colouring, combined with and inseparable from this gradation, give an effect of richness and splendour such as cannot be obtained by any one unbroken mass of colour, however brilliant that colour may be in itself.

SNOWDROPS

Except for the very early blooming shrubs, such as Chimonanthus and Yellow Jasmine, the Snowdrop is, for gardens in general, the first flower of the year; and for this reason and its own charm of modest beauty, it will always be one of the best loved of our garden flowers. It is a plant for many uses and is everywhere welcome, whether in little tufts in the flower borders or shrubbery edges, or better still where lawn merges into plantation, or in thin woodland. In such places, it sows itself, and in time will cover large spaces of ground. One of its best uses is on some bank or border that in summer is covered with hardy Ferns, or in any place where Ferns are specially grown.

Here will also be the place for Scillas and other small bulbous plants, the procession being headed by the Snowdrops. They are also charming in half-shady places where the ground is carpeted with the small wild Ivy, or breaking through a broad flat Ivy border. Compared with other species and varieties now in cultivation, our common kind, *Galanthus nivalis*, always retains a certain liveliness of appearance from the wide spreading of the outer petals; they are carried more horizontally and with an air of strength and energy that is wanting in those that have a more drooping habit. The Italian Snowdrop, *G. Imperati*, is held by botanists to be a form of *G. nivalis*; it is larger than the type, and has some fine varieties.

Of other Snowdrops in cultivation, perhaps the best known is *G. Elwesii*, a native of Asia Minor, which shows distinctive green markings on the inner perianth segments, a character that is also conspicuous in *G. Fosteri*, one of the handsomest of the more recently cultivated species.

It would be interesting to know how and when the capital name Snowdrop came into use. To the old herbalists it was known as the Bulbous Violet, and was classed with the Snow-flakes under the botanical name Leucojum, which now belongs to the Snowflakes alone.

SPRING CROCUSES

The Crocuses of our gardens, commonly known as Dutch Crocuses, are derived from three species, namely, *Crocus* *vernus*, *C. aureus* and *C. versicolor*. *C. vernus* is a native of the whole European mountain range from the Pyrenees to the Carpathians; the colour of the flowers is purple or white only. It has become naturalised in some parts of England; at Warley Place* it is beautiful and abundant. Here it has long been established and is always spreading by natural increase. *C. aureus* is a native of South-eastern Europe, and was one of the earliest species in cultivation; the garden kinds of which it is the parent are all yellow. *C. versicolor*, a plant of the Maritime Alps and another of the species of earliest introduction, has given us some of the finest of the purple and white varieties in cultivation, many of them beautifully striped and feathered with deep purple markings.

Among some others of the early Crocuses, *C. Sieberi* is a flower of singular beauty and charm. It is not large like the Dutch kinds, on which we depend for brilliant effect, but has qualities of distinction and refinement that are extremely attractive. It is a plant for a very choice place in the wild garden. It comes from the mountains of Greece and the Greek Islands; in colour it is a soft lilac with a yellow base and conspicuous orange stamens. *C. chrysanthus* is a deep yellow-coloured species from South-eastern Europe, and is variable in size and habit. A fine variety of *C. chrysanthus* has been raised by Messrs. Van Tubergen, who have given it Mr. Bowles's name. *C. biflorus* is found throughout a wide geographical range, from Northern Italy to the Caucasus. The colour is anything from white to pale purple, with striped and feathered markings on the outer sides of the perianth segments; it varies much both in size and colour. *C. Tomasinianus* is a plant of the Dalmatian coast, with rather long-shaped flowers of lilac colouring. To these may be added, as among the best of the early Crocuses, *C. suaveolens*, a native of Italy, and *C. banaticus*, a Hungarian plant with deep purple flowers, which botanists place very near *C. vernus*. The foregoing species are among the

*The garden of the late Miss Ellen Willmott.

best for careful naturalisation in half-wild places. Here they would be better seen than in the garden proper, for their more modest beauty would not come into immediate competition with the greater size and more powerful colouring of the Dutch kinds. But, in common with all wild gardening, the way of the planting should be very carefully considered. Where bulbous plants grow naturally they always seem to place themselves rightly and beautifully. Even when they grow in almost uninterrupted sheets, as *Crocus vernus* does at Warley Place, they thin out beautifully at the edges and so gradually merge into the grass. One has seen places absolutely spoilt by a bad planting of Crocuses or Daffodils in awkwardly shaped, stiff blocks or rigid circles round trees. As a general principle in planting it may be suggested that the best form is that of long-shaped drifts thickening a little in the middle of the length, such as may be described as a long, fish-shaped constellation with a thickened middle nebula, and that such forms should follow one another, not in parallel lines, but, as soldiers would say, in echelon. Afterwards, when they increase naturally, they may be trusted to do it rightly.

SPRING CYCLAMENS AND GRAPE HYACINTHS

Some of the hardy Cyclamens flower in the late autumn, but there are two species that are essentially flowers of spring. *C. coum*, a native of Asia Minor and Southern Europe, is in bloom in February and March. It is a short-growing plant, scarcely over three inches in height, and has dark crimson flowers and leathery, roundish leaves, which, though they are faintly clouded with lighter colour, are wanting in the distinct whitish marbling that is so attractive in the foliage of some of the other species. There is also a good white variety. *C. ibericum* is a larger plant, with better marked leaves and rose-red flowers that have deep red-purple colouring at the base. It is thought by some to deserve specific rank, but botanists consider that it is a form of *C. coum*. In the open garden the plants should be in a sheltered nook in rockwork where there is thorough drainage, and it is all the better if they can have some kind of overhead protection. The tubers root from the base, and should be planted from two to three inches underground. *C. repandum* is the pretty species that was commonly called *C. vernum* in gardens. It grows in the hilly wastes of Southern Italy and is in bloom from March to May. The flowers of the type are pink or rosy, with bright purple at the base. There is a good white variety. It roots at the base of the tuber, and should be planted three to four inches deep.

It is always a delight to see in February the closely packed heads of *Hyacinthus azureus*, quite surprising in their clear brightness of light sky-blue colouring. This class of Hyacinth is so closely allied to the Muscari and so nearly resembles them in form and general appearance, that they may be considered as one class of bulb for garden purposes. Of the true Muscari there are two that stand out as the most desirable. The first is *M. botryoides*, with its well-filled spikes of bloom and neat leaves carried upright, a distinguishing character in this species. It is in three varieties, all of value, namely, the type (blue-purple), a paler blue-purple, and a capital white. The second is *M. conicum*, and especially the fine garden variety called Heavenly Blue, a remarkably good garden plant. The foliage has not the brisk, alert carriage of *M. botryoides*—it is longer and more lax; but when a patch is well established, the mass of large bloom a foot high, of splendid purple-blue, is an arresting sight. These two are by far the best as garden plants. There is the well-known *M. racemosum*, something like a smaller *conicum* and very sweetly scented; this is the one most commonly seen, but in some soils it increases so fast that it becomes troublesome. It is more a plant for the wild garden. There is the humble looking Grape Hyacinth *M. moschatum*, that should be grown for the sake of its powerful fragrance. It has no effect in the garden, but the roundish head of bloom is interesting to examine closely in the hand because of the curious gradation of clouded colouring of purplish and greenish yellow.

LENT HELLEBORES

The Lent Hellebores are by no means so generally cultivated as their undoubted merit deserves, for at their time of blooming, from the end of February to nearly through March, they are the most important of the flowering plants of their season, both for size and general aspect. They are well suited to some place where wood and garden meet, and are also good at shrubbery edges, for they hold their foliage all the summer and are never unsightly. One would like to plant a whole garden of them in the nearer part of some wood where Primroses and Bluebells come naturally, in cool soil enriched with its own leaf mould, and to have them grouped with a following of hardy Ferns, sheltered by Hazels and occasional Oaks. In my own garden I have them in borders of a nut walk, a place that suits them well, for by the time the young foliage is growing the leaves are coming on the nuts and giving just the amount of shade that is most beneficial.

I doubt whether any of my plants are the true species. They came originally as a handful of small seedlings from the late Mr. Archer-Hind's garden in Devonshire, and were given me by Mr. Peter Barr—now many years ago when his nursery was at Tooting. He had just received from Mr. Archer-Hind such a liberal gift of seedlings that there were some to spare for a keen amateur. Their original parentage was somewhere within these Caucasian and near East species—*colchicus*, *orientalis*, *caucasicus* and *abchasicus*—with flowers for the most part of a low-toned reddish purple, but some with pure white varieties and many with gradations between purple and white. They vary in height, from compact plants rising about ten inches to more spreading ones whose height is anything from eighteen to twenty inches.

Lent Hellebores in the Nut Walk

The rare double white Hepatica

The early flowering ANEMONE BLANDA

It is interesting to observe the large variety of colouring and marking, for even among the purples alone there is considerable difference, though what is most usual is a finely splashed spotting of a darker colour. In general the purple flowers have a lustreless surface, in many cases with a faint film of plum-like bloom. Their spotting is only on the front or inner side, for turning the flower over, the back shows only a straight veining.

The pure whites are charming flowers. A mature plant carrying a quantity of bloom is a striking object in the still wintry woodland or in some sheltered garden corner; an occasional tinge of green only serves to make the white purer. Sometimes there comes a remarkable break––a pure white flower heavily spotted inside with dark crimson. When this occurs the spots show faintly through to the outside. There are a number of plants showing intermediate colouring. Some have a rather coarse habit of growth, but are well suited for woodland planting; they have large leaves and light-coloured bloom. Some gardeners or growers might think them worthless because of the undecided colouring, but to anyone with a trained colour eye they are charming and full of interest, with their tender flushes of pink, suffused with a still tenderer hint of green, and sometimes a thread-like picotee edge of rosy red.

What appear to be petals in the Hellebores are not petals but sepals. The true petals are quite small, barely a quarter of an inch either way. They are set in an overlapping ring in the base of the flower, and are like little triangular flattened bags, closed at the mouth and running down to a fine point at their insertion. The age of the flower may be known by the development of the central organs. At first the clear, warm white stamens are closely packed, but as the flower develops those at the outside separate themselves, and the filaments that carry the pollen-bearing anthers increase in length. These are followed by the next, and at the moment of full development they all stand out slightly apart, making a handsome centre to the flower.

It is often thought that the Lent Hellebores will not last in a cut state. It is true that if they are put in water without preparation they soon droop and fade, but they last well if they are properly treated. As soon as they are cut, they should have the ends of the stalks slit up from one to two inches, and should then be plunged right up to the flower in a pail of water, to stay there all night, or at least for some hours. They can then be arranged with any suitable foliage, preferably warm-tinted Berberis, and will last as well as most flowers.

THE EARLY ANEMONES

The race for precedence in time of flowering among the early Anemones is between *blanda* and *Hepatica*; both may be looked for in February. *Anemone blanda* is a small Greek plant with much the same character as the larger, later and more free growing *apennina*, but it keeps closer to the ground, the usual height being from three to four inches. The flowers are of a deep blue colour. In our gardens it likes a warm bank or sheltered piece of rockwork, where it is an admirable companion to the various kinds of early Iris and Crocus. In cultivation it varies in colour to paler shades of blue and even to white, but none of these are equal in value to the colour of the type. *A. Hepatica*, more commonly called *Hepatica triloba*, is a native of the Alps and Southern Europe. It is a very old favourite in gardens. Parkinson, writing near 1629, describes ten varieties, of which two, a blue and a purple, are double. A double white has appeared from time to time; it is considered a great rarity and is always much prized. When the double white form does appear, it seems never to be of strong constitution, and it would not be surprising if it died out and did not occur again for many years. The best growers offer some six varieties of Hepatica, of which there are two doubles, a red and a blue. They all enjoy a rich loam or chalk, though they have been well grown at Wisley in light soil, planted with the roots tightly pressed between pieces of sandstone. A stronger plant altogether is *A. Hepatica angulosa*, a native of Transylvania, a handsome thing that soon grows into strong tufts. The flowers are of a fine light blue colour, as large again as those of the ordinary Hepatica, and the leaves are better borne up by their stems, so that the whole plant looks more stronger and more prosperous, and rises to something near a foot in height.

A. stellata is a frequent plant in vineyards and on hilly ground on the Mediterranean coasts and islands. It is always a charming plant in these rocky wilds, not large, but with a distinct vivacity of its own. In colour it is extremely variable; it may be anything from nearly white to a deep red, besides many tints of lilac and purple. In our gardens it likes a place on a sunny bank or in a well sheltered bay in the rock garden.

A. fulgens, usually appearing before any of the *A. coronaria* varieties are in bloom, has the distinction of being the only true scarlet flower of its season. It is a native of Southern Europe. There are varieties with a warm white ring at the base of the petals that helps to set off the central tuft of black stamens. There is also a Greek form with large flowers of good substance and of a deeper and more intense colour.

A. Pulsatilla is a beautiful low-growing species of our wind-swept chalk downs, where the whole plant is only about three inches high. It gains much both in height and size in the shelter of our gardens, where the better development of the silky sepals gives a softened quality to the rich but quiet purple of the blossom.

MISTLETOE AS A SPRING PLANT

We are so much accustomed to thinking of Mistletoe in connection with Christmas and its decorations and festivities that it is natural to suppose that the berries are then at their best, though, in fact, they are neither fully matured nor fully coloured till three months later. It is only at the end of February and up to the middle of March that they come to their full development and are quite ripe. The full-sized berry measures nine-sixteenths of an inch in diameter; that is, a good bit over a quarter of an inch, or the size of a large white currant. The colour and texture of the berry are both so subtle that they would be difficult to describe to anyone to whom they are not familiar, but it may be said that it would be somewhere between a colourless pearl and a white currant—not so shiny and transparent as a currant, but a little more translucent than a pearl, and with a dim high light on a surface that has only a faint polish, something like the gloss on an eggshell. The faintest possible whitish lines run like meridians of longitude from pole to pole; five tiny dark dots mark the top. The berries are firmly seated, without stalk, at the extremities of the twigs, between the short, terminal growths of last summer, either singly or in groups of three. At their base is one, or may be more, of the little green snouts that are the fertile flowers and that should form the berries of next year, and the same, either in pairs or threes, are between the two leaves at the ends of the twigs. The yearly joints average an inch in length. The flowers are now (in the second week in March) ready to receive the pollen. The pollen bloom is quite different, opening flat, with the yellow grains quite visible and the whole deliciously scented. As Mistletoe is dioecious and I have no male plants on my ground, and none conveniently accessible, some twigs of pollen bloom come to me from a kind friend in Ireland. When the parcel arrives the strong scent tells me what it is before I have opened it.

IBERIS SEMPERVIRENS AND OTHERS

A well-invented spring garden is likely to have some rocky incidents, for so many of its occupants, other than bulbs, are plants of low stature for which a mild rocky treatment is indicated as the most suitable. Angles where paths join, or any little promontories, may well have bold masses of stone, and where this occurs will be the place for *Iberis sempervirens*.

Planted at the back of a stone or the top of a rock wall, the roots soon find their way down and cling gratefully to the cool underground rocky surface. Year by year the plant grows into a larger sheet until it hangs well over the front. A plant of Iberis will stand for a number of years, but it is well after three or four, in order to renew its energy, to cut back some of its exuberant growth; this is best done by cutting away, nearly to the root, under the front edge. Not only is it one of the best of the spring flowering plants, but it well deserves its name of *sempervirens*, for the tufts of wholesome-looking deep green are as good in the winter as in the summer months. In rock and spring gardening it is well to plant this good Iberis freely enough for it to become a distinct feature, carrying it right along a ridge of rock, letting it here and there bulge into a clump, and then having another ridge roughly parallel, or more than one if space allows. For there is no other rock plant of its dense and almost prostrate habit that makes so fine a show as a plant, even when not in bloom, or that forms so good a background for frailer flowers in their blossoming time, whether it is dressed in its robe of white or clad in its deep and sober green. It is, in fact, a plant of so many uses that it is hardly out of place anywhere in the garden. Often a flower border has a rocky front edging; and, if one edging plant is desired, there could be no better choice than this evergreen Iberis, good alike at all seasons of the year and a sheet of white bloom in spring. In such a case as that of a special garden of Irises it will again serve not as edging only, but also for running up between the Iris drifts, varied by other plants good for the same use, such as Asarum and *Heuchera Richardsoni*.

For retaining walls and all rocky wall-like places it should be used boldly. Often walls are planted with too large a variety of plants that are in sight at the same time, with no particular thought as to their suitability as companions; a case of want of judgment that spoils many a garden. For whether it concerns flower borders or rockwork or watery places, the same main rule is one that is safe to follow—that is, to have only a few kinds of flowering plants at a time in view together, and that those few should be chosen for their pleasant interharmony, to be quietly enjoyed before passing on to another satisfying association. In rockwork or planted dry-walling some such vigilance is specially desirable, for the vertical presentment arrests the eye more readily than the horizontal, and therefore demands the more careful consideration. In massing plants in such places it does not matter how common the plant may be, so long as it is placed with forethought and definite intention and some kind of consideration for colour harmony. For instance, nothing is more usual than to see a mixture of Aubrietia and yellow Alyssum, a garish contrast that no doubt gives pleasure to many who may not, either from endowment or cultivation, have acquired an eye for colour in the more refined sense. But if the Aubrietia is in two shades of colour, such as four-fifths of the typical warm lavender tint and one-fifth of one of the fine dark purples, and it is grouped with double Arabis, there will be a beautiful garden picture worthy of being framed by a rich, dark setting of the evergreen Iberis. These plants are all the more suitable for associating, because not only do they flower at the same time, but they are botanically related, being all within the Wallflower order of Cruciferae.

Iberis gibraltarica, lilac tinted and rather tender, is inclined to be straggly in the type form, but for garden use this weakness is corrected in the form *gibraltarica hybrida*, in which it becomes an excellent and well-furnished plant.

The handsome *Iberis coronaria*, with its bold, upstanding spikes, is not so often seen as it deserves. It may be that it is overlooked, because for its best development it requires to be sown in autumn.

Perhaps there is no white flower whose white is of such a pure and solid character as may be seen in some of these Candytufts. It is specially noticeable in *I. sempervirens*, where the white is of a curiously hard quality, White chalk is dim

"It is with . . . variations of plants and colour that the floor of the wild garden is most suitably covered. It is not enough to say that in a wild garden anything looks well, even indiscriminate planting. Successful planning and grouping of varieties and colour forms will turn even a dull stretch of thin woodland into a place of beauty." A wild garden in spring.

when set beside it, just as a white cat looks grimy in snow. This hard white can only be matched by some kinds of crockery; possibly its unity and absence of all gradation may be caused by the thick texture of the petals.

PRIMULAS FROM A GARDEN POINT OF VIEW

When we consider the main uses of our garden Primroses we find that they fall into three groups, namely those for borders, those for the rock garden, and those for boggy ground. The border kinds alone need a further sub-division, suggesting distinct ways of use, for there are what we call the true Primroses, namely those that are all on single stalks; there are the Polyanthus or bunch Primroses; then the old florists' Polyanthus, the double Primroses, and the border Auriculas. They all agree in preferring a soil of light loamy character with some leaf-mould, and a place where they are never dried up, and where they can have either slight shade or at least a non-sunny exposure.

The native Primrose of our woods, one of the most charming of flowers, is no doubt the origin of the coloured Primroses. If one might have a perfect place for them it would be a partial clearing in just such a region as the natural haunts of the wild plant—a wood of Oaks with an undergrowth of Hazel, such as occurs in nearly every farm and private property throughout the land, and not infrequently adjoins the garden. A path slightly depressed, leaving irregular, shallow banks on either side and passing through the wood in easy sweeping lines, would provide the best possible way of growing and enjoying the Primroses; for though they are also indispensable in the actual garden, they are rather more rightly placed in the setting of woodland. It will be all the better if the plants of the main sub-divisions are kept quite distinct, either by following one another along the length of the path or by having a separate little path for each kind. This is the more desirable because the varieties are so easily mixed by chance pollination by bees. Indeed, where the Giant Cowslips are grown their influence is so strong that they must be kept quite away from the bunch Primroses, and can hardly be admitted in the same garden.

The earliest to bloom will be the true Primroses. Even these, if the best effect is desired, must have some kind of division in colour grouping; for they vary from palest pink to richest crimson, and from faintest lilac to deepest purple, thus at once suggesting two distinct colour groups. And there will be found a third group of warm colouring, of which the strongest are of a red approaching scarlet, which will agree with neither of the others and must be treated by itself. It was from a purple Primrose, with a colour inclining to violet, that Mr. G. F. Wilson raised his blue varieties. These again must be kept distinct from the rest, but they group charmingly with the very useful early blooming white, seed of which can be found in the trade lists.

In these days when good hardy flowers are so much prized and so well used, it is difficult to account for the general neglect of the fine old double Primroses. They should be in every garden, except those on light soils, for in these they do not flourish. In any soil of a loamy nature the double lilac, white and pale yellow, will grow freely and are among the best of spring flowers. The crimson and some other shades are a little more exacting but are well worth trying. The equal neglect of the old florists' Polyanthus is more easy to understand, for, though it has much charm, it is rather a thing to look at in the hand than of value as a conspicuous plant for the garden; still, without considering the show points of special marking and lacing of edges, a free growing strain of these might well be among our early flowers, and, planted rather closely and fully set with bloom, would have an effect of richness that would be of marked value among the flowers of spring.

Following the true Primrose in time of blooming are the large bunch Primroses, and of these, though there are also fine

"With April the spring flowers come crowding in. Planted dry walls and rock gardens this month and next are full of bloom, and hosts of . . . plants are in flower."

things among the pink and red colourings, the best for garden effect are the whites and yellows. Carefully grown strains, the result of nearly a lifetime of watchful selection, have produced beautiful flowers of large size and handsome habit. Stalks a foot long and individual blooms two inches across are by no means uncommon, and yet there is nothing of coarse appearance about the flower. Among the whites and yellows alone there is an extraordinary variety of detail, which, while it is not apparent in the mass, makes the plants extremely interesting as individuals; hardly any two that may be seen near together having the same physiognomy. The disparity is mainly in the form and disposition of the petals, for some are smooth-edged and others largely or finely notched; some stand clear while others are imbricated; some are flat and others waved. The old florists' distinction of pin-eye and thrum-eye also alters the character of the flower, for though it is not noticeable or of any importance when the plants are seen in the mass, yet, when the individual bloom is observed, the single flower and the whole truss gain by the thrum-eye, where the anthers rise above the pistil and form a symmetrical centre, and especially when this is further enhanced by a raised, fretted ridge at the edge of the tube, forming a kind of crown and giving the flower what is called a rose-eye. In the pin-eye the pistil rises above the anthers and shows alone, and the more ornamental detail is wanting.

In a woody garden where some thousands of these bunch Primroses are grown the effect is extremely striking. The yellows have developed to a tint of the deepest orange, which gives great richness to the mass of full yellow colouring and additional value by contrast to the tenderer tones of pale yellow and white that are seen in the more distant stretches of the garden.

At the time of fullest bloom the best are marked for seed, and every year some thousands of seedlings are raised; one portion of the garden being given to the divided plants and another to the seedlings. In the case of a good loamy soil the seed may be sown at once, but in lighter soils it is found better not to sow till spring. In stronger soils the plants may also stand two years if it is desired, though it is generally safer to divide yearly.

Border Auriculas enjoy a rather stiffer soil, and especially one that contains chalk. They are derived from natives of the Alps and are in beautiful ranges of colouring of purple, crimson and yellow. The border varieties are commonly called Alpine Auriculas to distinguish them from the show kinds, though the name is ambiguous and even misleading, as there are several Primula species of the Auricula class, natives of the Alps, that are grown in rock gardens. The most showy and easily grown of the border Auriculas are some very large forms having yellow and brown-bronze flowers with a white eye that have been raised in Scotland.

The second group of Primulas for popular use—namely, those best suited for rock gardens—will partly overlap the first, for all the border Auriculas will be in place in the lower rocky regions, while the best of the true Alpine species, with their white varieties and a number of natural hybrids, will find places in other cool rocky clefts and hollows. The prettiest of these will be among *Primula Allionii*, *P. glutinosa*, *P. hirsuta*, *P. integrifolia*, *P. marginata*, *P. minima* and *P. viscosa*; the planter bearing in mind that some of these belong to the calcareous and some to the granitic regions. Thus *P. auricula*, *P. integrifolia* and *P. minima* will be thankful for lime in any form, and, for preference, limestone rock; while *P. hirsuta*, *P. marginata*, *P. glutinosa*, and *P. viscosa* will flourish in sandy peat with granitic rock or sandstone.

The Primulas that, from the garden point of view, it is convenient to put in the third division are those that may be regarded as bog plants. These will include the pretty little *P. farinosa* of our own northern moors and of Alpine marshland, three Himalayan species, and one from Japan. The

Himalayan are *P. involucrata*, a beautiful little Primula, quite easy to grow and strangely neglected; the early-blooming *P. rosea*, with buds of brilliant crimson followed by the full bloom of rosy pink, and *P. sikkimensis*. This, when well grown, in a fairly large mass rising from black boggy ground, and seen in shade, is a wonderful picture of plant beauty; the full heads of hanging sulphur bells having that curiously luminous quality that is only observed in this and one or two other flowers of this rare colouring. Lastly, of the well-known bog Primulas there is *P. japonica*. The type colour is a rather rank magenta red, of a quality that does not please a critical colour eye, but there is a good white variety and many intermediate shades of pleasing pink.

It is still well-grown at Wisley, but it was a wonderful sight to see it for the first time some twenty years ago, when it was a comparatively new garden plant, as grown by the late Mr. G. F. Wilson, by the side of a shallow peaty ditch in shade in the lower ground. It showed a fine plant in good quantity, so placed that it could develop to the utmost its capacity for the display of beauty and the evidence of well-being. It was one of the many good lessons taught by Mr. Wilson that one is thankful to remember and glad to acknowledge.

MUNSTEAD BUNCH PRIMROSES

It must have been quite forty-five years ago, sometime in the early seventies of the last century, that I came upon a bunch-flowered Primrose in a cottage garden. I was familiar with the old laced Polyanthus, and had seen some large flowered ones of reddish colouring; but one of a pale primrose colour—something between that and white—was new to me, and I secured the plant. The next year, from some other source, came a yellowish one, much of the same character. They were of a quality that would now be thought very poor, but they were allowed to seed, and among the seedlings some of the best were kept. Gradually, from yearly selection, the quality improved, and, as the grower's judgment became more critical, so more and more of the less satisfactory Primroses were discarded. It was an immense pleasure, as the years went on, to see the coming of some new type or some new degree of colouring, and to watch for the strengthening of some desired quality. The strain is kept to whites and yellows only, and though confined within the limits of these colourings, the amount of variation in size, habit, marking and shade of colour is quite remarkable.

The rule for a Primrose is to have five petals, with a distinct notch in the middle of the outer rim of each. This is varied in this strain by some of the flowers being nearly circular and without notch, while others, on the contrary, have the effect of having frilled edges. This comes about, not so much by the edge of the flower being actually 'snipt', as the old herbalists say, but by the petal being of unusual width—sometimes as wide as a full inch—when, it will be readily understood, it has to be folded, or rather frilled, so as to fit into the circumference of a Primrose flower. In many examples there are six wide petals, closely ridged and waved, making a flower of rich detail and incident. Some of the most striking flowers among the whites—a pure white is rare; the white is nearly always of a warm tone—have a splendid blotch, large and of the deepest orange colour; deeper, in fact, than anything that can properly be called orange—something very near the pure orange scarlet of red lead. Others that most readily catch the eye are the strong yellows, some of pure, strong chrome colour with darker eye, and, deeper still, many of a soft dark orange colour, with here and there the orange inclining to apricot. Among these there are some that are almost self-coloured. The variation in the form of the eye is also considerable. The little raised ridge that borders the throat, called the crown, is always yellow, and one looks through this into the greenish yellow hollow of the throat, either to the group of anthers just within that forms the 'thrum', or to the slightly projecting pin-head of the pistil. Next to the crown comes the blotch, one to each petal, more or less five-sided in the more regular examples, but joined at the base. In some it flares away, clear and pointed, into the middle of the petal, but is often suffused in an even gradation, especially in the case of the deeper yellows.

It is these strong yellows and the whites with orange eye that are the showiest; but the ones that personally give me the greatest pleasure are some of those with the more tender tinting. There is one great favourite that I call Lemon Rose; it is of a pure primrose colour, with six wide petals that have handsomely waved edges and a pale lemon blotch; a flower of refined and yet rich effect. Another beauty, called Virginie, is flat and white, with an eye that may be called citron, for it is paler than any lemon colour. Then there is a whole range of purest canary, many of them as nearly as possible self-coloured, the blotch either disappearing entirely or remaining only as the softest suffusion of slightly deeper colouring. It seems curious that, as they must all have been originally derived from the common Primrose, the pale greenish yellow of the type flower should be the rarest colour among them, but so it is. Doubles occasionally appear; there is one this year with ten petals, but I have not yet had a double that was a really good thing or worth keeping. I have never very seriously regarded the florists' dictum that a good Primrose must necessarily be thrum-eyed. I perceive that the thrum eye is a rather better feature in the individual pip than the pin; but my aim has been to produce handsome garden plants rather than to consider niceties of show-table dogma, and if a Primrose has a good display of fine trusses, well carried, and is a beautiful thing in the garden, whether the pip is pin or thrum seems to me a matter of but slight importance.

The Primrose garden is in a region where there are a few Oak trees and where some additional Nuts and Hollies have been planted. It has large, continuous beds with narrow paths between all arranged on the easiest lines that would suit the ground. In a former home it was in a prettier place, a more natural bit of woodland with groups of Birches, where the Primrose masses seemed to flow between in wide streams and were lost in a mysterious distance. However, the present place is not unbecoming, and, though retired, is easily accessible.

The seed is kept till the next spring, when it is sown and the seedlings pricked out into shaded beds or empty frames, to be finally planted out in any suitable weather in the later summer. Some are of opinion that the seed should be sown as soon as ripe. I have tried both ways and find that the spring sowing is the more suitable in my garden. The soil is naturally a poor sand, but has been gradually enriched by constant working and fresh manuring, with cow manure when procurable, before each replanting. The Primroses do not seem to mind being in the same place year after year. Drought is a great enemy; a rather unusual degree of success this year I attribute to the good spring rains that came at just the right intervals.

EARLY IRISES

Even before the New Year there will have been bloom on the ever welcome *Iris stylosa*. The more proper specific name is *unguicularis*, but it will probably retain the name *stylosa* for garden use because it is so obviously descriptive. What one takes for the flower stem is only the elongated style, so that if in the later time of the year one looks for the seed, the pods will be found close down to the root. It is well to remember, when planting this Iris, that it not only likes a dry, sunny place, but one where the soil is not rich. If it is planted in ordinary good garden ground it will make masses of over-long leaves but hardly any flower; but in poor soil at the foot of a south wall it will be sure to bloom well, and the foliage will be of moderate length. The white variety is a beautiful thing, and there are several other garden kinds with larger flowers and

IRIS HISTRIOIDES

IRIS STYLOSA *against a dry wall*

ANEMONE PULSATILLA *with* A. BLANDA *etc.*

Solomon's Seal in a shady border

with colour varying to deeper purple or towards blue, but the type plant, with its delicious scent, is as charming as any. There is a clean, smooth look about the flower, trim and fresh in its light blue-purple dress with the lower half of the falls neatly striped with purple on white, and a middle stripe of pure yellow. It is good to see it growing wild in the Algerian hills, in scattered tufts about the stony ground often in company with *Iris alata*. This is rather shorter growing, but the flower is even handsomer. It has rather wide, pale-coloured leaves with a glossy surface something like that of a Leek. The bloom is of a paler and slightly bluer colour than that of *I. stylosa*, but is widespread and altogether larger. The edges of the falls are jagged with large teeth here and there, and have so much full-ness that they are necessarily deeply waved and have the appearance of being boldly fringed. This character is more distinct in wild plants than in those in cultivation, and is further accentuated by the tender flowers being so often torn and tattered in their native windy heights. *I. alata* is hardly a plant for the outdoor English garden, though it has been grown in sheltered places against a warm wall. But it has never taken to our gardens and multiplied as *I. stylosa* does so readily.

Among some of the best of the small bulbous Irises that we can bloom in the open in the earliest months, *I. reticulata* is the central plant of a group that are natives of the Caucasus and the northern mountains of Asia Minor. The bulb is covered with a brownish netted coat, which gives the meaning of the specific name. Both in flower and leaf, it is distinguished by a singularly upright carriage. The colour of the flower is a violet purple of the fullest strength and the purest quality, which is enhanced by a patch of bright orange at the base of the lower petals. In the beautiful variety *I. r. cyanea* the colour is a greyish blue; in *Krelagei* it is a strong reddish purple. *I. his-trioides* is another bulbous Iris of much beauty, nearly related to the *reticulata* section, but with larger flowers, which are

handsomely blotched on the falls with white and purple.
I. Danfordiae is a delightful small kind, of yellow colouring
with brown spots at the base of the falls and stiff, upright
foliage, a pleasant variety from the greater number of these
small Irises, whose bloom colour is for the most part some
kind of purple. There are also the dwarf purple *I. balkana* and
I. Bakeriana, an Armenian species with light bluish standards,
and falls, which in this case are carried nearly erect, prettily
blotched and edged with purple.

All these smaller bulbous Irises will succeed in warm,
sheltered spots in the rock garden. The fact of their small size
would naturally point to the desirability of raising them above
the ground level, a position that also tends to their well-being,
as mountain plants requiring absolutely good drainage.

There is, of course, always the element of risk in our
variable climate of sudden damage by snow or hail, or something disastrous that may either destroy the little flowers or
check their full development. Though the pleasure of growing
these little gems of the earliest months of the year is worth the
risk, there is always the alternative, which ensures their perfect
safety, of giving them the shelter of a cold house, when their
fullest and most perfect growth is secured, together with their
longest duration in good order. It would be extremely interesting to have them in the same garden under both conditions.

THE IRIS GARDEN

When we speak of Irises, and especially of those that are
best suited for use in quantity, the name is generally understood to mean the flag-leaved or bearded Irises. In many gardens, fifty years ago, there was but one of this class, the old
purple early blooming kind that does so well in London. This
is *Iris germanica* of botanists, an inaccurate name, for though
it is a native of Central and Southern Europe, it is unknown in
a wild state in Germany. From this specific name the term

Munstead Bunch Primroses

Two views of the spring garden. The bold-leaved plant in the right foreground is VERATRUM NIGRUM

German Iris, formerly in common use, became attached to the many flag-leaved kinds, though it has now been dropped. Recent years have seen a remarkable advancement in the cultivation of this grand summer flower. From the pioneer days of Sir Michael Foster to the nearer and always progressing labours of Messrs. Vilmorin of Paris, and Mr. R. Wallace, Mr. Dykes and others at home, we have now only too many good things to choose from. To do justice to them a considerable space of garden ground would be required, for they are plants that are of specially good effect when placed in masses or, better still, in long streams or drifts; and though in the case of the newer and choicer kinds one may have to be content with a few only, they are best seen in a much larger quantity. But until price comes down, or is not a deterring influence to the rare garden lover who has a well-filled purse, there are such fine things among what are now the older kinds, that for a general good effect the newer and costlier ones may be done without. Indeed, there are many of the older Irises that in their own way cannot be beaten. When one thinks of the stately *I. pallida dalmatica*, the pure pale yellow *flavescens*, the deeper *variegata aurea*, the tall and charmingly pencilled Mme. Chereau, the fine whites Princess of Wales and Mrs. H. Darwin, and the early grey-white *florentina*, with Sultana, purple and white, and some of the best of those that we knew as *squalens*, one finds that there are already enough first-rate kinds for any garden of moderate extent.

We owe to a commission of enquiry of the Royal Horticultural Society a new and much simplified classification of these Irises. It was found impossible, owing to both natural and intentional hybridisation, to determine the many kinds as within distinct species, and whereas we formerly floundered about among *neglecta, amoena, squalens, plicata* and the rest, we are now allowed to discard these names altogether, and to group our garden Irises according to colour and habit; and though some of us may like to keep in mind the older garden botanical name and to trace its use by eye in the hybrid forms, yet the newer way is certainly the more generally useful. Thus in *I. pallida dalmatica*, one of the parents of so many of the grand new flowers, the presence of the papery spathe and the persistent foliage will always point to the relationship.

Many successful examples of bearded Irises grown in quantity are to be seen. In some cases, the Iris garden is kept a little way away from the nearer pleasure ground, because it is for June only, and the foliage of the greater number of the flag-leaved kinds goes off and becomes unsightly in the later summer; but there is no reason why this should not be corrected in the gardens of the future by a space being left between the ranges of Iris for the planting of something that will follow, and that, without actually overshadowing the earlier plants, may so far veil them that the dying foliage may be, if not actually hidden, at least rendered unobtrusive. This is the more to be desired if the place of the Iris garden is one whose paths would be fairly frequented at other times in the summer. There are a certain number of plants of rather a dry character, such as *Epimedium pinnatum* and Woodrush (*Luzula sylvatica*), Gypsophila and hardy Ferns, that would come in well for this use. The common male Fern does not object to a rather dry and open place.

There is a widespread belief among those who are not better informed that Irises must have damp ground. It is true that there are a number of species that require a cool or damp place, but it is not so with the kinds we have been considering. On the contrary, they do best in a position that is dry and open. The Italian *I. florentina* is often seen on the top of walls. In fact, bold rockwork would suit them well and though Iris gardens have usually been planted on the level, they would be all the better in rock garden form, not much raised, but showing distinct rocky ridges. An ideal place for a more comprehensive garden would be one which had an upper part raised and dry and rocky, coming down gradually to a stream or pool, with ground quite damp or boggy at the lowest level. This would not only give the interest of a much larger choice of species and their varieties, but also a much longer flowering period. It would begin in April with the quite dwarf kinds in many cultivated varieties, impossible to define botanically, but having a probable derivation from *I. Chamae-iris* and possibly *I. pumila*; in colourings of yellow, an indefinite white, purple and, in the case of the so-called Crimean Iris, sold as *I. pumila coerulea*, of the nearest colour to blue, except perhaps *I. persica*, of any of the family. For though among the flag-leaved Irises one hears talk of blue, it is always some kind of purple, whereas the colour of the little Crimean is of quite a distinct character, a soft greyish blue inclining towards that of Love-in-a-mist. Next to these little kinds in time of blooming are some very beautiful and useful hybrids, known in the trade as the May-flowering kinds, for the origin of which I believe we are indebted to Mr. W. J. Caparne of Guernsey—some whites and yellow of moderate height, a very good shaded purple and a later one or two more distinct purples, followed by a tall and extremely graceful one of light lavender colour.

There are something like twenty Iris species that can be used to good effect in our gardens. Of these a few, other than the flag-leaved kinds, stand out as specially desirable. Of the smaller Irises one of the first to bloom is the splendid purple *I. reticulata*, flowering in March or even earlier. The intense colour of the flower is accentuated by the middle flash of pure deep yellow. As the bloom passes, the tuft of grassy leaves shoots up to a foot in height. *Iris Cengialti*, an Italian species, is a charming plant with pale foliage and bluish lavender flowers shaded with darker colour. It has been widely used with good effect in hybridisation. *I. Tolmeiana* is a little beauty of upright growth and, smallest and neatest of all, *I. cristata* is a perfect gem, rejoicing in a sunny rock shelf in almost pure leaf-mould. Whereas the main occupants of the Iris garden are for large effects, these little Irises well repay a close examination of the individual flower for the enjoyment of the miraculous beauty of their various striping and shading and individual markings. *I. cristata* is specially interesting for the little white serpent that wriggles down the middle of the lower petals. They should be near at hand, with perhaps a seat not far off from which the general effect of the garden can be seen at ease. *Iris graminea* should not be forgotten, for though the red-purple bloom is not specially showy and is for the most part hidden by the tuft of grassy leaves, yet it should be among the Irises for special examinations for the sake of its delicious scent, exactly like that of the best possible ripe plum.

Some generous tufts of the native *I. foetidissima* should not be forgotten, for though the modest size and colouring of the flower make it almost inconspicuous, a visit to the Iris garden in November will show a wealth of its handsome pods of orange-scarlet berries, useful for indoor winter decoration. It is one of the Irises that is abundantly self-fertilising, a quality almost wanting in the flag-leaved kinds, although these respond readily to artificial inoculation. On the other hand, *foetidissima* is remarkable for being quite unwilling to hybridise with others of the family. It is a native of chalky soils, but does well in any rich loam; in poor ground it has to be encouraged either with manure or a strong limy dressing. It likes a cool but not necessarily damp place, preferably in shade.

Coming now to the lower and cooler part of the ground, where the soil is never droughted and the water edge is near, there is a whole range of fine things in *Iris sibirica* and its varieties, including the closely related *I. orientalis*, which for garden purposes is an enlarged *sibirica*. Among the cultivated varieties of *sibirica* there is a fine large white and a splendid deep purple, also of unusual size. They can be planted right to the water's edge. Here also will be the place for the two nearly related Japanese species, the violet *I. laevigata* and *I. Kaempferi* in a varied assortment of colouring—white, blue-purple, lavender and purplish rose; many of them blotched with yellow

and some double, when they look like Clematis. In rather damp
loamy soil is also the place for the tall and handsome *I. aurea*,
deep yellow, and the equally conspicuous *I. ochroleuca*, a tall
plant with clear white and yellow bloom. The native *I. Pseudacorus*, with its bright yellow bloom in June, should not be forgotten. If the Iris garden be bounded by a stream it would look
well if planted in some quantity on the further bank.

A general mention of garden Irises would be incomplete if
I. unguicularis, perhaps better known by its older name of
I. stylosa, were omitted It is difficult to know whether to class
it as a flower for the end or the beginning of the year, for its
first blooms come in November and its flowering season goes
on in all open weather till the middle of April. It should be
grown in the sunniest places, either at the foot of a wall or of
steep rockwork, and is all the better if it is raised above ground
level, both for the certainty of good drainage and for the
advantage of some degree of summer root-baking. The soil
should not be rich or it will make a mass of foliage and give
but little bloom.

IX

SOME HARDY FAMILIES

AZALEAS
The Garden, December 28, 1918

A YOUNG HEATH GARDEN
The Garden, June 17, 1916

THE GUELDER ROSE
Country Life, July 8, 1916

EREMURI IN THE WILD GARDEN
The Garden, June 21, 1913

POPPIES
Country Life, August 2, 1924

HOLLYHOCKS
Country Life, February 25, 1911

MICHAELMAS DAISIES
Country Life, November 5, 1910

IX

Some Hardy Families

AZALEAS

IT IS well to remind those who have to garden in light ground that some of the hardy Azaleas will do well in soil of this nature under fairly favourable conditions. Rather moist peat suits them best, but they will thrive in sandy soil with leaf-mould slightly enriched with thoroughly matured manure. Among seedlings of the Ghent Azaleas there are so many beautiful plants unnamed that it is best to visit a nursery at blooming time (the first week of June) and to mark the desired plants; but, failing this, a reminder of some good kinds may be of use. The hardy Azaleas have a character so much their own that it is well worth while to give them a separate place of their own, some place for preference between garden and woodland where they can have plenty of space. Although they do well quite in the open, providing that the roots are never dried up, yet, in places where natural moisture at the root is not present, it is well that there should be some passing shade during a part of the day, a condition that also prolongs the duration of the bloom. Such a place is provided by an opening in woodland, where they also look their best. The garden Azaleas have one great advantage over their near relations the Rhododendrons, in that there are no colourings that absolutely clash. From pure white to deepest red there is none that is unpleasantly inharmonious, though a careful arrangement for colour is an undoubted advantage. Such an arrangement has been made in the garden in which these notes are written, commencing with the beautiful *Azalea Daviesii*, a white flower slightly toned with yellow. It is a starting point for others of tender colouring, on the one side leading to pink and red, and on the other to yellow. Of these the first is the pale yellow double *narcissiflora*, then another well-known kind named Nancy Waterer, a large flower of a full soft yellow; then comes another, of much the same colouring, but with flowers backed with bronze. This is followed by Princeps, deep yellow with red rube, leading to the glorious deep orange Gloria Mundi. The lighter coloured of this yellow group are backed by bushes of the sweet old yellow *A. pontica*.

Starting again from the white *Daviesii* and going the other way, we come to a pale pink and a series of tender pinks chosen from among a batch of *Azalea rustica plena*, growing in the nursery of Mr. Anthony Waterer. Among these a beautiful named kind is Bijou de Gendbrugge, and another good pink, Marie Ardente. These lead to the splendid old Fama, a full rosy pink, always smothered with bloom with, a little way beyond, a glowing mass of reds.

A YOUNG HEATH GARDEN

It is not yet three years since the ground was cleared, and already the Heath garden has a look of young maturity. Its site was a woody place with a thin sprinkling of Oaks; the soil is sandy, and there is a natural undergrowth of Heath, Bracken and Whortleberry. The space cleared of trees measures about 300 feet one way by 200 feet the other. All around is the natural woodland of Birch, Oak, Holly, Juniper and Spanish Chestnut. The part where the Heaths were to be planted was cleared of all other roots and dug over—not trenched; trenching would have brought pure sand to the top, whereas plain digging kept the thin skin of peaty soil within root reach, and provided depth enough for the needs of the Heaths. In some places, tongues or promontories of the natural growth were left; they are of long shape, running down obliquely with the line of the path.

Their value is apparent in that they so well connect the wild ground with the planted, that no line of junction can be seen, the planted Heaths having the appearance of being there naturally.

A careful selection of cultivated kinds was made, of not too many varieties. For winter bloom there is *Erica carnea* and *E. darleyensis*, and near them the tall *lusitanica* and *arborea* and the fine hybrid *Veitchii* with the rather tall growing *E. stricta*. The *carneas* are planted so that they will shortly form a continuous mass; the others are in informal groups, one group thinning out at the edges to join in to the next. The general form of the groups is that of longish drifts following each other in a quite uneven succession, varied by thicker or thinner patches, and here and there entirely broken by the projecting promontories of natural Heath and Whortleberry. Near the front are rather extensive patches of the beautiful white variety of Menziesia, the Irish Heath, followed by the rather rare native *E. ciliaris* and its Portuguese congener, *E. Maweana*.

E. ciliaris is one of the best of Heaths, with its large pink bells and downy foliage with ciliated edges, and has the further advantage of a long succession of summer blooms. It is so good that it is remarkable that it should be so generally neglected in gardens. Also in front are the varieties of *E. cinerea*, pale pink and white—the white very good. These are followed by the Bell Heather or Cross-leaved Heath, *E. Tetralix*, in nature growing preferably in wettish ground, though fairly contented in dry. These are backed by a good planting of the Cornish Heath (*E. vagans*) in three varieties that will form thick, bushy masses two feet high. At the further end of the Heath garden are several of the many varieties of *Calluna*, of which the tall whites, *Hammondii* and *Serlei*, are of special beauty.

When the Heaths were placed, the ground was by no means covered with the nursery plants, but, except for some spaces left for other suitable growths, it was more or less filled with young plants of the three wild Heaths common in the district.

Places in the neighbouring widespread heathy wastes, where four years before there had been a great Heath fire, were newly covered with a prosperous growth of young plants, and by the permission of a friendly Lord of the Manor we could collect what we might want. In this way delightful young tufts of *E. cinerea*, *E. Tetralix* and *Calluna* could be had, and were filled in between the nursery plants. There are some wild things common to Heath land that we thought it desirable to add. These are the Wood Sage (*Teucrium Scorodonia*), with small Sage-like leaves and spikes of Mignonette-coloured bloom; Harebells, and the very pretty blue Sheep's-bit Scabious (*Jasione montana*). These give just such points of interest as constantly arrest attention and compel admiration when passing over the natural wastes. For the rest, any remaining spaces of ground are toned down into harmony with the whole by a short, furry growth of moss. The paths are covering themselves with seedling Heaths and Thyme and the natural peat-loving grass *Aira flexuosa*, whose tufts of hair-like foliage soon tread down into a short, close turf.

THE GUELDER ROSE

No shrub is more frequent or familiar in gardens than the Snowball Tree or Guelder Rose, but it is nearly always used in shrub masses among Lilacs, Laburnums and other old favourites. But there are other desirable ways of using it, for it is good as a partly trained shrub on a high wall, where it was placed with the intention that it should rise some feet above the wall and so give added dignity to the gateway. There are many places about the colder sides of houses, or where there are blank buildings or backs of sheds that would otherwise be unsightly, where a planting of Guelder Rose would convert ugliness into beauty. Though the wood is hard and unyielding when old, it is not difficult to train it as it grows into any desired form. It can be made into delightful arbours, or if several are planted on three sides of a square of anything from seven to ten feet, it can be trained to form a shelter that is a pleasant retreat on hot summer days. Guelder Rose is also one of the best things to form a shrub hedge, the natural twiggy growth being encouraged and regulated by clever pruning. Our garden shrub is a cultivated sport of the native *Viburnum Opulus*, the large ball shape of the flower resulting from the whole inflorescence being of the larger sterile florets only. In the wild bush the flower is flat, the sterile florets surrounding and fertilising those in the centre which form the berries. These are so abundant and beautiful in September that it is a matter for regret that the shrub in this form is so seldom seen. At its time it is one of the finest things in the garden, and it can be used in any of the ways already noted for the better known Guelder Rose. In fact, the support and closer training it would have as an arch or arbour would be an advantage, as the branches of splendid red berries are so heavy that the bush is liable to be broken down by their weight.

EREMURI IN THE WILD GARDEN

The larger of the Eremuri are fine plants for the outskirts of the garden, or preferably for well-sheltered, sunny places in thin woodland where this adjoins the garden. Their whole aspect is so surprising and the height of the giant flower-stem so great that they are out of scale with ordinary garden plants; moreover, the one that is most generally grown, *E. robustus*, has large roots that radiate horizontally, much like a cart-wheel without the tyre, so that each plant requires an uninvaded root space of five feet diameter. Although so large, the roots are of a brittle texture, easily broken; they are impatient of any disturbance and need careful handling at planting-time. This should be when the plants are not more than three years old. They enjoy deep, sandy loam, well drained and well enriched, and are thankful for a protective winter mulch. It is best, whenever possible, so to place them that the group tells more or less as one mass from the spectator's point of view. In the case of plants such as these, whose nature of root prevents their being planted near together, the effect of good grouping can be obtained by having the length of the group running front and back, or, better still, diagonally to the path from the chief point of sight, rather than at intervals along both sides of the path.

E. robustus rises to a height of ten feet. There are others of the genus that can also be grown anywhere to the south of London, and for garden grouping and good colour arrangement there are none better than *E. robustus*, flowers pale pink; *E. himalaicus*, with a beautiful white flower, seven to eight feet; *E. Olgae*, pink, about three to four feet high; and the yellowish *E. Bungei*, a Persian plant rather on the tender side and seldom exceeding about three to four feet high.

The strap-shaped foliage of the Eremuri is all radical, and does not in itself make much effect. It is well to group near them plants with leafage of a different class and of bold effect, and with flowers whose colour will neither clash with nor overpower the tender colouring of the giant spikes. Such would be the great Heracleums, of which *H. giganteum* is much the best, and the ornamental Rhubarbs. These should be at the back, and, more forward, such plants as the larger of the hardy Ferns, *Rodgersia podophylla*, with its handsome red bronze leaves of Horse Chestnut shape, and the bold form and tender pink bloom of *Saxifraga peltata*, with a background to all of trees of dark foliage.

POPPIES

Poppies provide our gardens with beautiful and brilliant flowers in a great variety of form and colour, both among the kinds that are of annual lifetime only and those that are perennial. Among the perennial kinds the earliest to bloom, flowering in the end of May and to the middle of June, is the

Oriental group; now, owing to the good work of raisers, in a large variety of choice. It is a plant that seeds freely and is easily crossed and hybridised. A few years ago it broke, from the usual scarlet, into fine forms of salmon-red colourings, and more recently there appeared a good pure white, in which the dark blotch and mass of purple stamens are extremely effective. An old but always useful form of *P. orientale* is known as *bracteatum*. The flowers are of a deeper scarlet than is usual among the ordinary kinds; by this and its stiff, upright habit it is most easily distinguished. This specific name *bracteatum* is convenient for garden use, though botanically the plant cannot be separated from ordinary *orientale*. Seed sown from a pod of *bracteatum* may give no *bracteatum* at all, but will probably produce some good forms of scarlet *orientale*. Any form of *orientale* hybridises freely with the smaller species *P. rupifragum*, and does so spontaneously in many gardens where the two Poppies are fairly near each other. This has happened so often that the hybrid, which in appearance is just intermediate between the two, has been given the suitable name of *ruporient*. *P. rupifragum* is a handsome plant with rough, hairy foliage much like that of *orientale* in miniature, and showy apricot-coloured flowers, carried singly on stems something over a foot high. It is useful in the flower border, but perhaps better in the rougher parts of rockwork. Another Poppy of rather the same class but with smoother, more glaucous leaves, is *P. pilosum*. The flowers have nearly the same apricot colour, but there are several on a branching stem about two feet high; an almost daily removal of the spent blossoms will prolong the time of blooming. Both these Poppies come freely from seed and should be renewed every two years, as they are not long-lived. The same thing, as to duration of lifetime, may be said of *P. nudicaule*, which is now obtainable in a good variety of colour. This pretty Poppy, with flowers set singly on stems about a foot high, has yellow flowers in the type; but by cultivation and selection the colouring has both paled to white and deepened to full orange and red-lead colour. One of its most beautiful and refined tints is a pale yellow that may be called citron. This Poppy is one of our hardiest plants, having wild homes well within the Arctic Circle. *Papaver alpinum* is a tiny form of the same plant; botanically inseparable from *nudicaule.* It has dainty, little, pale yellow flowers on stems three to four inches high, and finely divided foliage, and is a valuable rock plant. But if it is to be kept true, seed must be obtained from alpine sources, for if seed of English-grown *alpinum* is grown on, the foliage widens, the flower stems rise higher, and a further sowing of seed from this will be *P. nudicaule.*

Of the annual Poppies, there are, first, the grand forms of the Opium Poppy (*P. somniferum*) in colourings of scarlet, pink, purple and white. Among the finest is one with wide guard petals, but is otherwise fully double, but not overcrowded. The colour is a full pink of a soft, creamy quality. A double Poppy, like a double Hollyhock, may be stuffed too tightly with petals, and there are some that are quite unbeautiful where the bloom is a tight ball of narrow straps. When these and other flowers are being raised and improved by rigid selection, the best aim is to try for the most curious and unusual. Quite single Poppies of this class are also handsome flowers, but are extremely fugacious. Seed from a Poppy head bought at the chemist's will give single white flowers of much beauty. When the petals have fallen and the pod has swelled up a deep scratch or shallow cut on its surface is soon covered with a milky exudation, which dries a darker colour over the cut. This is opium in the rough.

Everyone knows the merits of the Shirley Poppies, the fine forms of the common cornfield Poppy (*P. Rhoeas*) raised by the late Rev. W. Wilks. Something of the same kind and de- rived from the same wild Poppy was formerly sold as French Poppies, but these have been superseded by the better forms of Mr. Wilks' raising and careful selection. To see them at their best they should be given a large space and should be well thinned, so that they stand at least a foot apart. There are two other annual Poppies of great value, namely, *P. umbrosum*, a scarlet flower with a black blotch, on stems about a foot high, and *P. glaucum*, the Tulip Poppy. The latter should be more generally grown, for it seems to be very little known. It is well named, for the brilliant scarlet flowers are like immense Tulips, the large buds and leaves are smooth and glaucous, and the whole plant is conspicuously handsome. It is about two feet high.

All hardy annuals are stronger if they are autumn sown, but of all that are sown at that season the earliest should be the Poppies. Whereas the first and second weeks of September represent a good general time, all the annual Poppies should be sown within August. So I was told by the late Mr. Peter Barr, that experienced seed merchant and true lover of good flowers, whose helpful friendship I enjoyed and much valued forty years ago.

It is almost impossible to sow Poppies thinly enough; the seed is small, and even when mixed with three times its bulk of fine sand, the seedlings will come up much too thickly. They must be vigorously thinned; the great Opium Poppies must stand at least a foot apart—eighteen inches is none too much —and the lesser kinds in due proportion.

HOLLYHOCKS

There are many who are deterred from growing these grand plants by the prevalence of the disease, or, more properly, the fungoid pest, that is likely to infest them, the same pest attacking more or less all the members of the Mallow family, of which the Hollyhocks are the most important of the garden representatives. But one may say that Hollyhocks are indispensable in the late summer and autumn, and they cannot be let go lightly. In strong soils they are nearly always healthy, a plant lasting for several years, throwing up several grand

Guelder Rose on door leading from border to spring garden

Munstead Cream Pink Poppies resembling double Peonies

spikes and being well clothed with foliage to the ground. The difficulty arises in the lighter soils, for the Hollyhock is what gardeners call a gross feeder, rejoicing in a soil either of loam or lime, in any case rich and deep and also well manured. There can hardly be a place whose conditions are worse for Holly-hocks than the present writer's garden—on a sandy upland, which naturally produces only Heath and Gorse. Here all flower borders have to be artificially made; but where Holly-hocks are to grow it is made deeper still, the sand taken out to a depth of three feet and the place filled with the best stuff we can get together, with the ashes of the fire-heap plentifully admixed and some good manure from a foot to eighteen inches down. It is true that the plants always lose their lower leaves and are not free from the rust disease (*Puccinia malvacea*); but as they are necessarily near the back of the border, it is a simple matter to make sure that some group of plants, of close habit or strong foliage, shall be just in front. The well-fed Holly-hocks will send up fine spikes, and the defect of bareness of the lower stem will not be apparent. The flowers will be so good that their absence would be a grievous loss to the garden, although they must not be expected to be so vigorous as they would be on a soil of a stronger nature. The pest can be kept in check, though not absolutely abolished, by frequent syringing with a weak solution of permanganate of potash as soon as the leaves have made some growth, or with any of the anti-fungoid preparations.

For flowering the same year, Hollyhock seed may be sown in heat as early as the first days of January; but it may still be sown now if the plants are pushed on as quickly as may be. There is a good deal in getting a strain of seed that will give the right-shaped flower. The florist's Hollyhock, so fully double that the whole flower is the same rounded shape all over and is equally tightly packed with crowded petals, is not the best for the garden; in fact, instead of being a beautiful flower it is rather an ugly thing. The best kind has a distinct guard petal or outer petticoat, and the rising centre is only moderately filled. In this case the colour also is much enhanced by the play and transmitted glow of light and tint within and between the inner petals. All this is lost in the round, tight flower, where the light can only play upon the outer surface.

There is much beauty of tender colouring among some of the single Hollyhocks, but of these the ones that are easiest to grow and are the most generally useful are the varieties of *Althaea ficifolia*, the Fig-like shape of the leaf accounting for the specific name. The best are those of sulphur and white colourings, which should be secured if possible, or there will probably be a preponderance of flowers of a poor, washy, purplish pink. But if mixed seed is sown, some will be sure to be yellow and white, and seed for further use can be kept from these.

MICHAELMAS DAISIES

In the early autumn, when the flower borders, if not quite done for, are at least at their last stage before final dissolution, it is a joy to come upon a well-planted border of the perennial Asters, with their clear fresh colouring all the more accentuated by contrast with the general sombre rustiness of the greater part of the neighbouring vegetation. For the extension of the time of enjoyment of hardy flowers, as well as for their own beauty, it is well worth while to have them in a separate border in some place rather away from other gardening. If a double border can be given to them alone, it is all the better, and it will add another month to the life of the hardy flower garden. In fact, it is desirable to have two separate double borders of Michaelmas Daisies in different places. There are now such large numbers of desirable kinds that the difficulty is to choose few enough, for, unless a Daisy border is of unusual size or length, a better effect is gained by using not more than twelve to fifteen kinds in bold drifts than by having a larger number in lesser patches.

OLEARIA GUNNIANA *with foliage of Funkia and Megasea*

A double border of Michaelmas Daisies and PYRETHRUM ULIGINOSUM

A limited number of good kinds having been secured, the whole effect of the borders will depend upon good arrangement and good staking. It is much best, as in all other flower-border work, to do it by a plan on paper. If space can be given for a border or double border for September and another for October, both should be carefully planned; then a good range of kinds, both early and late, can be used to advantage. There are such borders in the present writer's garden. As the one for September has a greater length than the later one, some other colours and kinds of plants are introduced, though the main effects are of the early Daisies. Here are Asters *acris* and *Amellus*, with low plants of whitish or glaucous foliage, chiefly Stachys and white Pink, near the path, with a rather thick interplanting of Ageratum; then the moderate-sized *A. vimineus*, and, further back, the taller kinds derived mostly from *Novi-Belgii* and *Novae-Angliae*. It may be as well to remind readers that *Novi-Belgii* accounts for the greater number of the tall and medium-tall kinds with smooth stems and leaves, and that *Novae-Angliae* is the parent of those, also tall and of middle height, that have the stems and leaves rough and hairy and a rather strong, characteristic scent, the varieties of *Novi-Belgii* being much the more numerous.

To return to the early Daisy border, among the kinds of medium height is the splendid N.-A. Ryecroft Purple. At the back is one of the best, the grand *puniceus*, with its large, closely clustered heads of palest grey-lilac, and a number of the tall varieties of *Novi-Belgii*, with some groups of white Dahlias. Throughout the borders are groups of plants with grey foliage, such as *Phlomis fruticosus*, Lyme Grass and *Euphorbia Characias*, pleasantly breaking the flowery masses. Some groups of flowers of pink colouring are admitted in this double border—Japan Anemone, double Soapwort and the large Stonecrop *Sedum spectabile*, the last always covered with bees and butterflies. Near the middle of the length of the border on both sides is a break of palest yellow. Here the flowers are Dahlias, pale sulphur African Marigolds, lemon-white Snapdragons and flowering Golden Feather Feverfew at the foot.

By the time the September borders begin to look a little overrun, the ones for the later kinds are brilliant with their clear, fresh beauty. Here there are no other coloured flowers; the Starworts are alone, with the sole inclusion of the great white Daisy, *Pyrethrum* (*Chrysanthemum*) *uliginosum*, whose time of flowering, being intermediate, serves equally in the borders of the two seasons. Here are all the best late varieties of the *Amellus, Novi-Belgii* and *Novae-Angliae* sections of moderate and tall growths and in all shades of mauve, purple, lilac and pink, a shade which in some is apt to be of a heavy quality. In soils of a light character and possibly in all, it is well to divide and replant the Asters every year, freshly preparing and manuring the ground. If they are left for two or three years they spread considerably; then the outward overgrowth, which contains the best material for replanting, is chopped off with the spade, leaving only the less profitable part of the plant. Besides a carefully thought-out plan with a generous admixture of the tall white Pyrethrum, the most important matter is careful staking. This must be done not later than the third week in June, when the plants are rather more than half-grown. Stiff, branching sprays make the best kind of support. When the sharpened butts are thrust into the ground between and among the plants, the growths are carefully fingered among the spray—in some cases tied—so as best to display the plant's natural way of growth.

At the same time, some of the bolder growing kinds and any of the white Daisies that come rather forward can be pinched back to half their length. This keeps them shorter and causes them to branch without delaying the flowering season. Only varieties of *cordifolius* and *Novae-Angliae* are not pinched, because the graceful arching form of *cordifolius* would be disturbed and because *Novae-Angliae* is found to be shy of blooming after being cut back. Before any shortening the borders should be surveyed from end to end and the pinching done where the eye requires that the plant should go back. It may be done a little more boldly than the appearance of the border actually demands in June, as the flowering sprays are apt to come forwarder than one anticipates when they are loaded with bloom and sometimes burdened with rain.

X

THE WINTER GARDEN

GREEN THINGS OF THE WINTER GARDEN
Country Life, January 29, 1916
EVERGREENS ON WALLS IN WINTER
Country Life, February 13, 1915
SWEET VIOLETS
Ladies' Field

CHAPTER X

The Winter Garden

GREEN THINGS OF THE WINTER GARDEN

WHEN THE leaves are down and the flower borders are bare one turns with a feeling of grateful admiration to the evergreen trees, plants and bushes. They are all the more to be appreciated because so many of them are now in their best and deepest coloured foliage. Holly, Yew, Bay and Box are clothed in a kind of subdued splendour that is not only grateful to the eye but gladdening to the mind when one thinks of their shelter and comfort to the life of birds and other wild things. Then all the greys and faint browns and silvery greens of tree-bole and branch, and the thin mist so frequent during the days of early winter, form just the right setting for the deep, rich colouring of the evergreens.

It sets one thinking how good it would be to have a good space set apart as a hardy winter garden; a space large enough to have a whole background of Yew and Holly, Cypress and Ilex, and again beyond that of Spruce or Scots Pine or any suitable hardy conifer in a good mass of one kind at a time. If it could be a rather hollow, sheltered place on the outskirts of the garden, leading from it to hilly woodland, with wooded rising ground protecting it from the north and east, the position would be as good as possible. Such a place would be truly enjoyable from the middle of November and onward all through the winter, besides being a green garden of no little beauty. It would not be entirely without flowers, for in a cool nook near the path there would be the giant Christmas Rose early in November, followed by the later-flowering kinds; and

"The greys and faint browns and silvery greens of tree-bole and branch, and the thin mist so frequent during the days of early winter, form just the right setting for the deep, rich colouring of the evergreens."

Effect of rime on foliage—(1) GAULTHERIA SHALLON;
(2) *London Pride* (SAXIFRAGA UMBROSA)

in another such place the Lent Hellebores blooming at a time when late winter joins hands with earliest spring. These might make a flowery undergrowth for quite a considerable space on the cooler side, while facing them on the sunny aspect there would be tufts of *Iris stylosa* flowering in all open weather throughout the winter months. If a rocky or sandy scarp of a few feet high should be there, the yellow Jasmine would find a place, and could be so planted as to fall in sheets over the face of the scarp. There are other possible flowering things, among which the Winter Heaths should be remembered, but there would be no need to strain for more flowers, for just these few would give enough points of interest, and, with the Holly berries, enough of actual bright colouring. In fact, the winter garden is all the better for the fewness of its flowers. The summer garden is only too full of brilliant objects of beauty and interest, and the winter garden should have its own rather contrasting character as a place of comparative repose of mind and eye.

If the winter garden is on a sandy or peaty soil it will perhaps have all the better opportunity, for then many more of the lesser evergreens can be employed, and a part of the middle background would be of Rhododendrons. When these are planted they are often considered as flowering shrubs alone, but, fine things though they are when in bloom, the flower is for summer weeks alone. For the rest of the year they are for foliage only, and it is as masses of rich greenery that they serve in the winter garden. For this it should be remembered that the best are the ordinary *R. ponticum* and some of the earlier hybrids. Their foliage is much handsomer than that of the more recent varieties that have more of the American *cataw-biense* blood. There is an old Rhododendron called *multi-maculatum* that has the best foliage of all; it is much to be regretted that it is now despised by growers, because the individual blooms are narrow petalled. But indoors, as a cut flower, it has, just for this reason, a distinction and charming refine-

ment that make it much better for this use than the greater
number of the massive blooms that alone satisfy the florist. It
is white—the soft, cool white of skim-milk, and the blotch is
a cluster of spots of a very beautiful rosy red. It should be in
every garden where good cut flowers and the best winter
greenery are desired.

The winter garden on sandy or peaty soil would have many
of the best sub-shrubs in quantity—*Gaultheria Shallon*, the
broad-leaved form of *Skimmia japonica*, with its handsome red
berries, and the still finer *Skimmia Foremannii; Kalmia latifolia*
and the flowering Tree Ivies, beautiful for massing and for
growing into large, wide spreading bushes. Then the dwarf
Rhododendrons and several of the Andromedas, especially
Pieris floribunda that grows into good sized bushes, and the
two species of Leucothoë, *L. Catesbaei* and *L. axillaris*. Another delight will be the Candleberry Gale (*Myrica cerifera*),
whose leaves when crushed or bruised give off a delicious
scent. Then there will be tufts of that plant of rare beauty, the
Alexandrian Laurel (*Ruscus racemosus*), superb in strong yet
delicate structural form, and the lower growing Megaseas, with
large, feathery leaves, and Asarum, also with deep green,
leathery leaves, but the foliage small, much like that of
Cyclamen.

Some of the native Ferns are true winter plants. Polypody is
at its best in the earlier cold months; the Prickly Shield Fern
holds its dark green plumes the winter through, and Male Fern
is often in good order until Christmas, and even for six weeks
later unless there is snow—but snow makes an end of it. Hart's-
tongue is grand all the winter; it is a lime loving plant and
should be planted largely in calcareous soils. Another lime
loving plant good for the winter garden is *Iris foetidissima*,
with its prosperous-looking sheaves of deep green, sword-like
leaves, and, in November, its large seed pods, swinging heavily
and opening to show the scarlet-coated, berry-like seeds.

EVERGREENS ON WALLS IN WINTER

It is only in the depth of winter that we fully appreciate the value of evergreen shrubs and trees. In woodland, in the colder months, there is often nothing green but Holly and Ivy. It is then that we see what precious things are these two native evergreens; not only beautiful in themselves, but giving evidence of comfortable harbourage to many forms of wild life. So also in gardens, the shrubs with persistent foliage, that in summer passed almost without notice, acquire their full value in winter, and are then in their richest dress.

In planting garden spaces against buildings the mistake is often made of having borders of temporary or summer plants only, especially in such places as narrow borders between house wall and terrace walk; but if these are filled with evergreens, such as Laurustinus, Rosemary, Lavender and Berberis, with, among them, a few points of interest as of China Rose and Lilies, there is a pleasant sense of permanence and a kind of dignity that is in harmony with the sentiment of a good building. When a garden is terraced, and there are retaining walls of solid masonry at the back of borders, the good use of evergreen shrubs is important, not only for their own display, but for winter clothing and as a background to the flowery masses of summer. There are many more shrubs suitable for such places than are generally thought of. Where walls are fairly high, there are such fine things as the evergreen Magnolias and Bay (no matter if they rise above the wall level), Myrtle, Azara and white Jasmine, for though Jasmine is not strictly evergreen, not only does it hold its leaves till Christmas, but the mass of green stem shows with a general green effect. Some climbing Roses have the same quality; Jersey Beauty is now (late in January) not only well clothed with its polished foliage, but is bearing such quantities of red hips in thickish bunches that its whole effect is highly ornamental. Reine Olga, that good red Rose that makes yearly growths twelve to fifteen feet long, will be in fine foliage through February and even later. Garden Ivies are only too numerous, but the very large-leaved *Hedera dentata* and the small marbled Caenwood variety are so distinct that they should not be forgotten. *Cistus cyprius* is a fine thing on a fairly high wall, its fragrant foliage turning strangely blue in winter. Shrubs with variegated leaves should be used with caution, to avoid the danger of a patchy effect; but where questions of colour are carefully considered and a harmonious background for flowers of bright yellow colouring is desired, it is well to train on the wall both the gold-splashed Elaeagnus and the Golden Privet.

Walls from five to seven feet high will take shrubs of medium height. One of the best is Laurustinus, excellent for wall training and yet but seldom used. All the three varieties well known in gardens are equally suitable, but of special beauty is the May blooming *Viburnum lucidum*. It is tenderer than the two other kinds, *V. Tinus* and *V. hirtum*, and is much benefited by being trained on a wall with a warm exposure. They are quite vigorous enough for high walls, but are perhaps better seen on those of lesser height. *Garrya elliptica*, with its pretty tassels of midwinter bloom, is also suitable for high or lower walls. Myrtles, in warmest places, should not be forgotten, and the handsome Box, *Buxus balearica*. *Escallonia macrantha* and *E. Philippiana* are both beautiful on walls, the latter flowering in late summer when shrub bloom is rare. *Choisya ternata* is one of the best of wall shrubs, and Rosemary, often seen on walls in Italy, should be so used at home. The grey, Sage-like foliage of *Phlomis fruticosa*, a shrub commonly grown as a bush in the open, is capital trained, and still better is the beautiful grey-leaved shrubby Groundsel, *Senecio Greyii*.

For lower walls there is still a good choice of evergreen covering, such as several of the lesser New Zealand Veronicas. The taller *Veronica Traversii* is of a size for the wall of medium height, but there is a dwarfer variety of this well suited for the lower terrace. Other New Zealanders, *Olearia Haastii, O.*

stellulata and *O. macrodonta*, will also be welcome; several kinds of Cotoneaster, *Euonymus radicans* and *Daphne pontica*, the last filling the garden with its sweet scent in April and May. Aucubas can be used in shady places, and *Cassinia fulvida* must not be overlooked. Its tiny gold-backed leaves, set on long sprays that quickly grow, make it one of the prettiest things to cut and put with winter flowers in the house. Even *Berberis Aquifolium*, so useful and frequent as a bush in every garden, can be trained on a low wall with singularly good effect.

SWEET VIOLETS

In wintertime nothing is pleasanter in a room than a bunch of Violets; indeed there is hardly any other product of frame or greenhouse that diffuses so welcome a perfume. Forced Mignonette is good and sweet, and in open winter weather one may have the highly scented, almost over-scented blooms of Chimonanthus. The greenhouse may also give us heliotrope and the excellent sweetness of the Indian Daphne, while of the strong rather rank smell of Hyacinth there will probably be only too much. But most people will agree that on coming into a room the scent of a fresh bunch of Violets is the most welcome of all.

An immense advance has been made of late in the cultivation of Violets and the production of larger varieties. One of the foreign raisers has more than fifty named kinds in his catalogue. But unless anyone wishes to make a speciality of Violet culture two or three kinds in each class will be ample.

It may be convenient to think of Violets as in four classes. First, the small hardy kinds known in gardens as Russian; second, the larger singles that may be grown out of doors with protection or in frames; third, the old hardy double Violets flowering in spring; fourth, the double frame Violets commonly known as Neapolitan.

The short-stalked purple Violet that forms dense flowering masses in April is a garden form of our wild Sweet Violet, indeed can hardly be distinguished from it. What a joy it was in childish days to search sunny banks and hedgerows for the sweet little blossoms. There was a dear birthday that occurred in the third week of March. It was a point of honour to find a bunch of wild Violets, a little gift of loving labour whose annual continuity was never broken for fifty years. What a hunt it was sometimes when the season was backward; perhaps only a few half-opened buds could be found, but the custom came to have so strong a hold upon our childish minds that nothing would have induced us to miss the presentation of the little offering. However poor and small it might be, however far we might have to ramble, the Violets for the birthday bunch must be found. And then what a pleasure the search was in itself—what pretty places it led us to. The sunny skirts of woodland we came to know were the likeliest places, where the heart-shaped leaves nestled among tufts of grass; the grass now short or bent down; for Violets like sun while they are flowering and shade for the rest of the year. What prickly places some of their haunts were, at the foot of close black-thorn scrub and brambly brake. But the little fingers cared naught for pricks or scratches if only they could find a good bunch to carry home.

So the wild Violet remains to those children, now in late middle life, as a thing of delight in itself and a source of tender memories and of grateful remembrance of its kindly teaching and leading into fair wild places.

The wild Violet is of several colours, purple of more than one shade, pure white, white stained reddish at the back, and a dull red or puce colour, deep or light in different examples. With the English wild Violet may be placed the pale blue St. Helena, identical with it in size but of a colour that is never seen in the wild or other garden kinds. These wild Violets have a tender-ness of fragrance that is quite their own, and even more delicious in its own modest way than the more penetrating scent of the larger garden kinds. In the garden they are best on half-wild mossy banks where they feel the sun in spring, but are protected from it later in the year by summer growths of taller plants or by the summer leafing of overhanging bushes that are bare of foliage at the time when they are in bloom.

The large single Czar Violet is no doubt a development of a good form of the common sweet kind. When it came out as a new plant, now a good many years ago, it was the only large single, and though there are now many larger, it is still indispensable, for many of the larger new kinds are not so hardy. Where no frame space can be afforded it is a precious thing, yielding its fragrant flowers throughout the winter in all open weather. A fresh plantation must be made every year in early April, either of divisions or the rooted ends of runners; or, better still, from the runners cut off late the last summer and grown as cuttings. The plants should be quite eighteen inches apart and so placed that while they are shaded from hot sunshine in summer they may yet have sun in early spring. Therefore it is best to have them in vegetable ground where a row of fruit bushes will be on their south side, or where they will have such temporary shelter as a row of runner beans; or they may be outside the northern boundary of a patch of Jerusalem Artichokes which will be cleared away during the winter. A movable winter shelter, such as thatched hurdles tilted over the plants, will increase the amount of winter bloom and also lengthen the stalks.

Where a frame can be devoted to single as well as to double Violets, some of the very large and sweet new kinds should be grown, Princess of Wales and La France being among the best.

The old hardy double Violet with its little round mops of flowers in March and April is now but seldom seen in gardens, but it is a good old flower and should not be neglected.

A good supply of frame Violets is one of the most important matters in the way of a provision of flowers for the house in winter. English gardeners always prefer to grow Marie Louise, and they have some reason for their choice in that this kind is certainly the easiest to grow. But we think that its colouring, half-way between a light and a dark purple, is far less beautiful than that of the paler old Neapolitan; moreover, the flower is nearly always defaced by some small abortive petals in the centre, of an inharmonious reddish colour, from which the pale blue Neapolitan and the rather darker coloured and more robust De Parme are entirely free. A useful proportion for frame work would be one half of a good French strain of De Parme and a quarter each of Marie Louise and White Brazza.

Rhubarb (Rheum) foliage with background of Ivy

XI

THE FERN GARDEN

NATIVE FERNS IN THE GARDEN
Gardening Illustrated, January 1931
A WILD FERN GARDEN
Country Life, May 27, 1911

The Fern Garden

NATIVE FERNS IN THE GARDEN

THERE IS hardly a garden where our native Ferns may not be used with good effect, either for the display of their own beauty or for filling up spaces among shrubs, or in various odd corners that would otherwise be unsightly or uninteresting. The Common Polypody (*Polypodium vulgare*) is one of the characteristic plants of our country, the south-west corner of Surrey, within a walk of Hampshire on the west and of Sussex to the south. There are many hollow lanes where it clothes the upper parts of the steep, almost overhanging banks, matting into the stumps of Hazels and clinging in dense fringes to the sandy, half-rocky cornices. We have it in a number of places in the garden; it is good to see how kindly it takes to its assigned places, and, further, how it finds homes for itself and flourishes self-sown. One picture shows a spreading patch at the upper end of the Fern Walk, one of the many quiet ways that lead into the woodland. Another prosperous patch fringes a little dipping tank; here, after some years' growth, the fronds seem to come over the edge in exactly the right way, for if they had been purposely arranged it could hardly have been done better. In one part of the garden there is a Mushroom house, partly underground, with three steps down to the door. In the short length of retaining wall to the left a few small roots of Polypody were built in with the stones; they took kindly to the place, and now form a complete clothing. In connection with the same building there is an outer stairway leading to a loft. Here little Polypodies are coming—self-sown in the joints at the foot of some of the

*A September border with Michaelmas Daisies, Grasses,
Dwarf Asters and Stachys in foreground*

VIBURNUM TOMENTOSUM PLICATUM *with Acanthus and other*
foliage plants

upper steps. They have also formed a prosperous and always increasing tuft at the lower edge of a tile-roofed shed and on another tiled roof near by. They are also quite at home in any joints of dry walling and spread into sheets at the foot.

The Hart's-tongue Fern (*Scolopendrium vulgare*) comes in for many uses in the garden. It is happiest in cool, shady places and northern or eastern aspects. It is not frequent in a wild state in our sandy uplands, only appearing in the upper joints of the brickwork of wells or other such masonry, where it has the benefit of the lime in the mortar, for it is naturally a lime loving Fern. However, in cultivation it accommodates itself to a soil that is not only lime free, but that is naturally of a sour, peaty nature, as we know only too well by the persistent and often rank growth of the common Sheep's Sorrel (*Rumex acetosella*). Hart's-tongue not only consents to grow in our soil, but where it is well worked and enriched with leaf-mould it may be said to flourish luxuriantly. It is in great beauty in several places in the garden, notably in a small, shady place that is called the Hidden Garden, where there are other Ferns and some Lilies and various plants that enjoy shade. Here it forms the middle ridge of a slightly raised mound, covering and hiding some large lumps of sandstone, and guarding a drift of Foam Flower (*Tiarella*) that flowers in May. Interspersed with it are some well-established plants of the Willow Gentian (*G. Asclepiadea*), whose long, arching wands of bloom are in beauty in September. Near the house is a square tank surrounded by steps and squares of pavement that lead to a lower level. In the joints of the upper wall there is a growth of Hart's-tongue, with some Polypodies and the little Spleenwort (*Asplenium trichomanes*) that form a pretty fringe to the head of the tank.

Among native Ferns nothing is more useful than the common Male Fern (*Lastræa Filix-mas*). Many an old corner that would either give the impression of neglect, untidiness, or some form of unsightliness may be redeemed by a bold planting of this capital Fern, always so strong and handsome, and easy to grow. It makes a capital filling among newly planted shrubs where, if these are placed at a proper distance apart, there must necessarily be considerable spaces between. It also shows to fine effect planted in bold masses in the edges of woodland where this adjoins garden ground, and in many places, both in shade and half-shade, throughout the wood; and it is all the better when, as in our heathy upland, it meets and is backed by the taller Bracken which is native to the soil. But it is not of value only in the wild and shrubby places, for it is ornamental in more formal places.

There are several paths leading from the lawn and garden to the wooded ground on a higher level. One of them that passes upward in the shade forms an informal garden of hardy Ferns. The ground is a little higher on the right-hand side, and it was prepared for planting by scooping out hollow bays a few yards across on this side of the path from the thick natural growth of Whortleberry, some of which is left in jutting promontories between the main plantings of Ferns. The soil is solid sand under a thin surface layer of dark, peaty earth only a few inches thick. A good deal of sand was therefore dug out and a bed of leaf-mould put in, the excavation being enough to let a place designed for Royal Fern (*Osmunda regalis*) be well below the level of the path. It was further arranged for its better comfort, as the conditions of our dry, hilly land are not much to its liking, that it should have the benefit of any heavy rains; a shallow channel was therefore cut diagonally across the path, hardly deep enough to be noticeable, but serving to guide any storm water coming down the path straight to the *Osmunda*. Lady Fern (*Athyrium Filix-foemina*) comes next, for it is one of the most-water loving of our native kinds. It is happiest of all when it can be planted at the extreme edge of a pond or any rather still water, or the bank of a wet ditch, so that its outer rootlets are actually in the water. It is one of the most graceful and tender looking of the larger kinds, its only fault being that it is one of the earliest to turn brown and lose its fragile beauty. One of the bays of the Fern Walk is given to a main planting of Dilated Shield Fern (*Nephrodium dilatatum*), to many Fern lovers and certainly to one, the handsomest of our native kinds. Not only is it beautiful with a grand form and a rare perfection of detail, but it carries itself with a kind of strong, graceful dignity that is as remarkable as it is admirable. We are fortunate in having it, with Male Fern and Polypody, as one of the natural growths of our woodland. The Prickly Shield Fern (*Aspidium aculeatum*) is not in the Fern Walk, but in a place of its own among shrubs in the garden. It is a handsome thing, but less desirable than some other Ferns, as the fronds are of a deep dark green colour with a rather heavy effect; but it has one merit peculiarly its own, that it endures almost unchanged throughout the winter; in fact, well into the spring of the next year.

The Ferns named as in the Fern Walk are not its only occupants, for there are drifts of Hart's-tongue, Polypody, and Hard Fern (*Lomaria spicant*) and among these, coming into bloom in May, are some fine clumps of Trillium, the valued gift of an American friend; patches of Sanguinaria, and some fringing groups, which sometimes want restraint, of the lovely little *Smilacina bifolia*. At the back are some bold plantings of Solomon's Seal, then wild Bracken and the bushy growths of the woodland, with a background of dark Holly and the gleaming shafts of the Silver Birches.

A WILD FERN GARDEN

The planting of hardy Ferns should be one of the most beautiful forms of wild gardening. Though they are well suited for many uses in the garden proper, yet for their full enjoyment in fair quantity, the sentiment of association with shade in woody places is the one that is most sympathetic. Therefore a copse, or any kind of woodland that adjoins or approaches garden ground, should form the most desirable setting for the

A shady spot in a woody place — an ideal situation for the full enjoyment of ferns which Gertrude Jekyll so much admired. She wrote: "A copse, or any kind of woodland that adjoins or approaches garden ground ... and has acquired a rich surface soil, precious for Ferns, from the accumulation of the decayed leaves of hundreds of years ... There can be no better place for the Fern garden."

Fern garden. Best of all would be some natural pathway in a shaded hollow. Such a place often occurs in wooded land— possibly a former pack-horse track, or some such ancient way, that has long gone out of use, but that retains its form and has acquired a rich surface soil, precious for Ferns, from the accumulation of the decayed leaves of hundreds of years.

There can be no better place for the Fern garden. The path is not exactly straight, but very gently winding, after the usual way of a wild path that goes with the natural swing of the ground. When such a garden has to be made, it is commonly dug out in some roundish or oval form, with a raised island in the middle; but if it is made like this it never loses that artificial appearance that is not quite in harmony with what is to be planted, whereas the wood-walk, with its shallow banks sloping up easily to the natural floor of the wood, provides exactly what is most suitable. If the banks do not exist and have to be made, it is better to dig out and remove the poorer subsoil than to pile anything on the sides. The labour is not formidable, for a depth of eighteen inches down to the path level is quite enough. Such a depth, with a path not more than four feet wide, and the banks rising on a very slight convex line for from ten to twelve feet, and then dying away into the natural wood level, will give a quite easy and informal look to the place. But there may also be subsidiary hollows running up into the bank, and in making these it will generally be found that they should not be hollowed straight out of the bank, but a little diagonally, according to the lie of the ground and its natural movement. If the wood path leads down to moister ground it is all the better, for though the greater number of the hardy Ferns, both native and exotic, will do well on the banks, yet there are some that are true bog-plants.

As in many other special kinds of gardening, there is no reason why, although the place is called the Fern garden, it should contain nothing but Ferns. The same conditions suit many other plants, some of them blooming in spring when the

Ferns have not yet made their fronds. Such are Snowdrops, Primroses, Daffodils, the many forms of Wood Anemone and the charming little Wood Sorrel. In early summer there should be the neat little *Smilacina bifolia* and the fairy-like Trientalis, and, a little further back among the Ferns, in specially made pockets of deep leaf-mould, groups of *Trillium grandiflorum*. The Spanish Squills, blue, white and pale pink, should also be among the Ferns, with *Uvularia grandiflora*, Dentaria and Woodruff, and further back, Solomon's Seal and white Foxgloves. The Ferns themselves should be in handsome masses, cleverly placed with single plants detached from the main groups. They will be mainly the native Male Fern, Hart's-tongue, and the singularly beautiful Dilated Shield Fern. The planting will have an all the more natural appearance if it is not upon the banks alone, but stretches away back into the wood. If the soil is light or peaty, and Bracken grows spontaneously, it will be all the better, the planted Ferns joining harmoniously with the wild.

The smaller kinds of native Ferns, such as the Oak and Beech Ferns and the pretty American *Dicksonia punctilobula*—a creeping, rooted kind that soon spreads in cool, peaty ground—would come to the front. Where the ground is moister it would be well to have large clumps of Lady Fern and Osmunda, with the European Struthiopteris, again Dilated Shield Fern, Blechnum and two of the American species, *Osmunda cinnamonea* and *Onoclea sensibilis*.

The greater number of our native Ferns are subject to variation of form, sporting into curious slashings, duplications and feathery crestings. Many Fern-lovers take a delight in getting these together and making gardens of them alone. Such a collection is less suited to the wild-garden treatment here advised, though in itself extremely interesting. Those who collect such varieties will find in C. T. Druery's *British Ferns and their Varieties* (Routledge) a complete discourse on a fully representative series of known varieties, copiously illustrated.

XII

A RETROSPECT

OLD-FASHIONED FLOWERS
Black's Gardening Dictionary

GARDEN PLANTS OF SEVENTY YEARS AGO
The New Flora and Silva, vol. i, 1929

XII

A Retrospect

OLD-FASHIONED FLOWERS

IT IS of interest to consider what were the flowers of gardens in the days of our great-grandmothers, or of about a hundred years ago, and to think how charming those gardens must have been, although many of the plants that we now think indispensable were then unknown. From the middle to the end of the eighteenth century there had been in operation that great change in the treatment of pleasure-grounds that involved the inclusion of much larger spaces. In some ways it was a wholesome innovation, for it gave a wider outlook in all senses; but, as with all matters of prevailing fashion, it had regrettable consequences, for there were then existing all over the country the small enclosed gardens of Manor houses and those belonging to many a modest dwelling of fairly well-to-do people; gardens that had remained unchanged since Jacobean and even Tudor times, but that must now be swept away in obedience to the new fashion of landscape gardening. But a few people were faithful to the old gardens, and to the old garden flowers also, and to this day these remain and retain a special degree of loving appreciation such as we do not extend to the many newcomers, however gorgeous they may be and however well fitted to take their place in our modern pleasure-grounds.

There were then, as now, special fanciers of one kind of flower, so that by long continued care in breeding or selection better varieties had been obtained; but these examples of what we should call florist's flowers were then confined to a very

few sorts. If one mentions Auriculas, Carnations, laced Polyanthus, and Tulips, it was about all. Pansies were the next to be
taken up. Then, about the middle of the nineteenth century,
came the use of tender plants for summer bedding. It was a
cruel blow to the old-fashioned flowers, for in many gardens
they were either abolished or so little considered that they
ceased to count. Happily nothing was absolutely lost, and we
have now made up, by restoring them to use, for the neglect of
those thirty or forty years when the bedding system was almost
exclusively in vogue.

We ask ourselves, 'Is it the force of old association, or is it
that our ancestors had the sense to get hold of the most delightful flowers?' We know not; but we only feel that what we know
as old-fashioned flowers have a kind of charm that makes them
more lovable than all the fair plants of more recent introduction. We cannot fail to realise this when we think of a few, such
as Honeysuckle, Jasmine, and Moss Rose.

To pass briefly in review, season by season, some of the
chief of the old-fashioned flowers—the earliest expected were
Snowdrops, then Crocuses, white, purple and yellow, in lines
or patches in flower borders; no one had then thought of the
better way we have now lately learnt of having them in grass,
nor were they in such numbers of varieties as now. Daffodils
also were but few, the one most general in gardens being the
old double yellow *Narcissus Telamonius*. Here and there one
might find an early form of *N. incomparabilis*, and perhaps a
few patches of *N. nanus* and the pretty little *N. minor*. Others
were known, such as the good double Queen Anne's Daffodil
and the white *N. moschatus*; but they were in special collections
only, not in general use. There were the sweet-scented Jon-
quils, both the true rush-leaved kind and the commoner
Campernelle, also the single and double *N. Poeticus*. During
January and February there were three good flowering
shrubs—Laurustinus, yellow Jasmine, and, almost more
generally than now, the sweet-scented *Daphne Mezereum*, a

plant beloved of cottagers, and never seen to greater advantage than in one of those little garden strips between road and cottage that do so much to give beauty and interest to our English roadsides.

In March there was that charming plant Blue-eyed Mary (*Omphalodes verna*) of creeping habit, with leaves of vivid green and pure blue flowers much like Forget-me-not—one of the best of spring flowers and much too much neglected. Then came double Daisies, red and white, of moderate size, favourite plants for edging, and better in proportion than the modern ones, in which size is greatly overdone. Violets were still of small size; the usual garden kind, known as the Russian Violet, was only a shade larger, if larger at all, than the deliciously scented purple white and ruddy forms of the wild plant. But there was a double purple Violet, fairly hardy—that was more fully double than the kinds now grown in frames, the bloom being almost globular—that has now become rare in cultivation. Rosemary, one of the oldest and most favoured of garden shrubs, is in bloom very early in the year; it was in every garden. And there were always two bulbous plants —blooming in March or earliest April—the Common Dog's Tooth Violet (*Erythronium*), with its dull pink flowers and beautifully spotted and marbled leaves, and the Purple Fumewort (*Corydalis*), also of a 'sad' pinkish colouring of the same class.

Primroses were always favourites, though the singles were in fewer kinds and colourings than now. But the pretty double Primroses, white, yellow and lilac, were then more grown, and much attention was paid to the laced Polyanthus. Wallflowers were always welcomed, though for a long time there were none but the brown. But there was a capital plant, now only lingering in cultivation and but rarely seen, that was formerly in almost every garden—the perennial double Wallflower. It is a bushy, half-woody plant that goes on for years; just a little tender, and likes to have its back against a warm wall.

The end of April brings the Poet's Narcissus, and its still better and later double kind; a flower unsurpassed for beauty and value by any of the more modern Daffodils. With it comes the sweet-scented leafing of Sweetbriar. Crown Anemones will have finished their bloom but, from the end of April to the middle of May, Tulips are in full beauty. The kinds are those that have of late years been searched out and restored to favour under the name general of Cottage Tulips, besides the Breeders and Bybloemens of the Dutch, and a number of the flaked and feathered named sorts of the Tulip florists. May also brings Columbines; they were of the short-spurred kinds only, in the purple, white and dull red colourings in which we still have them. Lily of the Valley and Solomon's Seal were in every garden, though we now plant them by preference in woody places. Pansies were already the subject of special cultivation, though the pretty kinds we now have with frilled edges and rich red colouring were not yet known. Then in May also came the Sweet Rocket, both white and purple. The excellent and still more sweetly scented Double Rockets, flowering later, were also old favourites; they are still to be had though they are no longer in general cultivation. The wealth of Flag Irises that we now have were not available three generations ago; the old blue Flag alone was in every garden, and the grey-white *Iris florentina* was not uncommon. Thrift was prized as an edging plant, also London Pride and the good old White Pink, and for this use we have not found anything better among flowering plants. The white Pink is in fact a better thing than the larger modern kinds that in so many gardens have taken the place of the old favourite, one of whose many merits is its close habit and good silvery foliage in winter. May also brought the grand old double Peonies, varieties of *P. officinalis*, in three colourings, crimson, deep rose, and pinkish white; these remain much as they were in the old days. May was always the special month for flowering shrubs, and white Broom, Deutzia, Guelder Rose, Laburnum,

Lilac, Ribes and Syringa (*Philadelphus*) were in every garden. Lilacs that have of late years been so greatly improved by the work of French nurserymen were then of two kinds only, namely, white, and the light soft purple that has made 'lilac' a colour word. The Honeysuckle that we know as Early Dutch was one of the old favourites, and was much used for covering arbours. Another old arbour plant was the Tea-tree (*Lycium*), still the best thing for forming a neat living shelter. One of the later of the flowering bulbs, the Feathered Hyacinth (*Muscari monstrosum*), was a favoured plant. The aromatic Southern-wood (*Artemisia Abrotonum*), though without flower in our climate, should not be forgotten, for it was much prized in cottage gardens, when it was commonly the custom for a spray of it to accompany the prayer-book to church, both being wrapped round in a clean handkerchief.

June brought Day Lilies and the great Orange Lilies, perennial Lupines, Pinks, and the Red Valerian (*Centranthus*) with all the old Roses. The Roses, in fact, began in May with the bloom of the Scotch Briars, white, pink and red, and the clear pink of the early bloom of China Rose. But in June came the Damask Roses, red, red and white, and the old garden Rose nearly related to Damask named Reine Blanche, creamy-white, with a narrow edging of red that makes the buds nearly all red. Cabbage Roses too and their crested varieties the Moss Roses; also a number of sorts of the old *Rosa gallica*, nearly all now discarded. There were also a number of climbing Roses, the Musk Rose and a number of those we know as Ayrshires, hybrids of *Rosa sempervirens*, many of which are still unbeaten in spite of the large numbers of modern kinds. There were also the Boursaults, Roses without prickles, derived from *Rosa alpina*. One of these, the Blush Boursault, has a purity of colouring, of milk-white deepened to a rosy centre, such as no other Rose can show.

With June and July came in the taller of the border Campanulas, *C. latifolia* and *C. persicifolia*, with Canterbury Bells

A corner of the wood with PIERIS JAPONICA *and a white Azalea*

Daffodils planted in drifts along a clearance in the wood

A Heath garden in the wood (MENZIESIA POLIFOLIA) *and low-growing Heaths in front with one of the tree varieties at the back*

A group of Munstead White Foxgloves in the wood

and Sweet Williams, also the rosy Everlasting Pea, the sweet, late Dutch Honeysuckle, Monkshoods, both purple and purple and white, several kinds of Stocks, and above all, Carnations. Of the last, the one most generally grown was the Old Crimson Clove, of hardy nature and sweetest scent. There was an old kind something between a Pink and a Carnation called Anne Boleyn, in colour soft pink with darker centre, and very sweet. This appears to be lost, as recent enquiries for it have been answered by an assortment of flowers bearing the same name, but in no way equal to the original. Then there was the old kind called Painted Lady, with the back of the petals almost scarlet, and so short and stocky in habit that it was difficult to layer. This still exists, but has become rare.

The White Lily (*Lilium candidum*) was one of the glories of the July garden, as it still remains, for, notwithstanding the introduction of a number of other splendid species, the White Lily, in its stately beauty and purity, always holds its own. The other Lilies of the old gardens were the purple Martagon, two scarlet kinds, *L. chalcedonicum* and *L. pomponium*, the orange *L. croceum*, already mentioned, Tiger Lilies, and the earlier *L. pyrenaicum*, not of any great beauty and with a rank, unpleasant smell.

Lavender was always one of the joys of August, precious for drying and as an ingredient of pot-pourri, and the same season brought the ever-welcome white Jasmine, a well-deserved favourite of all time. Then came Phloxes, few in number and very poor in quality compared with those of the present day; thin and narrow petalled and of straggling habit. There were also a few Snapdragons of what we should now consider wretched quality, some Dahlias of the old show kinds, and China Asters.

The September show of bloom was not of much account save for the continued flowering of the Dahlias, but there were also French and African Marigolds. Of other annuals there were certain old favourites; Sweet Peas in four sorts only, viz. white, pink and white, purple (light and dark) and the finely splashed mixture that may be called roan. But they were deliciously sweet, a good quality that has been in large measure lost with the improvement of the bloom and the increase in the number of the varieties. These annuals were also commonly grown: the always charming *Collinsia bicolor*, Convolvulus, both tall and dwarf, Cornflowers, blue and purple, Love-in-a-mist, Mignonette, Nasturtium, the pretty blue Nemophila, Night-scented Stock, Sweet Sultan and Virginian Stock. This brief account is by no means an exhaustive description of the resources of the old gardens, but it gives a fair idea of the flowers commonly in use about a hundred years ago.

GARDEN PLANTS OF SEVENTY YEARS AGO

There is now such a wealth of flowering plants available for our gardens that it becomes almost a difficulty to make a choice without leaving out a number of good things that may be considered essential. Seventy years ago it was quite another matter, and yet it seems strange that there are a certain number of highly desirable plants that were then in favour, and that we should still consider to be among the best, which have passed out of cultivation or can only rarely be heard of.

Prominent among these was the old Double Rocket, one of the handsomest and certainly one of the sweetest of garden flowers. It was in two colours, a purple and a white; the white was the one most esteemed. It is a double form of the biennial common Rocket (*Hesperis matronalis*) that is so easily grown from seed, and that gives off such a delicious scent in warm evenings of early summer. It may have been generally lost, because it wants some care to keep it going, and now that our lives are so full of rush and hurry there may seem to be no time that can be given to a plant that needs careful watching, and the doing of what is needful at the right moment. The massive spikes of double flower necessarily exhaust a good deal of the strength, and the plant remembers that it was originally only a biennial; but at the base of the flowering stem there are always one or two tufts of young green growths; these must be carefully taken off and grown on separately to form flowering plants for the next year.

Then there was the old double perennial Wallflower, with bright yellow, full double flowers. I believe there was another of the usual red-brown colour, but I never saw it. A plant of this old Wallflower would endure for several years, the lower part becoming hard and woody. It grew into quite good sized bushes, and was reputed to be rather tender, so that we always put it in a warmish place with a wall at the back. It was very sweetly scented and was easily propagated by cuttings.

There was another old favourite, a double purple Violet, that also seems to have gone out of cultivation. It was quite distinct from the double Violets that we grow in frames, such as De Parme and Marie Louise and some more modern varieties. It was quite hardy; it did not have the shiny leaves of the usual double kinds, but the dull-surfaced leaf of the wild, or the common Russian Violet. The flowers were fully double, making them look like little purple balls; the stalks were short and not very strong, so that they could scarcely bear up the heavy flower head; there was a special weakness at the point where the stalk joined the bloom, for I well remember how in making them up into little bunches a number of the heads broke off.

Then there were the old Sweet Peas, of that strong, delicious scent that seems to be largely lost, although the Sweet Pea as a flower has been so wonderfully improved both as to size and colour. The old Peas were in four colours only, one a mixture of reddish and bluish purple, another of rosy pink and pinkish white, a third of a kind of grey roan and a fourth white.

Roses of the then new class of Hybrid Perpetuals were but few in number, for it was a time even before that of General Jacqueminot and Charles Lefebvre and their contemporaries—Roses that are now almost forgotten. The only Roses of this class that I can remember were a red one called Lee's Perpetual and the pink Coupe d'Hébé, a charming flower to the present day.

Of climbing Roses there were the Boursaults, derived from *Rosa alpina*, and, like that species, without prickles. The Crimson Boursault was the one most generally grown and the most free flowering, but we had also the Blush Boursault, a charming Rose whose lovely colouring, of a skim-milk white shading to a lively rosy red in the centre, can perhaps not be matched by any one of the numberless Roses now grown. There were also some of the old Ayrshires, climbing, cluster Roses that for sterling merit compare well with the best of the many Ramblers we can now choose from. Happily there was always the Sweet Cabbage Rose and its mossed variety the Moss Rose, and Damasks and Sweetbriar and the double white Rose of cottage gardens.

In the greater number of flower borders there were only a few of the plants that we still use; the double Crimson Peony, Day Lilies, Spiderwort, Monkshood, perennial Cornflower, Everlasting Pea, Hollyhocks, and some very poor kinds of Phlox and Michaelmas Daisy. The only Dahlias then grown were the stiff-looking kinds that we now call show or florist's Dahlias, and those in a restricted number of varieties.

Shady arbours, well covered, were much liked in the middle of the last century and earlier. They were usually clothed with a vigorous growth of Honeysuckle, Jasmine and Cluster Rose. An old favourite for the same use was the Tea-tree or Box-thorn (*Lycium barbarum*), an accommodating plant that can be made to cover quite a large space, and is docile to any amount of trimming and training.

Of smaller garden plants, some of the old favourites now generally neglected were Anemones, Auriculas and Hepaticas. None of these are actually lost, but it is rare to see hardy Auriculas now in gardens, or the other old favourites of the Primula family, the curious Hose-in-hose, or the double Primroses in colourings of white, yellow, lilac and crimson; though it is true that these are not for everyone, as they only thrive in a strong, rich loam. The charming little St. Helena Violet, deliciously sweet and of a tender lavender colour, is now but seldom seen. It is a variety of the wild Sweet Violet whose white and reddish colourings are well known.

Stove and greenhouse plants were grown much as they are to this day, except for the advance in some of the more familiar kinds such as Primulas, Cinerarias, and show Pelargoniums, and the present interest in Orchids and their now extensive cultivation. Tender plants for putting out in summer were largely grown to satisfy the needs of the then all-pervading bedding-out system; plants that we have now learnt to put to good use by better arrangement and thoughtful discrimination. One old favourite, now rarely seen, deserves mention: the Balm of Gilead (*Cedronella triphylla*); not a showy plant, but with a curiously interesting, sweet aromatic scent. For garden purposes it may be classed with *Humea elegans*, for it has the same attribute of a distinctive scent without any particular flower beauty.

In the older days there were some plants specially beloved of cottagers that might often be seen in their windows. The most notable was the tender *Campanula isophylla*, often beautifully grown in pots, and forming cascades of white or purple flowers. The common Musk, now alas! scentless, was also prettily grown over a little scaffolding of sticks, and was a charming ornament in the cottage window. Another old favourite was a single plant of the annual *Alonsoa Warscewiczii* carefully pruned to form good bushy growth, and by the middle of summer a mass of its scarlet flower.

Of annuals, some that were much grown seventy years ago seem to be now almost forgotten. There was the soft rosy scarlet Collomia and the pretty purple and white *Collinsia bicolor*, and best of all, Venus's Navelwort (*Omphalodes lini-folia*). These are all still in seedsmen's lists and at low prices, but are strangely neglected and well deserve to be restored to favour.

In the older days Mignonette was in one form only; it had not yet suffered from the ill-directed aims of seed-growers, who, in the desire to produce something that might be called a novelty, have encouraged reddish tints that are quite foreign to the plant's nature. For Mignonette is and always should be a plant of modest colouring and sweetest scent; both these charming qualities belong to the older kind and have been lost, or at any rate regrettably reduced in the modern named varieties.

Epilogue

IN A PRIMROSE WOOD

IT MUST have been at about seven years of age that I first learnt to know and love a Primrose copse. Since then more than half a century has passed, and yet each spring, when I wander into the Primrose wood, and see the pale yellow blooms, and smell their sweetest of sweet scents, and feel the warm spring air throbbing with the quickening pulse of new life, and hear the glad notes of the birds and the burden of the bees, and see again the same delicate young growths piercing the mossy woodland carpet; when I see and feel and hear all this, for a moment I am seven years old again and wandering in the fragrant wood hand-in-hand with the dear God who made it, and who made the child's mind to open wide and receive the enduring happiness of the gracious gift. So, as by direct divine teaching, the impression of the simple sweetness of the Primrose wood sank deep into the childish heart, and laid, as it were, a foundation stone of immutable belief, that a Father in Heaven who could make all this, could make even better if He would, when the time should come that His children should be gathered about Him.

And as the quick years pass and the body grows old around the still young heart, and the day of death grows ever nearer; with each new spring-tide the sweet flowers come forth and bloom afresh; and with their coming—with the ever-renewing of their gracious gift and still more precious promise—the thought of Death becomes like that of a gentle and kindly bearer of tidings, who brings the inevitable message, and bids the one for whom it is destined receive it manfully and be of good hope and cheerfulness, and remember that the Sender of Death is the Giver of the greater new Life, no less than of the sweet spring flowers, that bloom and die and live again as a never-ending parable of Life and Death and Immortality.

Index

Acer palmatum, 227
Achillea, 148
Aconitum Napellus, 315, 318
Agapanthus Moorei, 177
— umbellatus, 70
Agathea coelestis, 164, 177
Ageratum, 122, 146, 150, 167,
— mcxicanum,179
Ailanthus glandulosa, 10
Aira flexuosa, 267
Ajuga reptans, 125, 161
Alexandrian Laurel, *see* Ruscus
racemosus
Alisma Plantago, 98, 106
Allamanda, 11
Alonsoa Warscewiczii, 146, 319
Alströmeria, 115, 121, 130
Althaea ficifolia, 115, 126, 139,
165, 178, 179, 182, 272-276,
318
Alyssum, 130, 161, 224,
— maritimum, 143
Ampelopsis, *see* Vitis
quinquefolia
Anagallis caerulea, 143
Anchusa, Dropmore, *see*
Anchusa italica
— italica, 121, 128, 130, 164,
171
Andromeda, *see* Pieris
Anemone apennina, 223, 236
— blanda, 236
— Coronaria, 126, 222, 237,
311
— fulgens, 126, 237
— Hepatica, 222, 236, 237,
318
— Pulsatilla, 237
— japonica, 115, 279
— stellata, 237

Anthemis tinctoria, 120
Anthericum, 162
Antirrhinum, 83, 121, 126, 130,
150, 164, 167, 179, 182, 280, 315
Aquilegia, 136, 311
Arabis albida fl. pl., 130, 224
Arctostaphylos, 104
Arctotis, 143
Arenaria balearica, 84
Argemone grandiflora, 142
— mexicana, 140
Aristolochia, 91
Armeria vulgaris, 83, 311
Arrowhead, *see* Sagittaria
Artemisia Abrotanum, 312
— lactiflora, 118, 119, 128, 171
— ludoviciana, 122, 177, 180, 182
— stelleriana, 122, 178, 180, 182
Arundo, 81
Asarum europaeum, 136, 239,288
Asperula azurea nitida, 143
— odorata, 26, 306
Asphodelus, 163
Aspidium aculeatum, 288, 303
Asplenium Trichomanes, 301
Aster acris, 121, 166, 178, 279
— Amellus, 115, 117, 121, 122,
130, 167, 171, 173, 178, 180,
276-281, 318
— chinensis,11,38,116,122,126
130, 146, 167, 175, 179, 315
— corymbosus, 180
— Novae-Angliae, 279, 280
— Novi-Belgii, 279, 280
— puniceus, 279
— umbellatus, 166, 180
— vimineus, 279
Athyrium Filix-foemina, 79, 98,
104, 302, 306
Atriplex hortensis, 128, 165

Aubretia gracea, 130, 161, 224, 227
— Dr. Mules, 161
Aucuba japonica, 291
Auricula, *see* Primula Auricula
Azalea, 14, 264, 265
— Daviesii, 264, 265
— narcissiflora, 265
— pontica, 10, 265
— rustica plena, 265
Azara microphylla, 289

Balm of Gilead, *see* Cedronella triphylla
Bamboo, *see* Bambusa
Bambusa, 81
— Metake, 206
Barberry, *see* Berberis
Bartonia aurea, 140, 143
Bay, *see* Laurus nobilis
Beech, for pergolas, 94
Beech Fern, *see* Polypodium Phegopteris
Bellis perennis fl. pl., 224, 310
Berberis aquifolium, 289, 291
— Darwinii, 227
— vulgaris, 85
Bergamot, *see* Monarda
Bignonia, *see* Tecoma
Blechnum, *see* Lomaria
Bog Asphodel, *see* Narthecium ossifragum
Bougainvillea speciosa, 11
Box, *see* Buxus sempervirens
Brachycome, 146
Broom, *see* Genista
Buddleia Veitchii, 166
Butomus umbellatus, 98, 106
Butter-bur, *see* Petasites
Buxus balearica, 220
sempervirens, 21, 27, 205, 284

Calceolaria amplexicaulis, 155, 165
— integrifolia, 11, 116, 155
Calendula officinalis, 165
Calluna Hammondii, 266

Calluna Serlei, 266
— vulgaris, 267
Caltha palustris, 105
Campanula alliariaefolia, 133
— carpatica, 133
— eriocarpa, 133
— isophylla, 319
— lactiflora, 122, 180
— latifolia, 312
— macrocarpa, 115
— macrantha, 115, 130, 133
— Medium, 121, 142, 312
— persicifolia, 115,130,133,312
— pusilla, 133
— pyramidalis, 116
— rotundifolia, 267
Canary Creeper, *see* Tropaeolum canariense
Candytuft, *see* Iberis
Canna indica, 78, 79, 115, 119 166
Canterbury Bell, *see* Campanula Medium
Cardamine pratensis, 105, 110
Carnation, *see* Dianthus Caryophyllus
Cassinia fulvida, 291
Catmint, *see* Nepeta
Ceanothus Gloire de Versailles, 122, 166, 179, 183
Cedronella triphylla, 319
Centaurea cyanus, 171, 316, 318
— montana, 11
— suaveolens, 316
Centranthus, 121, 130, 305
Cerastium tomentosum, 83, 166
Cheiranthus Cheiri, 83, 125, 126, 130, 161, 224, 227, 310, 317
Chimonanthus fragrans, 227, 291
Chionodox, 160, 222
Choisya ternata, 290
Christmas Rose, *see* Helleborus niger
Chrysanthemum, 130
— frutescens, 166
— maximum, 115, 119, 121, 166
— uliginosum, 167, 173
Cineraria maritima, 122, 166, 167,

178, 180, 182
— stellata, 11, 319
Cistus, 137
— cyprius, 290
— laurifolius, 206
Clematis, 82, 119, 130
— cirrhosa, 13
— Flammula, 79, 94, 115, 118, 164, 171
— Jackmani, 121, 167, 177, 179, 182, 183
— montana, 91
— paniculata, 94
— recta, 115, 116
— vitalba, 91
Clerodendron foetidum, 166
Cobaea scandens, 79, 150
Colchicum autumnale, 221
Collinsia bicolor, 316
Collomia coccinea, 126, 319
Columbine, *see* Aquilegia
Commelina coelestis, 164, 175
Comptonia asplenifolia, 103
Conifers, 284
Convallaria majalis, 11, 133, 311,
Convolvulus major, 95, 144, 316
Coreopsis lanceolata, 165
Cornflower, *see* Centaurea cyanus
Cornish Heath, *see* Erica vagans
Corydalis ochroleuca, 224
— solida, 223, 309
Cosmos, 145
Cotoneaster, 84, 291
Cotton-grass, *see* Eriophorum
Crambe maritima, 177
Crataegus Pyracantha, 94
Crinum Powelli, 79
Crocus, Autumn, *see* Colchicum autumnale
Crocus aureus, 229
— banaticus, 229
— biflorus, 229
— chrysanthus, 229
— Dutch, 158, 159, 221, 222, 228-230, 309
Crocus Sieberi, 229
— suaveolens, 229
— Tommasinianus, 229

— vernus, 229, 230
— versicolor, 229
Crown Imperial, *see* Fritillaria Imperialis
Cruciferae, 139, 140
Cyclamen coum, 224, 230
— ibericum, 230
— persicum, 11
— repandum, 230
— vernum, 231
Cynara Scolymus, 177
Cypripedium spectabile, 105

Daffodil, *see* Narcissus
Dahlia, 115, 119, 122, 164-166, 177-179, 279, 280, 315, 318
Daisy, *see* Bellis perennis
Danaë racemosa, *see* Ruscus racemosus
Daphne indica, 62, 291
— Mezereum, 158, 223, 309
— pontica, 291
Datura, 61, 145
Day Lily, *see* Hemerocallis
Delphinium consolida, 167, 177, 180, 183
— (perennial), 118, 119, 121, 125, 128, 130, 164, 171
Dentaria bulbifera, 306
Desmodium penduliflorum, 85
Deutzia, 311
— gracilis, 162
Dianthus, 130, 142, 146, 311
— barbatus, 142, 315
— caryophyllus, 315
— fragrans, 84
Dicksonia punctiloba, 306
Dielytra spectabilis, 162
Digitalis, 14, 130, 136, 162, 163, 306
Dimorphotheca aurantiaca, 143
— pluvialis, 143
Dog's Tooth Violet, *see* Erythronium
Doronicum caucasicum, 130
Doronicum plantagineum, 125, 130, 224
Drosera, 106

Dryas octopetala, 105

Echinops ruthenicus, 179
— sphaerocephalus, 130, 137
166, 167, 177, 183
Eleagnus pungens, 290
Elymus arenarius, 116, 279
Epimedium pinnatum, 258
Equisetum Telmateia, 108
Eranthis hyemalis, 155
Eremurus, 268, 269
— Bungei, 269
— himalaicus, 269
— Olgae, 269
— robustus, 268, 269
Erica, 103, 265-267, 287
— arborea, 265
— carnea, 266
— ciliaris, 266
— cinerea, 266, 267
— darleyensis, 266
— lusitanica, 266
— Maweana, 266
— Tetralix, 106, 266, 267
— vagans, 106, 266
— Veitchii, 266
Erigeron speciosus, 115, 121, 130, 166
Erinus alpinus, 83, 84
Eriophorum polystachyon, 106
Eryngium, 177
— giganteum, 121, 167
— Oliverianum, 117, 119, 121, 179
— planum, 179
Erythronium Dens-canis, 223, 310
— giganteum, 14, 223
Escallonia macrantha, 290
— Philippiana, 290
Eschscholtzia, 140, 142
Eulalia japonica, 82
Euonymus radicans, 291
Euphorbia Characias, 279
— Wulfenii, 166
Everlasting Pea, see Lathyrus latifolius

Ferns, 61, 137, 155, 160, 228, 288, 298-306
Feverfew, see Pyrethrum
Ficus carica, 68, 80
Fig, see Ficus carica
Flag Iris, see Iris Pseudacorus
Forget-me-not, see Myosotis
Forsythia suspensa, 85, 94
Foxglove, see Digitalis
Fritillaria imperialis, 224
— meleagris, 110
Fuchsia gracilis, 61
— Riccartoni, 166
Fumaria bulbosa, see Corydalis solida
Funkia grandiflora, 61, 79, 177
— Sieboldii, 177

Gaillardia, 121, 130
Galanthus Elwesii, 222, 228
— Fosteri, 228
— Imperati, 228
— nivalis, 222, 224, 227, 228, 309
— plicatus, 222
Galax aphylla, 104, 133
Galega, 115, 121, 122
Garrya elliptica, 290
Gaultheria, 104
— procumbens, 104
— Shallon, 14, 288
Gazania, 116, 165
Genista hispanica var. alba, 162, 311
Gentiana asclepiadea, 136, 301
— Pneumonanthe, 106
Geranium, bedding, see Pelargonium
— ibericum, 115
Godetia, 125, 167, 182, 183
Golden Privet, see Ligustrum ovalifolium aureum
Grammanthes gentianoides, 143, 146
Grape Hyacinth, see Muscari
Guelder Rose, see Virburnum

Gunnera, 82, 103
Gynerium argenteum, 82
Gypsophila paniculata, 115, 119, 121, 166, 178, 180, 182

Hedera dentata, 290
— Helix, 64, 228, 289
— — var. arborescens, 42
Hedychium, 61
Helenium pumilum, 115, 120, 130, 165
Helianthus orygalis, 115, 116, 118, 119, 130
— sparsifolius, 120
Heliotrope, 116, 175
Helleborus abchasicus, 158, 232
— atro-rubens, 158
— caucasicus, 232
— colchicus, 158, 223, 232, 287
— niger, 155, 284
— olympicus, 158, 223
— orientalis, 158, 223, 232
Hemerocallis, 11, 115, 121, 130, 312, 318
Hepatica, see Anemone hepatica
Heracleum giganteum, 110, 269
— Mantegazzianum, 103
Hesperus matronalis, 130, 311, 316
Heuchera Richardsoni, 125-128, 161, 162, 227, 239
Hippophaë rhamnoides, 122, 179
Holly, see Ilex aquifolium
Hollyhock, see Althaea ficifolia
Honesty, see Lunaria
Honeysuckle, see Lonicera
Hornbeam, for pergolas, 94
Humea elegans, 59, 319
Humulus japonicus, 95
Hyacinth (Hyacinthus orientalis), 21, 291
Hyacinthus azureus, 231
Hydrangea, 115, 116, 180
— arborescens grandiflora, 177
— paniculata, 177
Hydrocotyle vulgaris, 83
Hypericum calycinum, 85

Iberis, 161
— coronaria, 142, 240
— gibraltarica, 240
Iberis sempervirens, 161, 238, 239, 240
Ilex, see Quercus Ilex
— aquifolium, 205, 206, 284, 289
Impatiens glandulifera, 145, 148
Ipomea purpurea, see Convolvuus major
— rubro-coerulea, 144, 150
Iresine Herbsti, 128, 165
Iris alata, 13, 253
— albicans, 12
— aurea, 261
— Bakeriana, 254
— balkana, 254
— Cengialti, 259
— Chamae-Iris, 259
— cristata, 259, 260
— Danfordiae, 254
— Flag, see Iris germanica
— flavescens, 257
— florentina, 257, 258, 311
— foetidissima, 260, 288
— germanica, 162, 254-258, 311
— graminea, 260
— histrioides, 253, 254
— Kaempferi, 260
— laevigata, 98, 105, 260
— ochroleuca, 105, 261
— orientalis, 260
— pallida, 163
— — dalmatica, 177, 257, 258
— persica, 259
— Pseudacorus, 106, 261
— pumila coerulea, 175, 259
— reticulata, 175, 253, 259
— sibirica, 98, 260
— squalens, 257
— stylosa, 13, 250, 253, 287
— Tolmeiana, 259
— unguicularis, 261
— variegata aurea, 163, 257
Irish Heath, see Menziesia polifolia
Ivy, see Hedera

Japanese Hop, *see* Humulus japonicus
Japanese Maize, *see* Zea Mays
Japan Privet, *see* Ligustrum japonicum, 166
Jasione Montana, 267
Jasmine, white, *see* Jasminum officinale
— yellow, *see* Jasminum nudiflorum
Jasminum nudiflorum, 94, 227, 287, 309, 318
— officinale, 289, 315
Jerusalem Sage, *see* Phlomis
Juniperus Sabina, 84

Kalmia latifolia, 103-105, 287
Kerria japonica, 94
Knotweed, *see* Polygonum

Laburnum vulgare, 267, 311
Lady Fern, *see* Athyrium
Lapageria rosea, 11
Larkspur, *see* Delphinium
Lastraea dilatata, 98, 104
— Filix-Mas, 288, 301, 302, 306
Lathyrus latifolius, 115, 118, 119, 137, 165, 315, 318
— odoratus, 11, 142, 315-317
— pubescens, 144
— sativus, 144
Laurel, Common, *see* Prunus laurocerasus
Laurus nobilis, 166, 284, 289
Laurustinus lucidus, *see* Viburnum Tinus var. lucidum
Lavatera Olbia, 121, 167, 178, 179, 182
— trimestris, 145
Lavender, 85, 116, 136, 175, 177, 289, 315
Lavender Cotton, *see* Santolina
Ledum latifolium, 103
Lent Hellebores, 232-236
Leptosiphon, 144
Leucojum aestivum, 108, 221

— vernum, 222
Leucothoë axillaris, 288
— Catesbaei, 104, 288
Leycesteria formosa, 85
Ligustrum ovalifolium aureum, 165, 290
Lilac, *see* Syringa
Lilium auratum, 116
— candidum, 315
— chalcedonicum, 126, 315
— croceum, 115, 312, 315
— Harrisii, 79
— longiflorum, 61, 79, 115, 116, 117, 182
— pomponium, 315
— pyrenaicum, 315
— speciosum, 61, 79
— tigrinum, 315
Lily, St. Bruno's, *see* Anthericum
Lily of the Valley, *see* Convallaria
Limnanthes Douglasii, 144
Linaria maroccana, 126
Linnaea borealis, 104
Linum grandiflorum, 126
Lithospermum prostratum, 176
Lobelia cardinalis, 98
— Erinus, 154, 155, 164, 168, 171, 177
— fulgens, 126
Lomaria spicant, 303
London Pride, *see* Saxifraga umbrosa
Lonicera belgica, 94, 312, 315
— japonica, 84, 94
Love-in-a-Mist, *see* Nigella damascena
Luculia gratissima, 62
Lunaria biennis, 125, 145, 148, 227
Lupins, 121, 163
Luzula sylvatica, 258
Lychnis chalcedonica, 115, 126
Lycium barbarum, 305, 318
Lyme Grass, *see* Elymus arenarius
Lysimachia vulgaris, 108

Magnolia grandiflora, 64, 289

Maianthemum convallaria, 130, 133, 306
Malcolmia maritima, 316
Male Fern, *see* Lastraea Filix-Mas
Malva sylvestris, 173
Maple, *see* Acer
Marigold, *see* Calendula
Marigold (African, French), *see* Tagetes
Marsh Marigold, *see* Caltha
— Rattle, *see* Pedicularis
Matthiola, 11, 116, 130, 315
— bicornis, 144, 316
Maurandya Barclayana, 144, 145, 150
Meadow Cranesbill, *see* Geranium pratense
— Sweet, *see* Spiraea
Meconopsis, 136
Megasea ligulata, 158, 288
Mentha rotundifolia, 11, 165.
Menyanthes trifoliata, 108
Menziesia polifolia, 106, 266
Michaelmas Daisy, *see* Aster amellus
Mignonette, *see* Reseda odorata
Mimulus luteus, 11, 98, 115, 319
Mina lobata, 95, 150
Mistletoe, *see* Viscum
Monarda didyma, 126
Monkshood, *see* Aconitum Napellus
Morus nigra, 31, 80
Mulberry, *see* Morus nigra
Mullein, *see* Verbascum
Muscari, 130, 231
— botryoides, 231
— conicum, 231
— monstrosum, 312
— moschatum, 231
— racemosum, 231
Myosotis dissitiflora, 125, 130, 161, 224
— palustris, 98, 105
Myrica cerifera, 288
— Gale, 103
Myrrhis odorata, 125, 224, 227
Myrtle, *see* Myrtus communis

Myrtus communis, 21, 25, 289

Narcissus, 21, 130, 159, 218, 221, 309
Narcissus, Horsfieldii, 218
— incomparabilis, 218, 221, 309
— minor, 309
— moschatus, 309
— nanus, 309
— pallidus praecox, 218
— poeticus, 218, 221, 309, 311
— Telamonius, 309
Narthecium ossifragum, 106
Nasturtium, *see* Tropaeolum majus
Nemophila insignis, 316
Nepeta Mussini, 116, 130, 178
Nephrodium dilatatumm 303, 306
Nicotiana affinis, 148
Nigella damascena, 316
Night-scented Stock, *see* Matthiola bicornis
Nolana prostrata, 143
Nut, Hazel, 158, 160, 232
Nyctarinia selaginoides, 143
Nymphaea, 77, 202

Oak Fern, *see* Polypodium Dryopteris
Œnothera biennis, 120, 136
— fruticosa, 121, 130, 165
Olearia Gunniana, 162
— Haastii, 290
— Lamarckiana, 148
— macrodonta, 291
— stellulata, 291
Omphalodes linifolia, 319
— verna, 310
Onoclea sensibilis, 104, 306
Opium Poppy, *see* Papaver somniferum
Orchis latifolia, 106
Orobus aurantiacus, 133
— vernus, 133, 227
Osmunda cinnamomea, 306
— regalis, 104, 302
Othonnopsis cheirifolia, 166
Oxalis acetosella, 306

Paeonia albiflora, 162
— officinalis, 119, 121, 130, 311, 318
Pansy, *see* Viola
Papaver, 269-272
— alpinum, 271
— glaucum, 126, 144, 272
— nudicaule, 270
— pilosum, 270
— Rhoeas, 271
— rupifragum, 270
— somniferum, 126, 271, 272
— umbrosum, 126, 144, 272
Paris Daisy, *see* Chrysanthemum frutescens
Parnassia palustris, 106
Passiflora coerulea, 11, 79, 95, 150
Passion Flower, *see* Passiflora
Pedicularis palustris, 106
Pelargonium (bedding) 11, 59, 61, 116, 154, 166, 168, 319
— Paul Crampel, 126, 165
Peltaria alliacea, 163
Pennywort, *see* Hydrocotyle
Pentstemon, 115, 130, 150, 165, 166, 178
Peonies, among Roses, 162
Peony, *see* Paeonia
Pergolas, 86-96
Periwinkle, *see* Vinca
Petasites, 82
Petunia, 59
Philadelphus, 312
Phlomis fruticosa, 85, 116, 137, 279, 290
Phlox amoena, 224
— divaricata, 224
— Drummondii, 142, 146
— Nelsoni, 224
— perennial, 119, 126, 130, 139, 165, 171, 179, 315, 318
— stellaria, 224
Phormium tenax, 166
Phragmites communis, 108
Pieris, 103
— floribunda, 105, 288
Pink, *see* Dianthus

Plane, for pergolas, 94
Platystemon californicus, 144
Plumbago capensis, 177
Polyanthus, *see* Primula
Polygonatum multiflorum, 162, 224, 227, 303, 306, 311
Polygonum, 81
— baldschuanicum, 94
— orientale, 148
Polypodium Dryopteris, 306
— Phegopteris, 306
— vulgare, 288, 298, 303
Pomegranate, *see* Punica granatum
Poppy, *see* Papaver
Portulaca, 146
Prickly Shield Fern, *see* Aspidium aculeatum
Primula Allionii, 246
— Auricula, 246, 309, 318
— double, 139, 160, 318, 319
— farinosa, 246
— glutinosa, 246
— hirsuta, 246
— integrifolia, 246
— involucrata, 247
— japonica, 104, 247
— marginata, 246
— minima, 246
— (Polyanthus), 242-250, 309, 310
— rosea, 247
— sikkimensis, 104, 247
— viscosa, 246
Privet, Golden, *see* Ligustrum ovalifolium aureum
Prunus laurocerasus, 10
— Pissardi, 128, 165
Pulmonaria, 130
Punica granatum, 21, 25, 95
Pyrethrum, Golden Feather, 280
— uliginosum, 121, 280
Pyrola, 104
Pyrus japonica, 84, 85
— malus floribunda, 94

Quercus Ilex, 205, 206

Reseda odorata, 316, 320
Rheum officinale, 269
Rhodochiton volubile, 79
Rhododendron catawbiense, 287
— multimaculatum, 287
— ponticum, 10, 287
— praecox, 223
Rhodotypos kerrioides, 94
Rhubarb, *see* Rheum
Ribes, 312
Ricinus Gibsoni, 128, 165
Robinia hispida, 95, 166
Rocket, *see* Hesperis
Rodgersia podophylla, 82, 105, 269
Romneya Coulteri, 142
Rosa alba, 200, 206, 211, 318
— alpina, 198
— altaica, 197
— arvensis, 86, 187
— berberidifolia, 187
— blanda, 198
— bracteata, 195
— Brunoniana, 205, 206
— Californica, 196
— calocarpa, 196
— Caroliniana, 196
— centifolia, 200, 211, 215, 312, 318
— — muscosa, 200, 309, 312, 318
— chinensis, 65, 130, 163, 188, 202, 214, 289
— — pseudoindica, 191
— — var. semperflorens, 191
— cinnamomea, 10, 195
— clinophylla, 187
— damascena, 200, 312, 318
— — rubrotincta, 200, 211
— Ecae, 198
— Eglanteria, 31, 201, 210, 214, 311, 318
— Fendleri, 196
— foetida, 197
— foliosa, 196
— gallica, 199, 211-215, 312
— versicolor, 199

— gigantea, 193
— granulosa, 197
-- gymnocarpa, 196
— Hardii, 187
Rosa Harrisoni, 197
— Hawzana, 201
— hemisphaerica, 198
— hibernica, 198
— hispida, 197
— Hugonis, 198
— humilis, 196
— involuta, 198
— Iwara, 196
— laevigata, 193
— laxa, 195
— Lheritieranea, 198
— lucida, 85, 196, 207, 210, 214
— lutea, 197
— macrantha, 201
— microphylla, 195
— moschata, 188, 312
— multiflora, 91, 187, 188
— nitida, 196
— Noisettiana, 193
— ochroleuca, 197
— pendulina, *see* Rosa alpina
— persica, 187, 198
— pimpinellifolia, 197
— polyantha, 206, 208
— pomifera, 201
— pomponia, 200
— pratincola, 198
— provincialis, 200
— rubrifolia, 201
— Ruga, 188
— rugosa, 196
— sempervirens, 85, 187, 207, 312
— setigera, 191
— spinosissima, 197
— virginiana, 10, 196
— Watsoni, 191
— Webbiana, 196
— Wichuraiana, 85, 191, 207, 208, 210
— Xanthina, 198

Rose Aimée Vibert, 193
— Anemone, 195
— Austrian Briar, see Rosa lutea
— Ayrshire, 208, 215, 312, 318
Rose, Banksian, 193
— Bengal, see Rosa chinensis
— Blanc Double de Coubert, 196, 203
— Bourbon, 200
— Boursalt, 12, 198, 207, 214, 312, 318
— Burnet, see Rosa pimpinellifolia
— Cabbage, see Rosa centifolia
— Celeste, 206
— Celestial, 201
— Charles Lefebvre, 317
— Cherokee, see Rosa laevigata
— China, see Rosa chinensis
— Coupe d'Hébé, 318
— Cramoisie supérieure, 191, 214
— Crimson Rambler, 206
— d'Amour, 196, 214
— Dorothy Perkins, 210
— Dundee Rambler, 206, 215
— Fortune's Yellow, see Rosa chinensis pseudo-indica
— Garland, 206, 215
— General Jacqueminot, 317
— Hebe's Lip, see Rosa damascena rubro-tincta
— Jersey Beauty, 210, 289
— Lady Godiva, 202
— Lamarque, 193
— Lee's Perpetual, 318
— Macartney, see Rosa bracteata
— Madame Alfred Carrière, 206, 207
— Madame Sancy de Parabère, 215
— Maiden's Blush, 201, 206, 211
— Miss Lawrence's, 191
— Moss, see Rosa centifolia muscosa
— Penzance Briar, 201, 202
— Provence, see Rosa hemisphaerica
— Reine Olga de Wurtemburg, 206, 289
— Scotch, 197
Rose, Scotch Briar, 130, 207, 312
— Souvenir de Malmaison, 200
— Sweet Briar, see Rosa Eglanteria
— William Allen Richardson, 193
— York and Lancaster, see Rosa gallica versicolor
— Zephyrine Drouhin, 203, 204
Roses, 21, 22, 163, 186-215
— among Peonies, 162
Rosmarinus officinalis, 85, 116, 137, 289, 309
Royal Fern, see Osmunda
Rudbeckia speciosa, 120, 130
Rue, see Ruta
Rumex acetosella, 301
— Hydrolapathum, 106
Ruscus racemosus, 133, 288
Ruta albiflora, 116

Sage, see Salvia
Sagittaria sagittifolia, 98
St. Bruno's Lily, see Anthericum
Salpiglossis, 145, 178
Salvia, 116
— officinalis, 125, 161, 162
— patens, 164, 175, 177
— Sclarea, 121
— virgata, 119, 121
Sandwort, see Arenaria
Sanguinaria canadensis, 303
Santolina chamaecyparissus, 116, 122, 137, 166, 167, 180
Saponaria officinalis, 279
Satin-leaf, see Heuchera Richardsoni
Savin, see Juniperus Sabina
Saxifraga peltata, 105, 269
— umbrosa, 136, 311
Saxifrage, 84, 86, 136, 160
— broad-leaved, see Megasea

ligulata
Scilla, 160, 222, 228
— hispanica, 306
— maritima, 13
Scolopendrium vulgare, 79, 288, 301, 303, 306
Sea Buckthorn, *see* Hippophaë rhamnoides
Sea Kale, *see* Crambe Maritima
Sedum coeruleum, 143
spectabile, 167, 279
Selaginella, 61
Senecio Greyi, 166, 290
Shield Fern, Dilated, *see* Nephrodium dilatatum
— Prickly, *see* Aspidium aculeatum
Shortia galacifolia, 104, 133
Skimmia Foremanii, 288
— *japonica, 103, 288*
Smilacina bifolia, see Maianthemum convallaria
— racemosa, 104, 130, 303
Snapdragon, *see* Antirrhinum
Snowdrop, *see* Galanthus
Soapwort, *see* Saponaria
Solanum crispum, 95
— jasminoides, 79, 95
Solomon's Seal, *see* Polygonatum
Spiderwort, *see* Tradescantia
Spiraea Aruncus, 163, 164
Sparganium ramosum, 98, 106
Sphagnum, 106
Spiraea Aruncus, 99, 108, 130
— palmata, 98
— Ulmaria fl. pl., 98, 105, 108, 121, 130
— venusta, 98, 105, 108, 130
Squill, *see* Scilla
Stachys lanata, 116, 122, 166, 167, 178, 180, 204
Stephanotis floribunda, 11
Stock, *see* Matthiola
— Virginia, *see* Malcolmia maritima
Struthiopteris, 104, 306

Sundew, *see* Drosera
Sunflower, *see* Helianthus
Sweet Cicely, *see* Myrrhis odorata
Sweet Gale, *see* Myrica
Sweet Pea, *see* Lathyrus odoratus
Sweet Sultan, *see* Centaurea suaveoleus
Sweet William, *see* Dianthus barbatus
Syringa (Lilac), 203
(Mock Orange), *see* Philadelphus

Tagetes, 116, 130, 145, 146, 165, 178, 280, 315
Tanacetum vulgare, 108
Tansy, *see* Tanacetum
Taxodium distichum, 10
Taxus baccata, 205, 206, 284
Tecoma radicans, 95, 166
Tencrium Scorodonia, 267
Thalictrum acquilegifolium, 120
— flavum, 108, 120, 121, 130, 165
Thrift, *see* Armeria
Thunbergia alata, 143, 150
Thymus Serpyllum, 31, 267
Tiarella cordifolia, 133, 136, 224, 301
Tobacco plant, *see* Nicotiana
Topiary work, 21
Torenia Fournieri, 150
Tradescantia virginica, 11, 318
Trientalis europea, 104, 306
Trillium grandiflorum, 303
Tritoma, 81, 115, 120, 126, 128
Tropaeolum canariense, 95
— majus, 95, 126, 316
— polyphyllum, 116, 165
Tulipa Gesneriana, 161, 227
— retroflexa, 161, 224
Tulips, 130, 224, 227, 309, 311
Typha latifolia, 106

Uvularia grandiflora, 306

Vaccinium, 103

Valerian Red, *see* Centranthus
Veratrum nigrum, 125, 224
Verbascum, 115, 121, 136
— olympicum, 148
— phlomoides, 148
Veronica Traversii, 290
Viburnum hirtum, 290
— lucidum, 166, 290
— Opulus, 94, 267, 268, 311
— Tinus, 289, 290, 309
Vinca major, 85
Vine, Grape, *see* Vitis vinifera
Vines, for pergolas, 93
Viola (Pansy) 130, 136, 309, 311
— gracilis, 125
— odorata, 292
Violet, de Parme, 294, 317
— La France, 293
— Marie Louise, 293, 317
— Neapolitan, 291, 294
— Princess of Wales, 293
— Russian, 291, 310, 317
— St. Helena, 292, 319
— Sweet, *see* Viola odorata
— White Brazza, 294
Violets, 21, 175, 291-294
Viscum album, 237, 238
Vitis Coignetiae, 93

— cordata, 93
— quinquefolia, 64, 68
— vinifera, 25, 31, 68, 88, 93

Waldsteinia, 136
Wallflower, *see* Cheiranthus
Water Lily, *see* Nymphaea
Water Plaintain, *see* Alisma Plantago
Winter Aconite, *see* Eranthus hyemalis
Wistaria, 64, 91, 95
Woodruff, *see* Asperula odorata
Woodrush, *see* Luzula sylvatica
Wood Sage, see Teucrium Scorodonia
Wood Sorrel, *see* Oxalis acetosella
Wych Elm, for pergolas, 94

Yew, *see* Taxus baccata
Yucca filamentosa, 166, 182
— gloriosa, 166
— recurva, 166

Zaluzianskya, *see* Nectarinia
Zea Mays, 122
Zinnia, 146, 178